C000214635

B (AFTER DANTE)

NED DENNY was born in London in 1975 and has worked as a postman, art critic, book reviewer, music journalist and gardener. Carcanet published his first collection, *Unearthly Toys: Poems and Masks*, which was awarded the 2019 Seamus Heaney Prize for Best First Collection.

to the Maestro

NED DENNY

B

AFTER DANTE

CARCANET

First published in Great Britain in 2021 by
Carcanet
Alliance House, 30 Cross Street
Manchester M2 7AQ
www.carcanet.co.uk

A CIP catalogue record for this book is
available from the British Library.

ISBN 978 1 78410 959 2

Book design by Andrew Latimer
Printed in Great Britain by SRP Ltd, Exeter, Devon

The publisher acknowledges financial
assistance from Arts Council England.

+ LVCIS.ON[US] VIRTVTIS OPVS DOCTRINA REFVLGENS
PREDICAT VT VICIO NON TENEBRETVR HOMO[1]

---

1 This bearer of light is the work of virtue – with its shine it preaches the
doctrine, so that man shall not be darkened by vice.

We are therefore to recognize that the life of darkness is only a fainting poison, like a dying source; and yet there is no dying there. For the light-world stands opposed to the mirror of darkness, whereby the darkness is eternally in terror...

Jacob Boehme

CONTENTS

PREFACE

B is my second book of poetry and in many ways a true sequel or companion volume to my first – whose Dantesque opening poem was, in fact, written well before I encountered Dante. I began work on his arcane masterpiece one autumn morning not long after my fortieth birthday, *nel mezzo del cammin*, and ended up devoting the next few years of my life to it… eight initial months on each cantica, working seven days a week in the silent hours before dawn, and at least as long again on numerous redrafts. Having never read the Commedia in any of its English incarnations, the long labour was – line by line by line – also a voyage of discovery, albeit accompanied by a constant sense of prescience that was both encouraging and uncanny.

It should be made clear at the outset that I make no claims to strict fidelity. This is, rather, an interpretation and portrayal of the Commedia in the form of another poem, a subsidiary song, echo or counterfeit though it may be. In the manner of the poet-translators of the sixteenth, seventeenth and early eighteenth centuries, the maestros, it is at least partly aimed at those who know the original – a variation, one might say, on a familiar theme – and hence full of conscious expansions, explications, compressions and distortions. Whilst of course attentive to the original, in the end my loyalty was to the integrity and vigour of this love-child, these forged notes, this verbal cathedral, my impossible task.

What, though, of the title? It is a cipher implying that which precedes it, the white peak of Dante's immutable cry. It is Brunetto and Bernard, Babel and Bethlehem, Bonaventure and Boethius. It is Boniface, the archetypal unscrupulous pope, and it is the deathless emperor Barbarossa. It is birth, beauty, burial, breath, burden, betrayal, the lie of blasphemy and the truth of benediction, the memory that is blood and the labyrinth of the brain. It is beloved, balance, brutal, beyond; it is the bee, symbol of divine eloquence and the risen soul, and also the simplest yet most sublime command of all: *Be!* It is Dante's mother Bella, who died when he was young, and the bell that calls the sleeping mind to God. It is the unrelieved darkness of a B movie and the hidden treasure of a B-side. It is the Bethel stone on which Jacob's head lay when he saw a ladder linking earth and heaven, and also the very letter with which the Hebrew Torah begins. And behind all of this, at the bedrock of our languages, it is the Phoenician sign for *house* ("peace be within thy walls, and prosperity within thy palaces").

Last and perhaps most importantly, I should say that I regard the Commedia as something more than a mere work of literature in the profane current sense. The four levels of meaning[1] are all of course essential, yet it is the last and properly metaphysical one by which the other three are crowned and in which they have their justification – that higher perspective, common to all authentic traditions but alien to modern thought, that can conceive of a soul being "made holy and free" and see this supreme victory intimated in a symbolic narrative. Like any prophetic book, moreover, the Commedia's praises, teachings and denunciations have a truth and application that are perennial.

---

1 These are, insofar as they pertain to the poem: the *literal* (a journey through the three realms of the dead), the *allegorical* (a study of the various conditions of living souls – hell, purgatory and heaven understood not as places the other side of death but as states of egoistic delusion, ascetic striving and illumined awareness), the *moral* (a demonstration of the workings of divine justice, more fashionably known as karma), and the *anagogical* (the inner depths and heights that must be traversed by one who would regain man's primordial innocence and, beyond that, direct knowledge of God, the stages of awakening mapped onto the Ptolemaic model of the cosmos).

A BRIEF NOTE ON FORM

Rather than ape the Commedia's outward form, I have aimed to create a living equivalent *different from but parallel to* the highly structured and numerologically-minded original.[2] Each of B's nine hundred stanzas is a roughly 12 by 12 block, the ground plan of the Book of Revelation's radiant, "foursquare" city; line-lengths vary but no stanza falls short of or exceeds 144 syllables, this number evoking both the 144,000 who "sung as it were a new song" and the hours in the six days of Creation (and thus the end and the beginning of sacred time). With the addition of the single hanging line with which each canto opens and closes, this gives a total of 11,000 lines for the whole poem – transposing, in a sense, Dante's hendecasyllable onto the vertical plane.

---

2 "In what follows," writes René Guénon towards the beginning of his brief study The Esoterism of Dante, "we shall see clearly enough what fundamental importance the symbolism of numbers assumes in Dante's work; and even if this symbolism is not uniquely Pythagorean and reappears in other doctrines for the simple reason that truth is one, it is no less permissible to think that from Pythagoras to Virgil, and from Virgil to Dante, the 'chain of the tradition' was… unbroken on Italian soil."

BLAZE

And ill slant eyes interpret the straight sun,
But in their scope its white is wried to black.

Swinburne, *At Eleusis*

1.

In the midst of the stroll of this life that some call good

I came to my senses in a corpse-hued wood,
having strayed from or abandoned the righteous way.
Ah, that wood! Such rampant death as but to say
its grim and grinning names will summon back a fear
which made annihilation seem a mere idea,
and yet I need to treat of the dark before light.
There was little hope – I'd been so immersed in night
when my path was lost – of retracing with wide eyes
steps forced in sleep; I crept on; the ground began to rise,
and glancing up I saw the benevolent rays
of that planet which leads men through the deepest maze
minds can build, the glow the hillside wore like a cloak.

As a castaway whose very bones the seas soak
and then spit, his breath spent, upon a jagged shore
turns round and looks long at the grey and shifting moor
where he has roamed, so now my navigator's soul
gazed at that paralysing valley's tree-choked bowl,
the forest no flesh ever got out of alive;
I sat and rested there that my strength might revive,
then continued – firm foot hindmost – up the bare slope
until my circumspect tread encountered the lope
of a rosetted leopardess barring ascent,
her sleek face in my face whichever way I went.
It was dawn, when half-light and starlight are conjoined –

as they were at the holy time when Love first coined
the gold whose spinning holds us still – and it was spring,
and hour and season augured well of the leaping
of that printed beast. Next there came at me a lion,
his wild and oak-wide mane like some nightmare vision
but with undreamt fangs the air itself tried to flee,
and then a bitch wolf whose immense vacuity
declared a thirst for sweet meat no feast could sate.
At the sight of this final creature, such a weight
of ineffable dread oppressed me that my climb
felt hopeless; and, much as one who rides the time
dupes call boom then loses all in the scheduled bust

will sit and wring his thoughts in the city's cold dust,
the relentless approach of that hungering heart
pushed me back to the place where the sun's song falls quiet.
Down I sped, bounding at first then eager to slow,
my streaming eyes glimpsing a man amongst the low
shrubs and shattered rock of the arid wilderness.
I instantly shout out of terror's recklessness,
the blank despair that makes you pluck at ghostly sleeves:
"Man or spirit, have pity… help me, *please!*" Dry leaves
are thunderous when they delicately collide
compared to the rustle of the voice that replied.
"I am no living man," it breathed, "but one who lived,

and your live glance reanimates what of me has survived.
My parents were Lombards, their country Mantua,
and I was young on the day of Caesar's slaughter
and then a dweller in the Augustan city
when false gods flaunted their stone mendacity;
yet above all else a poet, and I spoke
of him who saved his father from the raucous smoke
of infiltrated Troy. Though why such stumbling haste,
such readiness to swap this spiritless waste
for the hill where every joy embarks and returns?"
I answered like some star-struck girl whose soft face burns:
"Are you really Virgil – the *great* Virgil – the source

of those works that branch like a mighty watercourse,
the illuminated one in a crowd of apes,
writer and director of the lighted landscapes
I have explored with equal diligence and love?
All that I know of how a flowing style can move
is derived from you, maestro… my soul's author, too.
But quick, the thing I ran from you see above you –
protect me from her, *vates*, show me this mercy
for my green veins tremble like a shaken tree."
"What you need is to take a different tack," he said,
considering my tears. "The predator you fled
will so exactly match your slightest feint and dart

that exhaustion kills you, she hinders with such art.
You won't leave this barbarous place in that direction,
her nature being one of pure destruction
impelled by a vast, ever-willing appetite
which appears not to lessen but grow with each bite.
Her emptiness seeks fulfilment in other ways:
the rutting nights are as loud as her gorging days,
and on and on this will go until the greyhound's
dawn makes her end in abject screams. He'll heal the wounds
of which Italy's heroes and heroines die,
and nymph-born Turnus of the folk whose sombre eye
burned within the forests before Aeneas came –

this dog that doesn't feed on lands or wealth or fame
but on true wisdom, love and virtue's excellence –
and he'll pursue her through the cities' violence
until she goes to ground in that unenlightened fire
her rancour took her from. Enough. You desire
my assistance and I'll give it, if you agree
to step into the house of dark eternity;
there you shall witness the disconsolate screeching
of ancient spirits crazed by remorse, jabbering
of the agony of the death that doesn't end;
and you will, perhaps, even come to comprehend
those who find a kind of contentment in the blaze,

thoughts set on one day being capable of bliss.
And, later, if you wish to taste that place or state" –
I see him still, a timeless second, hesitate –
"there's one more qualified to be your guide than me…
I must leave you with her then, and she shall be
with you. I'd not endure that clear metropolis,
where everything is living law and His throne is
each atom of elected flesh." "So let us go,"
I said. "In the name of the God you claim not to know,
take me from this spot which an absence devastates.
Take me as far as Saint Peter's twelve pearl-carved gates,
but before that reveal to me what the dead do."

He began to walk downhill, and I went too.

2.

It was dusk, when the dark earth stains the blueing air

and soothes bird in tall tree and beast in silent lair;
I alone amidst all that hush of soil and leaf
prepared for the war of the way and the way's great grief,
of which an undistracted heart may speak or sing.
Ingenious muse, native wit, help me to bring
forth what my sight's laser burned into my mind
or that which that same sight projected on the wind…
your blood is of the highest descent, so show it.
"You who are now my guide," I then commenced, "poet,
be sure I'm strong enough before the depths begin;
you wrote of when devout Aeneas swanned right in
to the immortal realm still in his sensing skin,

and that the giant adversary of all sin
took good account of who and what he truly was –
this clearly, to one of understanding, because
those who live within the bright pyre that does not burn
had chosen him to sire the empire that in turn
would shelter the visionary key – and of how,
on that journey, his listening eyes came to know
secrets that give us victory. I've also read
how Paul rode the sunset to reach the penned undead,
putting what he saw in a book laid down like wine;
but me, I'm no Chosen Vessel or half-divine,
no confirmer of the faith and the ways that save,

so why should *I* presume to go there, and by whose leave?
I count myself as nothing. Others think likewise,
and to commit my days to those buried skies
would, I fear, be madness and cause of madness too.
Yet you know more than all this talk… what should I do?"
Thus did I, on the world's gloom-overtaken shore,
cunningly unwill what I had willed before
and withdrew from a beginning back into my ideas.
"I hear the speech," that crag-high mind replied, "of fears
which infest your soul and not your soul itself.
The sheep that imagines a shadow is a wolf
is bitten nonetheless. I can, however, free

you from these hollow-bellied thoughts. Now you hear *me*,
and learn the reason I am here and what I know
of your life that grieves my heart. I was in Limbo,
where souls float on a crow-black ocean's foaming hem,
when the fairest face out of heaven's diadem
called to me with such a call as makes a man kneel.
Then she spoke, her enunciation like the peal
which draws to worship, her eyes' shine like dawn's sole star:
'O courteous spirit, whose utterances are
mellifluous and lasting as the spoken world,
a friend of mine – though not of fate's – is on that wild
and empty coast where the path is blocked by terror,

and I dread that what I saw in bliss's mirror
I saw too late for me to light his way. So, quick,
go to him with your voice's disciplined magic
and all that is needed for his deliverance –
and know I am Beatrice, citizen of the dance
to which even now I hunger to go back to.
It is my love that moves me. Love made me speak to you'.
A silent space, like the mind of a cyclone,
preceded my reply. 'Lady, through whom alone
men can pierce that low heaven thick with cries of fear
contained by the rotation of the moon's close sphere,
to obey your least wish is such a pressing thing

that was it already done I'd still be lagging.
But how come you don't recoil from this dense centre,
fresh from that boundlessness you long to reenter?'
'As you sincerely wish to understand,' she said,
'I will tell you why it is I'm not affected
by such air. We can only fear what does us harm,
and God has so attuned me that the shrill alarm
of flotsam souls – this cold flame where they cannot drown –
seems barely there. Another, understand, looks down
with pity for that one with horror-shackled feet
who is, in his confusion, little more than meat,
herself seeking out the sweet saint of lucid eyes

who found me where I sat beside Rachel. *Beatrice*,
Lucia said, *God's loveliest praise, can't you hear*
his howling brain? Can you not see how fir-shagged fear
stalks him by a stream the sea's shimmer cannot claim?
Why don't you hasten to the one who shone your name,
whose love for you was such he chose to walk alone?
Her last words were hanging as I dropped like a stone,
descending from that unimaginable height
to find you here… to seek your speech'. Those eyes were bright
with tears. What could I do but move as fast as her,
plucking you from the horizon of the monster
tasked to stop your scurry to the radiant peak?

Yet why are you so dull, so silent? Speak, child, speak!
Why does cowardice squat in the mansion of your heart?
You should be bold – a *free man*, noble and apart –
and all the more so given that a triple grace
favours you from heaven's court." As the dawn's clear gaze
unclenches the tall mimosa's fern-frail hands
night had closed, now I was like a cripple who stands
and marvels at powers that he had long thought lost.
"Wondrous the one who pitied my staggering ghost!
And you too, whose response to her mouth's true music
brought words which have recomposed a soul that was sick…
one will unites us. Go. I follow." Off he strode,

and thus began my sounding of the savage road.

3.

As if inked with night itself, these lines flared above me:

I AM THE WAY TO THE EVER-WAILING CITY
BEYOND THIS POINT BITES SORROW'S NEVER-MELTED FROST
WHERE LIES THE KINGDOM OF A PEOPLE WHO ARE LOST
MY MIGHTY MAKER MOVES TO THE DRUM OF JUSTICE
TRANSCENDENT POWER FASHIONS ME WITH THAT WHICH IS
ALL-WISE AND THE DEEP LOVE ALIGNED WITH ORIGIN
I RAGE IN MY ICE BEFORE THE AGES BEGIN
AN ENDLESSNESS NONE CAN ESCAPE OR UNCREATE
DISCARD YOUR WRETCHED DREAMS AND YOUR HOPE AT THIS GATE
"The dismal glow," I said, "of these words fosters doubt."
"From now on," he replied, adept, "you go without
imaginings and fears or you don't go at all –

we have come to the house of grief, of those whose fall
is consequent on hearts that cannot understand."
His features strangely joyous, he grasped my hand
and led me in among the secrets of the dark.
Perfect blackness. Fetid air. A lone bark
starring the deep, a bark that as I listened became
an almost human voice shouting an almost human name
and then a thousand voices raised yet not together:
rantings, bayings, thick gibbers, the evil blether
of dialects no living man has ever heard,
and mingled there the sound of flesh hitting flesh hard.
What could I do upon that threshold but weep,

sensing a billion souls fly as black snowflakes sweep
when death's blizzard breathes? "Maestro," I asked, my soft hair
bristling like a dog's, "what's this horror that I hear?
Who are these people pain appears to overwhelm?"
"The inhabitants of this melodious realm
are those who, when alive, blew neither cold nor hot;
amongst them are the tepid angels that were not
majestic either in devotion or revolt,
the merely self-involved whose unambitious guilt
would have nonetheless contaminated bliss…
yet there's no place either for them in the abyss,
where their meagre radiance would cast a dazzling light."

"This anguish that they retch out feels infinite,
but why?" "I'll tell you," he replied, "and make it brief.
Such music has no end. Oblivion's relief
denied them, their blind existence swells vast envy
of what they conceive others' lives or deaths to be.
Their very names are lost like some trumpeted book
the quick world eats; mercy and justice shun them, so look
and let us pass on by centred in our silence."
I turned round and saw, madly flapping, two immense
banners branded all their length with letter and sign,
the arabesque and stillness-scorning flick and twine
chased by a mob whose sheer extension stunned the eye

(I never dreamed the collateral was so high).
In this great shadow-play were faces that I knew,
and among them the drawn features of the one who
shied in his timidity from his sacred task;
I realised then, with the clearness which does not ask
but *sees*, how these are the lily-livered all despise:
as loathsome in the night's as in daylight's eyes.
So protective of their lives that they never lived,
their pale nakedness now endured the unrelieved
kisses and light footwork of flies and white hornets;
tears and blood trickled down in branching rivulets,
slicking leeches fastened on their legs like gross stones.

Peering into the distance, I spoke. "And those ones,
who seem from what I seem to see through this dim air
as if eager to be over the slow flood where
they gather… what custom grips them?" "All will be clear,"
he said, "when we reach the edge of that sad river."
Eyes downcast like a scolded hound's, I gabbed no more
until our feet sank in Acheron's reed-blurred shore
and there suddenly loomed from the marvellous dark –
the shock of his antic hair like the starry mark
on a horse's brow – a squalid troll who droned this:
"You twisted souls who'll never know what heaven is,
I come to transplant your cries to the other side

where flame's deepest layer is ice, where total shade
glares. And you – one life yet lights, a trespasser here –
keep away from the dead. This is *their* frontier."
But when he saw that I would not be driven off,
he spoke again. "Take instead some deft-built skiff
and sail another route. Depart a different port."
"Easy, Charon… this has been willed," replied my escort,
"where love and strength and wisdom join. No more commands."
At that – reluctant, though like one who understands,
reddish flickers circling the twin void of his stare –
the forest-bearded pilot of the bruise-blue mere
was quiet, while around us those bared and brutal souls

flashed teeth and rainbow hues like Amazonian shoals.
As if stung awake by Charon's tongue, each cursed
its parents and God, humankind itself, the first
time the first man and woman kissed, the nameless sperm
that sparked the growing crisis of its mother's term –
and then, moving as a herd of protestors moves,
they swept back to the foul shore where, with sobs and shoves,
they awaited what awaits those who have no awe.
He beckoned to them then, ember-eyed, his bone oar
punishing stragglers with precise violence;
and as, in November, summer's tattered raiments
fall leaf by leaf by leaf until the bare tree sees

its gaudy riches constellate the earth, so these
wicked seeds of Adam leapt seawards one by one,
each doomed as a panicked bird rising to a gun.
"Before they've even half-crossed," the maestro said, "new
crowds of refugees will be gathered here, all who
struggle out of bodies His wrath incinerates;
holy law so drives them that things a sound man hates
or fears – crossings such as this, say – are hungered for.
This way is never taken by souls that are pure,
hence Charon's snarls." Suddenly, that benighted plain
juddered as if shocked (at these words I sweat again);
the ground which oozes tears roared wind, a red light blazed

and I knew no more like one dreams have amazed.

4.

The grave reverberation of sky-wide thunder

rolled through my brain, and I stared with the bleak wonder
of a baby ripped from sleep. Standing upright,
I shone the beam of my invigorated sight
in order to see where I had awoken –
and praise God I did, considering the broken
brink of a colossal gulf was at my very toes,
echoing and booming with electrical sorrows
and so dark and cloud-trailed that vision itself might drown.
"Now we start," said the poet, ghost-white, "our climb down
into blindness. I will lead. Follow closely."
"How," I said, noticing his colour, "can I be
other than in doubt when my comforter's afraid?"

"The suffering," he replied, "of that low brigade
drains my features with pity you misread as fear.
But come, our great work calls us… we can't linger here."
He walked on then, and we entered the first circle
ringing the abyss. There, the air a ceaseless tremble
of mournful whisperings too faint to be laments,
were multitudes of men and women and infants
keening softly. "Why don't you ask," the maestro said,
"what spirits you see? Know before we press ahead
that those are not sinners but the unbaptised,
strangers to the mystic bath where faith's alchemised;
unillumined by the true and bodily light –

and such includes me – the dimness of their veiled sight
inhibits higher love. Only through these failings
are we lost, not guilt. No hope but infinite yearnings."
A sorrow clenched my heart when I was told this,
for many good souls endure the grey suburbs of bliss.
"Tell me," I said, "dear maestro. Tell me, O signor,"
(desirous of that certain faith where love is law)
"if – through his actions or another's – anyone
ever left these vague purlieus and climbed to the sun?"
"When I was yet new to this state," he replied,
alert to such phrases that disclose as they hide,
"there was a being came down here crowned with a sign

of victory – a mighty being, leonine –
and took from us the shadow of our first father,
and Abel, and that old scanner of sea-weather,
and Moses who hid and watched the light's dwindling back,
and Abraham and David (God's own Bacharach),
and angel-pinning Jacob with his tribe of twelve
and the lovely-limbed and duplicitous Rachel –
all these and many more he raised to bliss's court,
an unprecedented act." As I was thus taught,
we were not idle but proceeding onward through
thickets of ghosts dense as earth's primal forests grew;
and not too far away from the cliff where I woke

I now saw a ball of flame, a luminous yolk
hemisphered in a blackness it seemed to repel,
which despite being some distance off I could tell
was the home of souls of surpassing nobleness.
"You," I said, "who value the sacred sciences,
tell me who these are whose merit sets them apart."
"The names of these men," he answered, "whose virile art
resounds through the house of life and shall never die,
draw down grace and mercy from the inspiring sky."
As he finished talking, I heard somebody call:
"Praises to the seer who stands above us all,
returning as stealthily as he slipped away!"

In the silence which succeeded that sweet voice, they
approached – four shadows each as stately as a tree,
expressions poised between the poles of grief and glee –
and my guide spoke. "The one in whose hand shines a sword
is the foremost of these unfolders of the Word,
the sovereign poet Homer; next comes Horace,
then Ovid who portrays love's metamorphosis
and chaos-timbred Lucan last. We share the name
they called me by, that vision which gives poets fame."
And so I saw the fluent school unite once more,
gathering round the ocean king whose cantos soar
deeper than minnowed shores could ever guess or dream.

They conversed with strange sounds then beckoned me to them –
the maestro's face bright with kindness – and honoured me
by anointing me sixth of their sage company,
which moved in unison towards the radiance
whilst singing things that reduce these words to silence.
We soon arrived at a fabulous castle's base,
encircled by a river our harmonic pace
crossed as if on grass, and went through seven portals
in seven curved walls to fields in which immortals
die their lives. Eyes possessed by a solemn slowness,
the figures that I saw moved little and spoke less
and when they did their tones were quiet and debonair;

withdrawing to a tall space, a star-glazed niche where
all those set in emerald could be distinctly seen
as they walked or appeared to walk the perfect green,
we viewed such fine elaborations of His breath
as merely to have witnessed counteracts my death…
I saw Electra in a cloud of companions,
of whom I knew Hector of the nine brave ones
and Aeneas and Caesar with his falcon's gaze;
Camilla was there, she so quick her feet just graze
the trembling wheat-tips as she hums across a field,
and the Amazon queen forthright Achilles killed
then found he loved; and there sat that primeval king,

and his daughter Lavinia whose hair's flaming
predicted war; there was Brutus who kissed the earth
his grave mother, initiating free Rome's birth,
and Lucretia and Julia and Cornelia –
and, brooding alone in a honeycombed corner,
I recognised the warrior Salah ad-Din.
Then, lifting my eyes above this world-crazed scene,
I saw the great master of those who *know* and *are*
surrounded by his kindred like rays of a star:
Socrates and Plato the closest to the light,
then Democritus who considered that midnight
is where truth gleams; Zeno next and god-hemmed Thales,

Diogenes – Anaxagoras – Empedocles,
and oblique Heraclitus who declared the All
was a child at play with a coloured ball;
Dioscorides was there, the wise herbalist,
and Orpheus who made the cold stones immodest
and Linus who taught those unearthly melodies;
I saw soul-cleansing Galen and Hippocrates,
and Cicero and Euclid and stern Seneca –
sky-versed Ptolemy – Averroes – Avicenna –
and much which this brief commentary can't express,
compelled as I am by my dark theme's lengthiness.
We were two once more. A door opened on a night

that seemed to shiver, not the faintest star in sight.

5.

And so I stepped down from the outermost ring

into a second and smaller one, tightening
by a notch the belt that ratchets up the nightmare.
Here stood Minos, gave a warning growl, his coarse hair
rising like the vile hackles of a rabid dog;
he is this inverted court's examining god,
pondering the secret crimes of the arrivals
and passing sentence with the coils of his scales.
When each skull-whelped soul appears before him, I mean,
all that it is and all that it has done is seen
by the priestly eyes of a connoisseur of error,
after which he declares to what grade of terror
it has been assigned by how many times his slim

lizard-bright tail girds him. These antiseraphim
jostle there always, sliding forward one by one
to show themselves and hear judgement and be thrown down.
"You who dare approach this stricken inn," Minos cried,
turning from the role whereby he was justified,
"be careful what you enter... who you choose to trust.
Do not be deceived by the fact the foyer's vast."
"Your snarls as well? Just step," my guide said, "off the path
decreed where will and fate are one. And save your breath."
Now I began to hear the signs of untold pain,
now there started pressing at the gates of my brain
grey hordes of lamentations mouthing that we'd come

to a land where the articulate light is dumb –
the house in which a cyclone's self-divided force
is close contained – a room that sees all hell's remorse
break loose – an ice-cold atom where a tempest
whirls dead souls inside a vortex that will not rest
but torments them like a rapist who mocks as he plays,
such being this breeze which brawls as if to raze
the mind itself. When they stand before the ruinous
blast nothing can withstand, their shrieks are piteous
and drenched with hate for the One whose merest breath it is:
this is the condition of those whose lust urges
love to capitulate to a taste for skin.

As a blue flight of birds on glassy porcelain
is tousled and torn at by an eternal wind,
they hurtled with the frozen haste in which they'd sinned –
here, there and everywhere, and everywhere nowhere
but the same zone of unassailable despair,
then suddenly resembling when some veered our way
a line of cranes booming their strange, archaic lay
as they ride the turbulence of the upper air.
"Who are they, maestro," I asked, gripped with sudden fear,
"these souls the darkness beats as if to stun them clean?"
"The front one, breasting the gloom," he replied, "was queen
of multicultural Babylon, slum of tongues,

the empress of videoed flesh and preteen thongs
and the brave new and old world where deviance is law...
her name's Semiramis, the perennial whore.
Next is Dido, whose singing face the flames possessed
(*death invades me, its music is a welcome guest*),
and then rampant Cleopatra – and now see there
Helen who revolved whole zodiacs of warfare,
then Achilles whose last adversary was love
triumphant." And thousands more as they wheeled above
were pointed out, all them that romance despatched,
and, as I heard the great roll-call and as I watched
the cawing of those once-tender knights and beauties,

pity seized me. "Poet," I murmured, "who are these
two who are gliding with fingers intertwined
and seem to move as light would move upon the black wind?"
"You'll see with your own eyes as they approach," he said,
"and then just say the famous word by which they're led
and down they'll fall." I waited as the sky's current
swept them our way, then set my voice against that giant
roar. "Souls void of everything but *love*," I bellowed,
"come and talk with us if such contact is allowed!"
As doves, buoyed by the marvel of white, willing wings,
descend to the sweet site of their gentle couplings
on a half-parabola that desire describes,

so this pair detach themselves from Dido's lost tribes
and near us through the wholly evil weather
(such force has speech which is terse and warm together).
"Living man," they replied, their voices merged, "who bears
the inheritance of breath through these dim, spent airs,
who stoops to visit those who gored the blessèd day –
if the universal king was our friend, we'd pray
for your soul's peace since you pity our perversion.
But what we can do is to relate our version,
here where the wind's silence approximates a page."
Then the woman spoke. "I was born and came of age,"
she began, "in the city where the Po and its streams

surrender to the sea as a mind to sleep's dreams.
Love, who is readiest to bite where blood is pure,
filled this man with yearning for the flesh-mask I wore
till it was torn aside in that still-fresh attack;
love, who condemns the truly loved to love right back,
filled me with a holy thirst for his body…
an abandonment that will never, ever leave me;
mad love led us to this long and single death,
and Cain's cellar waits for him who stole our mingled breath."
These sounds shone like hieroglyphs in the tomblike air,
and I hung my head and gazed unseeingly where
two flies buzzed in unison. "I sense much thinking,"

my guide said. "Only," I answered, "how sad a thing
this is… innocent imagination sealed their fate,"
then turned to them once more. "Your words recreate,
Francesca, your pain so vividly it makes me weep.
But how, in those days of love's whispered semi-sleep,
did you receive the knowledge of your desires?"
"Lost and recollected joy's the fiercest of fires,"
she replied, "as he who conducts you knows full well.
Yet since you would hear where our love took root, I'll tell
as one whose agile tongue has been loosened by tears.
We were at a book some idle day, our eyes all ears,
learning of Lancelot and his doomed affair –

quite alone, barely suspecting what lips are for –
and now and again our illumined eyes would meet
then dart back to the page, an unaccustomed heat
pulsating in our smooth cheeks like a coral sea;
but it was only at a certain point, when we
read of how the wondrous spot where a smile takes place
was kissed and kissed to silence by the kisses of his face,
that a depicted world entirely mastered us:
he brought his mouth to mine then, tremulous,
a moment out of time which we have lived in since.
Our morning's reading ended there. Words made no sense."
As she finished speaking, the ghost whose hand she held

howled. I sank to the ground like a man the knife has felled.

6.

When consciousness returned, which like a sea anemone

had leapt into itself at the touch of misery,
I found my eyes walled by the mad extravagance
of wisdom devising ever-novel torments
for her ever-precocious daughters and sons. Third
circle, the code of intelligent life rain-blurred –
a rain chill, unending, onerous, accursed,
exact in its measurelessness as was its first
cruel drop; and not merely this, but golf-ball hail
suspending in ice the dregs of a shithouse pail
thundered down onto the miasma of the ground.
Cerberus crouches there, insatiable hound,
cracking the airy lash of his triple-throated bark

on the pale faces of the drowned; his dense beard's black
is congealed with fat, the bloodshot torch of his stare
crowning his gut and the talons that slash and tear
at what each spirit can remember of its flesh.
The rain seemed to stimulate them like round-lipped fish,
and they flickered and span and twitched as if the speed
of their frenzy would protect them. That centipede
glimpsing us, he opened his mouths to show his teeth
while countless legs drummed in weird rhythm on the earth;
without looking down, my guide spread and dipped his hands
and grasped and flung two gobbets of festering sands
into the singularity of those three throats –

and, as caged dogs will stop their ravenous shouts
the instant some meat is thrown, so the death-voiced fiend
was briefly unable to sound the notes that deafened.
We trod the profanities the grievous shower
hammered, and I marvelled as we did so how a
nothing or an echo can think itself alive –
the shades now prone beneath our ghost-stepping feet, save
one who suddenly sat up like a woken child
as he saw us pass. "You who amble undefiled,
he croaked, "through this nether deluge where none are cleaned –
recall me if you can, a man whose sorry end
coincided with your youth." "Suffering," I said,

"has perhaps so warped the proportions of your head
that the scannings of my memory find no match.
But tell me who you are then, consigned to such
a place whose fair climate is punishment enough."
"Your home city," he answered, "which evokes a trough
overflowing with the slops of mutual envy,
was where I was granted life's sweet serenity...
Ciacco is the name that they gave to my face.
For the error of my greed, as you here witness,
I'm strapped to the dissection table of the rain;
and I'm far from alone in my lengthy ruin,
all these others being under the same skilled knife."

Observing him withdraw into silence's nave,
I spoke. "Your afflictions, Ciacco, weigh on me
like a world of pattering sorrow, a tear-brimmed sea;
yet why not reveal, since you're tongued like a prophet,
what will happen to those in the city now split
between shadow and day... is no councillor pure
both in action and word? Why this uncivil war?"
"In time," he said, "white and black will be bathed in red,
the sylvan faction piling up the swarthy dead;
then, by the wiles of one whose craft now manoeuvres,
they must fall in the space of three sun-spun years
and the darkness shall hold its bland head in the skies

while its bootsoles trample the light, deaf to her cries.
Justice lives with two men whose voices go unheard.
Envy, pride and greed are the sparks that gut the heart."
Those words which resembled teardrops ended there,
succeeded by the noise of what descends forever.
"Speak to me more," I implored. "I want to know
of Jacopo Rusticucci, Mosca, Tegghiaio –
truly worthy souls, their minds wholly bent to good –
and Arrigo and Farinata too... I would
like to think they taste azure rather than this lake."
"Too bad," he scoffed. "Their crimes, like pocketed stones, take
them right to the shelves and canyons of the deep.

They flit with the blackest. As you fathom sleep
you'll reach them. For my part, I only ask you this:
when you're back in the world where but to breathe is bliss,
say my name." He glanced at me and lay down once more,
blind among the blind like a tile in a temple floor.
"He'll dream till the unimaginable angel
fanfares the stillness," my guide said, "and opens hell
to the dazzling tread of the enemy of sin;
each soul will then pull on its scarred and rumpled skin,
climbing up the melancholy steps of a tomb
to stand in the white flash of Love's eternal boom."
So we picked our slow way, over the ghostly loam,

touching a little on the life that is to come.
"Maestro," I asked, "when the surpassing passes sentence,
will these sufferings be less or as intense?"
"If you go back to your studies," he said, "you'll learn
that a perfected spirit is a thing we earn
by living through extremities of joy and grief;
though these shades shall never know the supreme relief
that heaven is, the pain will elevate them then."
And thus we returned to the curving path again,
discussing far more than I can say or recall
until we reached the place where it sloped downhill.
There Plutus sat on a suitcase fat with cash and gold,

the nemesis of all wealth hands can't hold.

7.

Oh, oh, Satan! O daddy mine… twoo-twit, twoo-twit!

Hooting in reverse through his whiskers' slick thicket,
owl-eyed Plutus screeched these words or something like them.
"Don't," said my gentle and sapient guide, "let him
stir up the terror that's his only weapon. Cock
of the walk is all his game… we'll descend this rock
despite it." Then, turning back to that swollen face:
"Silence, demented wolf! May your malice's force
strip the boughs of your bones like the sombre season;
this voyage into death also has its reason,
being willed at the altitude where Saint Michael's
vengeance was launched at the adulterous angels."
As sails big with the man-making, man-taking blast

collapse at once when the ship's spine snaps, thus the beast
fell empty to the ground. Skirting that ragged heap,
we entered level four of the multistory deep
which gathers to a dimensionless point
all time's wrong. Ah, justice of the omnipotent!
Who fits with untold novelties this bounding zero,
and how is it our decisions ravage us so?
Like two waves on the brink of a northern maelstrom
that clash and dissolve in their own private storm,
the spirits that I now saw danced in monstrous order;
ranged like battalions confronting each other
with the formal ferocity warfare allows,

they propelled giant boulders with their hellbent brows
and, as they collided, made brainsplitting cracks –
then, simultaneously turning a million backs,
they rolled those impediments the same way they'd come
whilst yelling *Blow the whole lot!* and *Hoard it at home!*
When they reached the far side of that black gallery,
the taunts rose again in a savage raillery
before they recommenced their rapid, swerving charge.
My heart stung by grief, I couldn't help but speak. "Sage,
tell me what this enmity is… and if the ones
on the left, the shaved ascetics, were devotion's
moneymen." "These insects," he replied, "spent their days

so in thrall to the perspective of a one-eyed gaze
that their wallets were as out of whack as their minds,
and misers goad spendthrifts as the war rewinds
again and again. The men you speak of were popes
and cardinals, souls which avarice wholly warps."
"Surely," I asked, "in that crowd of the infected
there'll be some I know?" "As easily," he said,
"tail a single larva through April's teeming lake.
Indiscriminate ways have made them all alike,
with features pinched and small as were their loveless lives;
imagine a tree that will not unfurl its leaves,
or lavishes death in June... an abomination

of that nature needs no words of condemnation,
so I won't waste them. This sterile battle will go
on and on, witnessing which should let you know
the folly of setting store by fleeting Fortune;
all the gold locked beneath the cold sway of the moon,
all treasure that ever was, can't buy these abortions
a moment's peace." "Tell me," I said, "if this Fortune's
the goddess whose secret grip holds the world's trillions
in reserve?" "So," he sneered, "say the craven civilians
of the city where ignorance waxes and wanes.
But now hear me describe the way she really reigns.
He whose mind is an overflowing fire

raised the invisible structure of the sky, a
boundlessness that's also a woven unity
due to those messengers which traverse instantly
its infinite span; through such unseen agents, all things
have an equal measure of the light that Love sings.
In similar fashion, the low heaven of earth
is ministered by one who is there at the birth
of far-marauding empires and their speechless end –
who sees the phantasms of pearl and jewel spend
no more than an instant in each almighty hand,
passing like daybreak from land to startled land
so that one race exults in the glory of the sun

while yesterday's heroes grope in night. This is done
by she whose ways are wise as a snake in the grass.
You can't contend with her whose graces surpass
your fool's science – a weighing hand, an eye that foresees,
a pace that outstrips like the gods of stellar seas
in their incandescent kingdoms, her changes quick
as the palms of a gypsy baffling with a trick.
Faces succeed faces as swift as shuffled cards.
Such is the one dogged by resentment and canards,
not honoured but reviled, yet who in her bliss
is deaf to all slander. She shares the happiness
of the primal ones, the aeons, and rotates life's sphere

and abides in joy. Now come, we can't dawdle here
for vaster griefs call. The constellations which rose
as I set out are already braving the sorrows
of the deep, and like them our light tread sustains us."
We crossed to the gulf's far side, where a tenebrous
rivulet of bloodlike water blacker than red
welled forth and trickled through a narrow streambed
leading down and on; dipping my ghost-white feet
in those occult ripples the glands of night secrete,
I followed the flow and my guide along turns and twists
to the rank marsh they call Styx. Naked pugilists,
wielding not only fists but shins and heads and teeth,

were fighting there knee-deep in mud. "This, child, is wrath,"
the maestro said. "You should also know," he added,
"that the constant bubbles are a sign of crowds hid
within the actual body of the bog. Spellbound
by the ooze they go on about how, *above ground,*
where the sun puts a spring in the step of each thing,
our hearts were smoke-stained rooms where no gladness could sing
and now, immured in slime, we're as miserable.
They think this a hymn but it's merely a burble,
sidling to the surface like the foulest of air."
While he was speaking we were slowly rounding the mire,
my eyes transfixed by a man whose sullen face

vomited earth. At length we reached a tower's base.

8.

As we had approached that monolith, our sight

was continually drawn to the daunting height
of its summit where a double blaze kept watch
(the huge flames appearing small, the altitude was such).
Far away in the distance, just discernible,
a third light blinked jerkily as though in signal.
"This is some kind of speech," I said, "responding to
the gaze that burns above," trusting that the deep blue
of my tutor's unruffled mind would make all clear.
"Enlightenment," he answered, "is already here…
across the greasy sheen of the waves it zooms,
visible to those whose eyes can penetrate the fumes."
Never did an arrow leap so fast from a string

as the kayak I saw that instant approaching,
its oarsman out and his mouth at my ear. "Child of sin,
he purred, "I have you now." "All your whispering's in
vain, Phlegyas. You only get us," said my signor,
"for as long as it takes to reach the farther shore."
Like someone who realises that he's been had,
he slunk away disputing with himself like the mad.
Following him down into his vessel, my lord
turned and beckoned. I stepped aboard – the heavy load
of my life weighing the craft that'd ridden light –
and the hideous prow moved off into the night,
half-submerged in swirling gloom. We'd not gone far

when there rose up beside us like some mud-fed tsar
a bloated man. "Who's this," he roared, "trespassing here
before his hour?" "A passerby without fear,"
I said. "And who are *you*, wallowing like a beast?"
"One that weeps. As your own eyes can tell you, tourist."
"And in this den of ceaseless weeping you'll remain…
I recognise you, fiend, despite the filthy mane."
He lunged for the boat with his barnacled fingers,
but Virgil kicked him off. "Back with the other curs,"
he spat, then threw an arm around my neck and kissed
me hard. "She who devised you within her be blest,
disdainful soul! This creature preened, proud in his bones,

yet did no good. And so his afterimage groans,
enraged that all that self-esteem has come to this.
There are many now above – the lit world's princes –
destined to end here like pigs snorting in a yard,
those celebrated faces turned to one smeared herd."
"I should love to see him dipped in this bouillon,"
I said, "this rich gruel, maestro, before we move on."
"The shore will not show itself," he replied, "without
your wish being fulfilled." And sure enough, with a shout
of pure bloodlust, a horde arrayed in rarest mud
gave him a beating for which I still praise the Lord,
that man whose steed would prance in diamond-studded shoes

taking in desperation a bite from his toes
and so on up until he crunched his own head.
We left him there, my open eyes forging ahead
and in the ear's spiral an innumerable cry.
"Now, my son," the maestro murmured, "there lies close by
the parody of a city which some call Dis,
the capital where there crowd the grave-eyed faces."
"I think I can already see its crimson mosques,
glowing as raked embers glow in November dusks."
"The remorseless fire that burns within them," he said,
"is next to heaven's lucid gold as dense as lead…
its blaze is unimaginably cold." Riding

the rapids into the first of the moats which ring
that kingdom of the unconsoled, its sides iron-clad,
we swept round once and our pilot stood. "Here," he cried,
"is the portal. Out of my boat." Raising my eyes,
I saw clustered at the gate like turd-thronging flies
more than a thousand of those torrential angels
angrily buzzing. "Who is this who'd enter hell's
sanctuary without taking death's holy test?"
My guide made a sign as if to say it was best
he spoke to them apart, and after some time –
quieter now – they droned once more. "Let the braggart climb
back the road he came, remembering his mad way

if he can do so, whilst you who've been his torch stay
on." Imagine, *hypocrite lecteur*, with what fear
I heard those phrases spewed forth by mouths black with fur,
and how I thought I'd breathed my last of this sweet air.
"Dear guide," I said, "you've saved me seven times or more
from dangers so profound my sole thought was to run –
if you desert me now I'm completely undone;
since we can't get past, let's retrace our double track
quickly together." "Relax," he said. "We turn back
for no one… nothing can hinder a footstep willed
by love, nor would I leave you in this sunken world.
Though wait here while I talk with the glittering swarm,

and feed your spirit with the hope which keeps hearts warm."
So the tender parent went once more from my side
and I was alone and in doubt, not knowing if I'd
ever been elsewhere than that godforsaken night;
a No and a Yes like a darkness and daylight
pursued each other round the planet of my brain,
and when at last they touched on dusk's blue counterpane
all was uncertain and wholly strange; a silence
that is something quite different from sound's mere absence
was born and killed its brothers and schemed and reigned,
the monstrous king. Yet time – as it must – rewakened,
the hum of a vast and grandiloquent wing

followed by the thunder of a basalt door slamming
and then the slow, returning tread of my friend.
His bold gait was gone and his eyes trailed the ground.
"Who are they," he muttered, "to lock this mournful house?"
Then, spotting me, he brightened. "If I seem morose,
don't worry. This is a fight we cannot but win,
whatever smart mechanisms death contrives within;
the arrogance of those who trust in coded doors
is built on sand, as the upper gate's mangled bars –
the entrance where the venomous sentences shone –
bear stark witness. Even now there descends the one,
speeding down the circles and each nocturnal bend,

by whom the stony soil of this land shall be opened."

9.

My face was so spectre-white from sheer cowardice

that, seeing it, he restrained the pallor in his.
He stood unmoving, head cocked, hell's dim atmosphere
compelling his body to be a single ear:
"We must not fail now" – I watched his lips – "otherwise…
how *long* it takes, the intervention of the skies!"
Despite the fact those first six unembodied words
were clothed by the spoken phrase that came afterwards,
his swiftly-hidden falterings fed my fear.
Maybe I read into them a sense that wasn't there.
"Do any ever come down from the first level,"
I asked, "to this low whorl of the echoing shell
where more than hope is lost?" "Very rarely," he said,

"although the crude witch who'd resuscitate the dead
once summoned me with a click of her vanished hand.
The meat-suit I'd called home had not been long unmanned
when she made me go within that terrible wall
to extract a spirit from the worst place of all,
the black nook furthest from encompassing light.
Have faith in me… I *feel* my way when the path's unlit.
As for this great swamp which exhales such evil breath,
it surrounds the sad citadel no devil's wrath
can keep us from." If he said more I can't recall it,
for my eye was that instant enthralled by the sight –
on the tower whose tip showed red like a fag –

of a diabolical and three-headed hag
whose lithe waist was belted with a hydra the shade
of May's just-published leaves. Round her pale temples played,
like rebel hair, miniature snakes with goatish horns.
The maestro, who knew the Queen of Lamentation's
shrill handmaid, now spoke. "Observe our gracious Fury –
Megaera, Alecto, and fair Tesiphone
between them." My teacher and guide was silent then,
and I stared as she tore her shapely breasts open
with long curved nails and beat herself with bloodied palms
and wailed like seven hundred thousand fire alarms
sounding at once. I drew close to him in terror,

and those lips curled down at us and hissed together:
"Let Medusa come and he'll be a man-shaped rock…
such vengeance should've paid Theseus's attack."
"Show your back," the maestro said, "and seal your living eyes.
If *her* head gets inside your head, you will not rise
again." Then he span me so that I faced away
from the thickening darkness and towards the day,
enclosing my mortal fingers with his light hand
to be triply sure; all who'd truly understand,
note the doctrine these elusive lines half-conceal.
Now there came a sound which at first you could just feel,
a nightmarish vibration that made both shores

shudder like the forest does when sudden wind roars
out of warring weather-fronts, pulling up trees
as we do weeds and then wheeling on – dust-veiled, at ease –
while panthers and panther-men cower in its wake.
Uncovering my eyes, he turned me round once more. "Take,"
he commanded, "a long, hard look across the scum's
fetid surface to where there drift the harshest fumes,
if your nervous glance can shoot that straight." As a snake
will send the cold frogs to the bottom of a lake,
so I saw thousands of those devastated souls
dive to escape the figure whose swift, bare soles
whirred untainted over the marsh. Tranquil but for

flared nostrils which showed how foul he found the air,
he was – it was clear to me – a being heaven-sent.
I looked to the maestro who motioned *Be silent*,
and then made a sign that I should lower my head
to the one who – the gesture calm yet revolted –
swung aside the weighty door with a blade of grass.
"Outcasts," he yelled at the dark, "despicable race
harbouring within you such baseless insolence,
why kick against that supreme intelligence
whose will has only ever intensified your pain?
Why butt your twisted horns against the fates again?
Think back and you'll recall how your own mongrel hound

received for such insolence a savage throat-wound."
At that he turned aside and was hastening back
as deft as he had come, a bright blur on the track
whose very substance flinched from him; not a word
was sent our way, and in truth he seemed a creature spurred
by concerns of which I could scarcely conceive.
I stepped through the pylon into the hall of grief,
all unopposed after that burst of melody,
invigorated now and desirous to see
the condition of those such a fortress would contain.
The rays of my darting eyes revealed a huge plain
bounded by that wall, an estate laid out by one

who meant to let disharmony reign. Where the Rhone
divides its diminishing force at star-tilled Arles,
between those blue arms being marshes where wild bulls
and horses roam – or at Pola, where an island-
studded gulf bathes Italy's shores and marks its end –
the ground is so thickly packed with the gaping dead
it bears distinctive lumps like a murderer's head...
such was this funereal landscape's character,
with the difference that each noble sepulchre
was blown upon by fierce flames whereby they glowed white
as vases in a potter's kiln; lids open wide,
there emerged from inside them an uproar which seemed

the grotesque miserere of souls that are maimed,
a cacophony ancient as femur-struck drums,
lamenting separation's horror and the worm's
fervid kiss. "Who are these ones, maestro," I asked then,
"whose panicked bellowing arises from within
the tombs that breast the rolling earth like broken arks?"
"This sound," he said, "is made by the heresiarchs
of every persuasion and by their followers,
the sects and divisions of spiritual wars
fought between pursuers of two sorts of riches.
Those stone ships groan with far more cattle than you'd guess."
Then he took a secret path that led to our right,

snaking past the shining graves and the wall's black might.

10.

"Sum of virtue," I began, keeping close behind,

"you who show my way down these gyres of the blind,
speak to me. Satisfy my curiosity.
The lids of all the tombs are raised, so can one see
those who cringe within them like grubs that hate the light?
The cells are unguarded yet no felon takes flight."
"Every last sepulchre will be sealed," he replied,
"when they return in the flesh they stepped from when they died.
Here bides Epicurus, a seducer whose whole
spiel was the myopic creed of the mortal soul…
now his friends and allies occupy these gardens.
But concerning your voiced and your unvoiced questions,
for I know you've a desire of which you won't speak,

all shall be revealed as we proceed." "I don't seek,"
I said, "to hide my heart but for silence's sake,
to which you have often urged me." "O you who make" –
these first words suddenly rang from inside a grave,
so that I recoiled – "death's pilgrimage whilst alive,
speaking with integrity in the midst of fire –
and in my own tongue too, so that I know you for
a native of that kingdom I perhaps misled –
will it not please you to linger here?" "Turn your head,"
said Virgil, "and see half-shown like a rough-hewn god
that citizen you once asked me of. Have a word
and make them count." Saying this, he pushed me toward

the plinth-like edifice where Farinata stood
with a look as if he held all hell in great disdain.
When I reached the sheer cliff of its base, he peered down
and scornfully demanded who my forebears were;
eager to oblige, I made a rapid answer
at which he raised his brows and considered and spoke.
"They," he said, "were the enemies of my kinsfolk
and of my faction, scattered twice by my own hand."
"And both times all who were driven out returned,"
I replied, "as unopposed as morning light…
your knights were not so hardy, if I remember right."
But before he could respond, a second spectre

showed his head and glanced round as if he'd expect a
traveller from the day to be accompanied.
Then, presuming me alone, he began to plead:
"If you pursue your way through this starless prison
by force of inner light, then where is my dear son?
Why's he not with you?" Each word rode a rolling tear.
"Another guides my path," I said. "He who led me here
waits close by, ready to take me onward to her
your Guido once wouldn't or couldn't honour."
I knew who he was by the nature of his penance,
and at my speech he reared upright. "But the *past* tense
when you tell of him," he cried. "His life so *brief*?

Is he not where the sun's sweet beams compel belief?"
In the momentary pause before I replied,
he fell backwards like a man who has doubly died
and was seen no more. That first fine soul had meanwhile
not moved so much as a ghostly hair, icy-still
as though he was sculpted from dark grey marble.
"If," he said, continuing, "they're that incapable
it hurts me far more than my bed's flame-feathers burn;
yet you yourself will find that the art of return
is the hardest to master, and it won't be long…
the cold face of the queen to whom these realms belong
shall not be reillumined more than fifty times

before you learn. If you'd go back to golden climes,
tell me why my line's so oppressed in our city."
"Because," I responded, "of an atrocity
and a river red with blood. Such rank slaughter's why
we pray for their banishment." I heard a deep sigh
and he shook his head. "In that I was not alone
or without cause… recall I was the only one,
when all had vowed to make a ruin of Florence,
to raise a human face in her fair walls' defence."
"I'll pray for your seed's peace. But help me with this knot
in which my mind is tied. It appears you cannot
see the present yet perceive what the future veils,

if I hear correctly." "That is true. We're exiles
from the fatherland that you call Now… eagle-eyed
for distant things, though squinting and stupefied
when it comes to what is near. The spark of the Lord
is feeble in us, and unless such as you bring word
of your human state it's not known to us at all.
Here is the very definition of hell.
It follows from this, understand, that the destined
time when nothing's hidden will make us wholly blind."
"In that case do tell," I said, conscious of a fault,
"the soul who just reentered his electric vault
that his son is still within the house of the living,

and that when I seemed as if hesitating
my thoughts were caught in the confusion you've made clear.
But please speak, lastly, of the others that are here."
I could see Virgil gesturing me to come away.
"There are many with me of whom the less I say
the better, the second Frederick and a certain
cardinal among them." And with that he was gone,
so I went back to where the ancient poet lurked
whilst pondering that speech and what it might predict.
We set off once more, and, looking askance at me,
he asked me the reason I paced that solemnly;
I told him what the shade had claimed, concerning both

his perceptions and my future… was this the truth
or a game of those beings that love to deceive,
eaten up by jealousy of any who live?
"Remember each word breathed against you," said the sage,
"but now give your attention to this single page
which surrounds us in its silentness" – his white hand
indicated the black wastes of that wonderland –
"and have faith that, when you finally stand before
the ray of her green and all-discerning eyes, your
days' strange meanderings will be made apparent."
Then he turned his feet to the left, and we went
down a track towards a valley which even from there

sickened with its vapours the already sick air.

11.

We soon arrived at the precipitous brink

of a ring of immense and shattered stones, the stink
exhaled by the abyss their leaning forms half-hid
so intensely foul we withdrew behind the lid
of a high tomb. *Here lies Pope Anastasius,*
my fingers read, *lured from the path of righteousness*
by the great adversary's Word-denying words.
"We must wait a brief while before going onwards,
or else – like an impatient diver whose ascent's
too fast – that air in your blood will do violence."
"Let's not let these minutes, like bubbles, fly empty."
"Your thought," the maestro said, "matches mine entirely.
So listen, my child, and I'll endeavour to tell

what I now know of the geometry of hell.
Within this ruinous circumference of rock
three diminishing levels rise, dense with livestock
in human guise… prepare yourself for that dread sight
by understanding how and why they're penned so tight.
All malice loathed by the light is injurious
to someone or something, either by fraud or force,
yet since only perverse mankind practises fraud
it is for that reason most hateful to our Lord;
in this upturned ziggurat, then, those who deceived
are nearer to the summit and hence more aggrieved.
Before them come the brutal, whose floor corresponds

in its triple structure to three different wounds
this sin can inflict – on oneself, on one's fellows
and on God. A man can be felled or killed by blows,
his property destroyed or made off with or burned;
both murderers and bludgeoners have therefore earned
a place in that first round, along with those who seize
what belongs to another. We may likewise raze
our works or the ivory tower of our bones –
so the second room resounds with the futile moans
of them who rob themselves of the sight of that Earth
surpassing any words, or waste the lesser wealth
man reckons on a hand, obsessing life away

when he should rejoice. Love herself becomes the prey
of fools who say in their dead hearts *There is no God*,
or who defile the living temple of His broad
world; the third and smallest of these metal rings, therefore,
stamps its family crest on Sodom and Cahors
and those who speak of sacred things with secret hate.
So much for the violent and what they create.
Fraud has rows of curved teeth which close on the conscience,
may be perpetrated on one whose confidence
the swindler has or one without that deeper trust.
In this latter instance, all that's turned to dust
is the bond of fraternal love which nature weaves;

and thus, in the following circle, squirm such thieves
as scam the credulous – the conman, the pander,
the drones who compose the age-old propaganda
that's sold as news, sly embezzlers, the litigious,
the ignoble shyster with his eternal ruse.
In the former case, not the trust with which we're born
but a loyalty cultivated by man alone
is taken foul advantage of and betrayed;
here is the reason that the treacherous are flayed
in central Dis… the universe's coldest point,
the inmost core of matter's unillumined flint."
"This account's as concise as I could wish, maestro,

and makes the architecture of the inferno –
the ranks of those possessed by fire – entirely clear.
Though what" – I asked – "of the unfortunates we saw
within the slimy bog, souls chastened by the rain
and spun in giant vortices time and again,
who have for each other not a single gentle word…
why don't they bellow with the scarlet city's herd
if high heaven's gaze sees them guilty of a fall,
or – if guiltless – then why are they there at all?"
"Your thoughts have walked back into a thicket," he said,
"beguiled by that ingenious dunce in your head.
Have you forgotten your *Ethics*, and him who writes

of the three dispositions that obstruct the light's
plunge and ascent – mad violence, cunning malice
and lack of restraint – and how this last failing's less
offensive to the godhead and incurs less blame,
sentenced to a cyclone but not the wheel of flame?
Consider that wise one's teachings, then call to mind
those we met whose penitentiary's the wind,
and perhaps you'll see why their spirits aren't ablaze."
"Sunlike man," I said, "you turn my dullard's nights to days
as the dawn's rays cleanse the waters of muddied sight,
the way in which you do so giving such delight
it has me almost glad of my disarrayed

brain. Allow me one more question. The point you made
about the sharks of Cahors, and how that practice
works on the budding land like a breath of ice…
why?" "Listen to the many-named philosopher,"
he said, "and you'll hear how the omniscient fire
unfolds and steers the cosmos, the supreme artefact;
how when you create, the supremely human act,
you take your cue from nature as she from the One.
God watches art, therefore, as a man his grandson.
The usurer – on the other hand – sets his mouth
on the warm neck of His earth and His earth's priests, both
growing pale while he gets fat. Now let us climb down,

for Pisces is tremulous on the world's horizon."

12.

The spot the good maestro chose for our descent

was raw as an alpine mountainside, violent
convulsions having thrown rocks as drinkers roll dice.
Something else made it seem a sacrilegious place
the mind and soul recoiled from, but first envisage
ruins of stupendous scale and inhuman age –
such as became of the vale of the Adige,
where once an entire cliff-face shouldered its way
from the eagled summit to the sleeping plain below –
down which, on titanic steps, you invent a slow
route from broken stone to stone; and then picture how
Crete's infamy, sired in an artificial cow,
stretched that disfigured form along the chasm's edge

and – seeing us – gnawed his arm in impotent rage.
"I expect that you suppose," sneered the mage, "the keen-
knived prince who hacked deep into your labyrinthine
room has come to part head and limbs a second time,
yet this one holds no thread and intends to free climb
to the night's upended peak. Now stand aside, freak."
Like a bull which has received a precise death-stroke,
crippled by its punctured heart but thrashing all ways
in hopeless freedom, so a calm and well-aimed phrase
unstrung the Minotaur. "*Quick*," urged my watchful guide,
"run for the pass… his fury holds him stupefied
and we can go in safety." Setting my bare feet

on huge pumices that rocked beneath my weight,
I began my wary, pensive descent. "Perhaps,"
he said, "you're wondering what made the cliff collapse.
The first time I ventured to this abysmal height
the precipice was sheer; if my sense of things is right,
it wasn't long before the Almighty's blonde beast
loped into hell and went off with those souls He blessed
that the whole nigredo shook to its hateful core –
it seemed to me then that our universe of war
thrilled to the touch of the Love that, as some have taught,
unendingly returns us to a brimming nought
the wise call Joy – and this ancient edifice was

tipped down. But cast your eyes below you now, because
we're approaching the turbulent river of blood
in which those whose rage harmed their fellow men are brewed."
Mania of anger and blind covetousness…
possessing the brief flash of our days, remorseless
in its aftermath! I looked and saw a broad moat
encircling the plain like a hand around a throat,
and in the space between that scarlet and the scree –
just as, when in the living world, they love to be
bent to the kill – an army of swift centaurs plied
the thunder of their hooves. Spotting us on the landslide,
three fitted feathered shafts to three giant bows

and galloped our way. "To which," the foremost bellows,
"torment are you headed? No further. Speak from there,
or this eager arrow will subdivide the air
and lodge in your voice box before you breathe a word."
"The one that talks is Nessus," the maestro murmured,
"whose overtures were stopped by Heracles's dart,
and with the parting gift of his infected shirt
had vengeance from beyond the grave. The next we see's
Pholus – dead of venom too – and then Achilles'
foster-father Chiron, he with the downward gaze;
they and a thousand avid others spend their days
patrolling the river's obscenely clotted shore,

and any soul which lifts itself an iota more
than its allotted inch above the febrile flood
feels an archer's sting." "It never did you much good,
my friend" – now he addressed the one who'd made the threat –
"that champing will of yours… I'll speak with the great
Chiron, Nessus, rather than to you." As we neared
those three outliers of the legendary herd,
Chiron took an arrow twice the length of a man
and, with its notch, flicked aside his beard; then, this done,
the cave of his mouth moved as if a mountain talked.
"Did the pebbles *shift* as the other one walked,"
he muttered, "as they don't under insubstantial feet?"

The brave maestro was now at that chest where there meet –
like the best of both worlds – the selves of man and horse.
"He is indeed alive, no smoothly-gliding hearse
with the corpse of a soul inside," my guide then said,
"and it falls to me to show his way past the dead…
urgent need drives us, this is not some feckless jaunt.
The one who I obey tore herself from a chant
prose can't express – the mad Word, the secret chord
sounded by the shining flesh of those who *see* the Lord –
and he is no burglar nor I a ghostly thief.
In the name of the breath which whirls me like a leaf
along this forest track, we ask for a horseman

to cross the torrent with… I'm a spirit and can
find toeholds in the air, yet that poet's leaden
limbs require a mount." "You – Nessus – you escort them,"
boomed Chiron, "and warn off any troops who approach."
And so we came down to the vermilion beach,
Nessus leading and my brain filled with the screaming
of souls like lobsters in an iron pot. "This king,"
he said, showing the bare crown of a half-sunk head,
"was a tyrant who once ground skulls to bake his bread.
Now he howls at the thought of his years of plunder.
And look… you'd never know it, but the boy wonder
of Macedon weeps beneath those crusted ringlets –

and all around him are the glorified bandits
whose rule was not from inner poise but force of arms,
no matter whether measured out in reigns or terms."
My eyes and those of Virgil met – "this savage creature,"
they seemed to say, "is in truth the better teacher,
so keep pace with him if you can" – and soon we came
to a crowd whose heads were fully clear of the stream,
one of them a moody figure standing apart.
"That man's knife," said Nessus, "had its way with a heart
whose precious drops the Thames's cool tongue still tastes."
Before long the spectres could be seen to their waists,
many I knew among them, and then a shallows

which only seethed and swirled around their tender toes
showed that we had come to a place where we might pass.
"The blood's pulse and heat," Nessus said, "gets less and less
in this direction; that way are the scalding pools,
the depths where there cook the marionette-like fools
who imagined absolute power was their own
(a tall shadow looms above each sublunar throne,
spurring the figurehead as a man spurs a nag).
There steeps Attila with his rancid saddlebag,
and there's room in this current for a whole lot more
puppet-despots of the interminable war
between the Serpent and the soul." We'd crossed the ford,

and he cantered off and left us in a trackless wood.

13.

As in a forest the hour before sunrise,

no green but a ghastly monotony of greys
hung motionless on every side; no smooth boughs
rose in calm strength, but knotted branches that sorrow's
sickening exhalations had stunted and coiled;
not one apple glowed in the twilight, a round world
ripening on the tree of night, but finger-length thorns
bristled along tortured trunks and dripped with poisons...
the tusked and cocksure beasts which devastate the crops
beside the Cecina have not so dense a copse
to snore in. This was the thicket where there roost
the harpies that snatched and shat upon the Trojans' feast,
driving them off with a dark annunciation

of worse to come, each tree as wild with lamentation
as in springtime earth's woods are blessed with lucent songs.
Peering up, I saw at all heights their loathsome wings
and – more eerie yet – on each bird a human face
cawing its hate. "Know," my guide said, "this fine place
for the brutal's second tier... look well and you'll see
things that if recounted would make you disbelieve me."
For now, though, it was my ears that were spellbound
by an undertone, subtle wails, a haunting sound
I couldn't tell the source of; the maestro, I think,
believed I imagined there to be behind each trunk
a spirit who'd been scared by our arrival –

"just break a twig from any plant," he said, "and all
will be shown far different from what your brain conceives"–
and I put out my hand and tore a dozen leaves
from the nearest growth. "Monster! You dismember me,"
shrieked a voice from the very substance of the tree.
"Have you no *pity*?" The fresh wound had welled with blood.
"We who were a crowd," it went on, "are now a wood.
Perhaps you'd be gentler with the soul of a snake?"
As there comes from one end of a still-green stick
drips and hissing air whilst it burns at the other,
so that ripped branch spat forth words and lymph together...
what could I do but drop it in dumb terror? "If,"

the good maestro said, replying on my behalf,
"he had given, mutilated soul, more credence
to the marvels in my verse, this act of violence –
an act which pains me too – would never have occurred.
Such is the gulf between what's seen and merely heard.
Yet why not tell him who you are, for then he might
make some amends when his mind regains the light
by reviving, in that distant realm, your name and fame?"
"Speech of such clear sweetness cannot but disarm,
and waken the long-buried eloquence in me.
I was the man" – the gash went on – "who held each key
to Frederick's sterling heart, keys so softly turned

he trusted no one else. In the end, though, weakened
by my restless dedication to that office,
I lost sleep and strength. Envy, the courtier's vice –
the whore who infected the house of my Caesar –
kindled flames in the thoughts of my enemies, a
conflagration which raced forth like a forest fire
until even the head of Augustus burned; far
from my former standing and held in contempt,
my impiety persuaded me to attempt
to kill the unkillable by dashing out my brains.
Spirit's not dependent on what the skull contains,
as I soon learned. But, fellow poet, take my word

that I never betrayed my honourable lord…
I swear by these feet that have grown so deeply strange;
and please, if either one of you ascends again
to that world where my reputation still lies stunned
in the mud where schemers kicked it, offer it your hand."
He fell silent then, and the maestro spoke. "Now
is the time for questions, *now*… what else would you know?"
"You talk," I said. "I can scarcely think for pity."
"Tell us," he began, addressing that twisted tree,
"so this man can do you the favour which you ask,
just how your soul came to have a trunk for a cask –
and whether, too, limbs of such elaborateness

are ever laid aside?" A wind stirred the branches
and turned imperceptibly back into a voice.
"When," it replied, "there blunders from its corpse a fierce
and self-evicted mind, Minos's snake-swift tail
whips round seven times and down to this brake we fall;
not, though, like a grain placed with a gardener's care
but as one remotely borne by casual air…
a speck of pure spirit which uncurls a seedling
frail as wild spelt, a plant that's soon the towering
tomb of a mighty thorn. The harpies peck at it,
grieving us yet also giving grief an outlet
in the form of slit windows where we sit and watch

the night. As for those priceless robes of flesh – garb which
we tore off our backs with such ungrateful fury –
were you to come here at the end of time you'd see
the whole wood decked with them, each on the jagged bush
of its disquieting soul." At that moment, the crash
of trodden branches broke the spell of his weird tale,
as if a boar and its pursuers sped pell-mell
within the undergrowth – and two figures appeared
rampaging through the brambles, naked and blood-smeared
from a thousand scratches on their virtual skin.
"Hurry, death!" cried the one in front. "O assassin,
release me!" "You weren't," yelled the other, "half so fast

at the battle when your lavish head was lost!"
Perhaps because short of breath, this one sought to hide
inside a shrub; a rash act, though, for right behind
was a black flood of hellhounds with serrated teeth…
and out he came with each limb in a different mouth,
separately writhing like sections of a worm.
My guardian then took me gently by the arm
and led me to that mangled and quivering plant,
which now rasped through its chewed twigs a feeble lament.
"Why try," it said, "to make a shelter of poor me?
What have *I* to do with his prodigality?"
"And who, pray, *were* you," asked the maestro, squatting down

so his face was level with that bleeding thorn,
"whose meagre words bubble forth mixed with bitter sap?"
"You who've seen," came the reply, "those nightmare fiends rip
from every branch my little leaves' delicate ears,
please gather them from where they flew. Observe my tears
and pity me. Mine was a town that honoured Mars –
keeping itself by this design immune to wars,
much as wise statesmen keep their enemies close –
until an emaciated image took his place;
for that infidelity, the red planet's art
reminds her of his presence by tearing her apart
time and again… even a pagan god is great.

I'm one who hanged himself from the spikes of his gate."

14.

Moved by love for the city where I too was born,

I placed the scattered foliage beneath the thorn
whose mournful recital had rustled to an end.
We then came to the verge of the violent's third round,
a chilling scene only His justice could contrive.
Picture a Saharan immensity, alive
with wavering heat that suffers no tender thing
to thrive, a fierce day girdled by the wooded ring
as the wood itself has an outline of blood;
this was the terrible threshold on which we stood,
the unsteady dunes high as those the elephants
of Cato once struggled through. Eternal vengeance
of the Lord, how your intelligence is made plain

to the eyes of a man who learns to *see* again!
I now had before me vast herds of naked souls
and could hear their strange and multifarious calls
shimmer in the warping air, each an expression
of sovereign law. Some sprawled in the position
of a corpse or drowsing beast, some crouched, but most went
dumbly on like creatures in a withered torrent
going nowhere fast; and over all this, more slow
than through an alpine stillness comes the blessèd snow,
there span down kaleidoscopic flakes of fire
such as – in the Indian wastes – Alexander
had his troops stamp out before they were sent insane…

these always-falling flamelets ignited the plain
unceasingly, like winking bulbs in darkened cities,
yet just to increase the exquisite agonies
of the souls whose hands blurred in a feverish dance
as they tried, in vain, to stop the blaze's advance.
"Father and teacher," I began, "whose sole defeat
was when demons swarmed round the hieratic gate,
who is that haughty one the drops seem not to scorch?
He lounges as if heedless of their white-hot touch,
his features gripped by a look of infinite scorn
as though no rain could ripen him." The ghost had seen
the movement of my lips, and shouted aloud

before my guide could speak. "I'm no more craven dead,"
he roared, "than when I was living. Jove might exhaust
the smith who shaped the bright bolt with which I was pierced,
then drive the other hammerers in Etna's forge
till they beg for mercy – hurling at me one huge
light-shard after another – and still revenge's
joy would not be his." With a force and distinctness
I had never seen before, the maestro replied:
"And your punishment, Capaneus, *is* this pride
which rages like the blizzard of crystalline flame;
what torment but that of your foul mouth's sound and foam
could equal the fury that simmers in your deeps?"

"He was," he said to me, "with the seven at Thebes
and has no – and never had – reverence for God;
as you heard me saying, he produces his mad
implements of torture with the heft of his tongue.
But follow me closely now… our path leads along
the border of the wood where your soles will not burn."
We went on in silence until we reached a burn
which trickled from amongst the trees – that shade of red,
it makes me shiver still – then into a stone bed
that cut across the desert sands and seemed to be
our way. "Observe this stream," said the poet, "and see
how the space above the flow is quite clear of flame –

and know this, more than all you've witnessed since we came
through the wide-open and inevitable gate,
for a highly noteworthy, significant sight."
These were his exact words, and they gave me a thirst
for understanding I implored him to slake. "East
of your country," he began, "is a dead land. Crete.
Time was sacred when its first king reigned, complete
and pure. Things basked in the light of what they truly were.
A mountain stands there that was once loud with water
and the voice of countless leaves, now quiet and bare…
this deserted spot is Ida, and it was here
that Jupiter was cradled in a grove of noise.

Within the peak's a venerable man – his gaze
fixed upon the city where he views his mirrored
self, the mystic palms of the Egyptian seaboard
at his back – whose head and face are living gold, sheer
wonder to behold. He is silver from shoulder
to arms and chest, then brass as far down as his waist;
the twin towers of those great legs are iron shafts,
yet the foot on which his weight rests is hard-baked earth.
A fissure wet with tears divides the parts beneath
the countenance's sun, and these slow drips become
a seam that wears its deft way from his hidden room
(making use, as it were, of a ladder of stone)

to our crucible. That stream's the source of Acheron,
Styx and Phlegethon – the three rivers we have passed –
and feeds through this small canal into the last
and lowest watercourse… you'll see with your own eyes
what manner of pond divine Cocytus is,
defying any speech." "How can it be," I said,
"if the mother-rill wends from the living to the dead,
that we haven't crossed over its track until now?"
"This house is a round house," he replied. "That much you know,
and though you've travelled hard and far – always tending
to the left as you descend the sonorous ring –
your footsteps have not as yet described a full

turn. If we glimpse bizarre things, don't gape like a fool.
Your eyes shall hear a voice before you. This is the way."
"What of Phlegethon and Lethe? The first, you say,
is fed by the tears of those who grieve in the sun…
of the other you don't speak." "I'm well pleased, my son,
by such curiosity. You've forded one, though
I didn't name its boiling flood; you'll judge, when we go
onward from hell's chasm to the mountain where
repentant souls bathe themselves in remorseless air,
the river of holy forgetting for yourself.
But it's time we left behind this unkempt gulf.
Keep to the channel's marble brink, which will not sear

your pale skin. Stay close to me. Come, set your foot here."

15.

Now a stone margin as cool as it was hard

sped us smoothly forth, plumes of steam making a shade
the flurries of garish flame couldn't penetrate.
Like those on coastal Flanders, where the desolate
chaos of winter surge is kept at bay by dikes –
or as along the Brenta, where that torrent aches
to warm its freezing body at each firelit inn –
so here two solid bulwarks hemmed the red swirl in.
The edge of the wood we'd left had fined to nothing
when we came upon a troop of souls, all gazing
our way (as, at twilight, an adventurer peers
at indistinct figures when the moon's spine appears
in lilac sky) and knitting their brows like an old

tailor threading a needle's eye. A voice then called,
tugging at my sleeve. "What wonder," it cried, "is this?"
I turned to the speaker, fixing my eyes on his
features baked as brown as a handsome Bedouin
and striving to view the soul through the craggy skin.
"Dear Brunetto," I whispered, my hand at his face,
"is it *you... here*?" "My boy," he said, "I'll ease my pace
if it pleases, the caravan can struggle on
and I'll walk a while at your side." "But let's sit down,"
I urged, "and talk. My heart could wish for nothing more."
"If any of our herd," he replied, "lingers for
so much as an instant, he gets a century

of celestial snow playing on his body
with both hands tied. So let's move together, and there'll
be time to join my tribe and their protracted wail."
I went with bowed head like one who does reverence,
for I feared to step off the dike. "What weird events,"
Latini began, "bring you here before your
ultimate breath, and who is your navigator?"
"Up there," I answered, "where the days are calm and clear,
I awoke in the black vale of my midmost year.
I sauntered up out of it yesterday morning...
he appeared as if from thin air as I was running
back to its embrace, and now leads me home by this

dubious passage." "The port will be glorious,"
he said, "if you set your course by the heart's pole-star.
On earth, where beauty's essence breathes and moves, I saw
all of this... how the constellations wrought your good,
and had death not taken me from you when it did
I could have better prepared you for the great work.
Your days' regal face is clear as a watermark
in a note raised to the light, so hear me out.
That slave-race whose mind pulsates with envy and hate –
vermin ever, despite their wealth and urban airs –
is your natural enemy; and with ample cause,
for the sweet fig and bitter sorb are mismatched trees.

They'll loathe you as a blinded man loathes one who sees,
greedy and resentful as their reputation
has them. Keep yourself apart from the contagion
of their ways, for a time will come when every side
will want a piece of you... the mad goat, though, is tied
and cannot reach the grass. Let the degenerate
be each other's fodder, while the inviolate
acacia in which true treasures of empire glow –
if such a plant can yet find sustenance to grow –
builds its radiance on the scrapheap of the world."
He paused briefly, and I spoke. "Were my prayers fulfilled,
Brunetto, you would not be exiled from the joy

man is meant for. You taught when I was just a boy
(your fatherly face still smiles within me, and now
the dear image leaps from my head to my heart) how
we may, whilst caught in time, make ourselves eternal...
and for *that* my tongue will tell how much I'm grateful,
so long as it lives. Your vision of my future
I jot and keep for one who – if I ever reach her –
shall elucidate all the prophecies I've heard;
but my conscience is clear, and what's more I'm prepared
for anything Fortune has in store. Such dark talk
I have become quite accustomed to on this walk,
so let her spin her wheel as the yokel child

his top." At that the maestro turned sideways and smiled,
regarding me. "He listens well," he said, as though
to himself, "and makes good notes." Meanwhile, Brunetto
and I spoke on. "Which of the nomads," I asked then,
"you were with when we first saw you are worthy men?"
"There are a few among them," he said. "For the rest,
considering the little time we have, it's best
I keep silent. Suffice to say that they were all
habitués of that metropolis some call
Sodom, an immortal city reborn from fire
whenever a people succumb to strange desire –
for union without love, coldblooded intercourse

warmed by exotic drugs, for the taking by force
what must be shared in joy, or for tasting the more
or less than human (the plastic mob at Lot's door,
baying for angel flesh) – and every perversity
flaunts what it's got. Both church and university
make generous contributions to this starry crowd;
I'd gladly elaborate, but a svelte dust-cloud
approaches like a wraith... beneath it drum the feet
of some it'd be catastrophic I should meet.
All that was truest in me survives in my book,
so treasure it as you would a living soul. Look
to the jewelled skies." He turned and ran from me,

and his stride seemed not so much defeat as victory.

16.

Soon we came to where the almighty resonance

of headlong waters – a sound like the measured dance
droning deep within a hive – declared that the pit's
horrendous brink was near. Seeing us, three spirits
detached themselves from a group battling through the rain
and sped our way. "A figure," they cried, "this urbane
surely has to be from our own vibrant city!"
The thought of their appearance fills me with pity
still, for the burn marks that graffitied their skin
were layered like scrawls on the door of a latrine.
Turning to me, unperturbed, my teacher spoke. "Wait,"
he said. "With these men we must be considerate,
courteous. Were it not, in fact, for the luminous

snow – the expression of the place's genius –
I'd say that haste was less needful for them than you."
By now they had arrived, and, just as wrestlers do
before a fight takes hold – stripped and oiled and twitching
and hungry for the first chance – they started circling
round us at the steady pace of a pagan chant,
their legs ever-prowling but their six eyes intent
on mine. "Though," one said, "this wide misery of sand
and these brows ravaged and spectacularly tanned
cast derision on us and on our desert prayers,
say – for our reputations' sake – who is it dares
trespass with light feet in the leaden underworld?

He in whose tracks I step, his blisters' blisters peeled,
was as good in counsel as he was with a sword –
Guidoguerra is the name to which he answered.
I am Jacopo Rusticucci, and the third
whirling Arab's Tegghiaio… a voice unheard
when it lived and unheard now. My shrew of a wife,
mark you, condemned me to this zone of endless strife."
I was ready right then to jump down, and merely
the thought of the blizzard and my own skin stopped me –
to leap in their midst and fling my arms around them,
and I think that healer and guide in his wisdom
would have let it be; yet desire was checked by fear,

and so I spoke instead. "The instant my emir
hinted," I began, "that the approaching shadows
were men such as you, not derision but sorrow's
leechlike mouth battened on my hot and restless heart…
impossible to dislodge as the winged boy's dart.
I'm also an inhabitant of that city,
and your stories and renown are known to me
like a drawing you trace and then feel it is your own;
bitterness is behind me, but I must go down
to the world's utmost centre and touch the black sun –
or thus declares my punctilious companion –
before the unearthly fruit of bliss can be mine."

"Long may your spirit lighten you, your grave limbs shine,"
he replied, "and when they fade let fame travel on.
Though tell us… does it still breathe or is it now gone,
the valour that in our day somehow yet endured?
For there's a new arrival in our barren horde
whose grim report inclines us to suspect the worst."
Hearing that, I raised my face to the skies and cursed.
"Usurpers and degenerates," I cried, "you've bred
such excess, such vulgarity, that even dead
souls can scent your fool's gold and your fool's arrogance!"
The three glanced at each other, much as men will glance
when the truth is revealed and nothing can be said

or need be. "If in hard times to come," they added,
"you can face interrogation at such small cost,
count yourself blessed. And when you steal out of this vast
and shadow-barred dungeon, feet on the earth once more
and your head buried deep in the sung stars' wonder –
when the simple notion *There I was* will be
the sweetest thing, knowing that hell's eternity
is behind you forever – speak of us then." They whirred
away, legs swift as the arms of a hummingbird,
and before you could say Amen we were alone –
pressing on again to where the waters intone
their roaring silence, a place we shall scarcely hear

each other think. Now calamitous falls drew near
(like those of the river which is first to strike east
from Monte Veso to the Adriatic coast –
called Acquacheta in the heights, the 'silent stream',
before it descends to men and outgrows that name –
whose broken reverberation batters the ear
by San Benedetto, an aqueous thunder
consequent on its taking in one immense leap
a thousand-stepped staircase of stone) where down the steep
slope the dark onslaught wheeled its limbs in sudden air.
There was a little belt or cord I used to wear,
and with which I had once intended to garrotte

the leopard in her hooker's coat; tying a knot
in its length and handing it to the maestro –
when a priest of Ceres says "do this," one does so –
I watched as his sturdy arm swung it round, then hurled
it far into the fathomless depth of that world
we had still to sound. "A sign," I mused, silently,
the words formed in my mind, "that's followed by the eye
this closely, this intently, must herald things new
and strange." Ah, stay on your guard around all those who
can read not just externals but the thought within!
"What I'm looking for," he said, "and what you imagine,
will surface any moment now… something only

dreamt shall become something seen." They say you should be
cautious when a truth is so inconceivable –
less like plain fact than myth, hence unbelievable
in most men's eyes – that the blind crowd will claim you lie;
yet here I must recite or sing my comedy,
in the hope its uneasy music's built to last,
and thus I swear, friend, that what I saw rising fast
through an air as dense and black as the North Sea's dregs –
like the diver who returns, fluttering his legs,
from his risky task at a rig's forested base
and a weak light begins to show his upraised face –
was a figure so marvellous that the hardest

heart would tremble in the high castle of its chest.

17.

"See," my pale duke cried, "the beast with the venomed tail,

for whom a mountain range is no barrier at all.
No wall can keep him out, no missile wound him…
see the subtle one whose diabolical scheme,
honed over centuries, now ensnares the whole world!"
Having reached our stone causeway's end, Virgil signalled
to that living image of fraud to come ashore;
at which the risen thing beached head and chest, the lure
of its agile stinger still pulsing in the dark,
and showed a face like the face of a patriarch
benevolent and just – or so, in its gracious
outer aspect, it seems. It held on with vicious
claws attached to arms that were tensed their hairy length,

and its scaled torso rippled with a python's strength.
Along the huge bulk there shone and danced a pattern
like the ones which wise village crones in Pakistan
weave into life (and yet, somehow, surpassing those
with the magic of its weird tones lit like windows)
or the lurid web transfigured Arachne shapes
in planetary skies. Like tide-stranded ships,
their sterns buoyed by water but their prows sunk in sand –
or the beaver who squats on the riverbank and
flicks his cunning tail in the clean current below –
so this repulsive prodigy rests a suave elbow
on the marble rim that edges the Sahara

of fire. The face was calm but the tail aquiver,
continually arching so its pointed tip
reared scorpion-style. "Now," my guide said, "we must step
to the right, as far as the steed which awaits us here."
Just ten paces upon the verge, keeping well clear
of the incandescent sands, took us to the spot
where the reptile beamed; beyond it appeared to squat
yet more desert dwellers near the dunes' ruled brink.
"To complete your knowledge of this circle, I think
you need to take a close look at that shifty tribe.
Consider their condition, the distinctive garb.
Though keep any talk brief," he added, "and meanwhile

I'll endeavour to parley with this creature. We'll
have to use his strong shoulders if we're to proceed."
And so I went alone along the unsullied
margin of round seven, where that miserable
troop fretted like flies on a dazzling white table.
No one spoke and yet their eyes left nothing unsaid,
as they turned and tossed like a child whose fever bed
is sharper in its softness than a nail; their hands
moved perpetually, now cushioning the sands
and now as though pulling an imaginary sheet
over supine heads, like the dog whose savage feet
spend whole summer days in hot pursuit of fleas

they never quite reach. Not a single one of these
faces in the whirl of incendiary snow
was known to me, as if somehow they possessed no
distinct identity, but then I saw each wore
around his neck a pouch of specific colour
and odd design. One portrayed an azure lion
on a yellow ground, and another was crimson
emblazoned with the virginal form of a goose
(a place is saved for a philanthropist whose gaze
shall feast upon a red shield and the bird set there).
A man tagged with a smiling sow, seeing me near,
bestirred himself and spoke. "Young intruder," he whined,

"go back to the house of breath. Many of my kind
continue death's vital work in the midst of life,
fastened on the golden sun." He gaped as to laugh,
but out came a tongue as gigantic as a cow's
with which he wiped his eyes and mopped his sweating brows
and licked deep into his nose. So I turn away –
revolted, yet also for fear a longer stay
would anger the one who had told me to be quick –
and hurry back to where that utter lunatic
is perched upon the anaconda's rainbow bulk.
"There are," he shouted, "no more stairs by which to walk.
Be intrepid now. It is time to take the snake

into crueller seas. Here, climb on our flying ark.
Sit in front of me and I'll shield you from the sting…
the sole way home is this demon's downward circling."
Like a man so near an ague's re-recurrence
that his nails are blue and he shudders all at once
at the mere sight of shade, the maestro's dark command
made my every bone quake; though somehow, as the hand
of a true king quietens his massed and nervy men,
his presence (and my own shame) steadied me again.
When I was aboard, I tried to say "hold me tight"
and yet – as a fiend-hunted dreamer slurs at night
the urgent word he meant to cry out loud – my tongue

but groaned in the close room of my mouth; as among
other perils, however, dear Virgil almost
seemed to read my mind, clasping me as just the ghost
of a poet can. "*Move*, Geryon! Off we go…
and let your descent be both gradual and slow,
for you bear the strange freight of a bodily soul."
Manoeuvring careful as a jet-strewn vessel,
Geryon reversed away from the shore until
he felt himself in clear air then turned so his tail
stretched and wriggled eel-like near where that head had been;
his paws, meanwhile, beat at the black empyrean,
and I felt as great a dread as Apollo's son

when he lost control of the spacecraft of the sun
or Icarus when the beeswax began to run.
Spiralling and deepening the monster swam on,
and nothing could be seen to determine how fast
we travelled (though the chill wind said our speed was vast).
After some seconds or eras had passed, I saw
beneath us fires like city lights and heard the roar
of wails and waters interlaced; my fear grew more,
but now – as the weary bird, when the falconer
whistles, wheels its disdainful way down through the sky
then stands in the next meadow, staring moodily –
our dragon landed by a cliff of jagged stone

and, unburdened of my heart, kicked once and was gone.

18.

There's a place in the blaze I shall call Hell's Trenches,

and the diorite wall which encircles it is
a polished grey variegated with rust-red flecks
(the same obdurate matter the entire complex
was sculpted from, though with what tool no man can guess).
In the centre of this space there glares an abyss
whose inner structure will be detailed in due course,
and between that evil void and the stupendous
rockface, the cliff where we'd been shaken off like fleas,
you've a belt divided into ten great valleys.
As a sacrosanct castle which with concentric
rings of golden water guards its hoarded magic,
the form of a mandala when seen from the sky,

so this terraced chasm presented to the eye
a ground plan that looked intelligently designed –
and as such fortresses beyond the north wind
have bridges that link them to the fallen world of men,
from where we now stood to the whirlpool's heart there ran
high ridges of raised stone. Resuming our leftward way,
we beheld in the trench to our right a melee
of all-new scourgers, all-new anguish, all-new pain
as densely crammed as the worn furrows of a brain
are with trudging thoughts; the souls were stripped quite bare,
approaching us on this side with the haggard stare
of office-goers in a February dawn,

whilst crowds in the far lane flowed the same direction
as we did although with more rapid, stranger strides
(a double line of metal barricades divides
the road, I recall, much the same as the ones they
put up in the city streets on carnival day).
Upon the ledge of tomb-dark rock, antlered demons
were stalking and lashing out with whips and truncheons
if ever a commuter dared to ease his pace…
and how a single touch made those spectral feet race!
Suddenly in the midst of the swift throng I see
a pair of brown eyes that are momentarily
fixed on mine, and I slow my step to follow up

this flash of recognition. My guide let me stop,
even let me retrace my way a little bit
to peer at that harried soul of whom you might spit
here's a face which makes the mind practically gag.
By now – as a woman pretends to search her bag
to avoid being seen by someone she once knew –
he walked with a frowning, lowered gaze. "I *see* you,"
I cried out. "What brought you into this human sauce,
and such an extremely pungent one that tears course
down your cheeks? You're Venedico, if I'm not wrong."
"I despise speech," he said, "but your clear dialect
revives the memory of a world as perfect

as a bowl of a master potter of the Song.
I am the procurer, or so the story goes,
who induced Ghisolabella to arch her toes
above whatever marquis felt a need for her…
there are numerous more of my fellow pimps here,
who laboured to feed their undying thirst for cash
by means of such trysts, such illicit love." A lash
of a dispassionate whip then silenced those lips,
and my tender guide and I advanced several steps
to where a kind of stone spoke or goddess-hewn bridge
protruded out from our austere Egyptian ledge;
scrambling up with dextrous feet, we made a right turn

and left these spirals of the eternal return
behind us. Near the bridge's centre, where the arch
gapes like a black and reeking cave behind a beach,
the maestro paused. "Wait," he said. "You can see from there
the ill-conceived faces of the spirits which were
flowing next to us when we strolled the circle's edge" –
and so we stood and watched the devil-goaded surge,
passing unrelenting as a train packed with coal.
"Look," he suddenly whispered, "at that noble soul
who doesn't shed a tear in spite of all he feels,
a king among men. This is Jason, he whose wiles
and wise heart discovered or created a way

to the golden fleece of which there are some might say
its light is the light of the spiritual sun.
When he docked at the isle of Lemnos, everyone –
or, to be precise, all those with balls – had been killed
by the flabby, pitiless and perversely willed
women of the place; a certain Hypsipyle
had hidden her old father from that butchery,
and Jason with his twinkling eyes and tricked-out speech
duped the duper and left her sown and in the lurch…
this tableau is expressive of his sense of guilt,
subsumed now in a torrent of those who have dealt
in romance as in cattle or costly goods. So

much for trench one of the towering inferno,
and the souls its granite jaw munches tenderly.
As always, though, penance and crime match exactly."
We'd now reached the spot where our razor's edge of stone
arched a second time, and heard from trench two a moan
as of self-hating pigs (if you can imagine
such a stupid thing). The steep sides were covered in
a mildew loathsome to the nose as to the eye,
which seemed the excrescence of the bestial sigh
breathed from beneath, and were moreover cut so deep –
just as a feeble yet inexorable drip
wears a groove in a cave's unassailable rock –

that you had to mount the arch and then crane your neck
to view them; you could also see, upon that bridge,
that the moat below was awash with raw sewage
through which more gentlefolk were struggling to proceed
as if running late. Peering into the filth, I spied
a man whose head was as populous with turds
as, in April, pondside stones crawl with swollen toads;
close to this monstrosity, sunk by his own tongue,
a bent hag apart from the hurrying throng
stood and then squatted then stood but to squat again
and scratched with shit-encrusted nails. "That vestal virgin,"
my guide said, "was once the pert, exquisite Thais.

Come. Such sights taint the living waters of your eyes."

19.

All those degenerate enough to be fooled

into thinking potency can be bought for gold,
as if the highest things were a sordid affair,
are the subject of my trumpet's next fanfare.
I was now at the third gutter or seething tomb,
marvelling again at how an unsurpassed wisdom
manifests itself in the tectonics of the blaze
as much as on earth and through Love's palatial skies –
and wondering too at His evenhandedness.
The moat's floor and sides were riddled with numberless
zeros cleanly cut in the drill-blunting stone,
and all an identical size and every one
more perfect a circle than is made on a pond

by touches of rain (the time a child nearly drowned
beneath my beautiful San Giovanni's dome
and I broke him out and sent a living boy home
instead of a corpse, and some said I'd a hoodlum soul,
it was from inside exactly such a hole).
At each burrow entrance there showed, like twin serpents,
a pair of legs writhing with dreadful violence
on account of the fact that their soles were alight
with quavering flames. "See that creature, neophyte,
who burns with redder-looking fire than his fellows" –
here spoke the maestro who inevitably knows
the words the heart frames before my mouth calls them out,

his will being my own – "and whose feet thrash about
with a matching wildness... if you let me bear you
down this slope you can ask his name, his crime's name too."
And so we stalked into trench number four, turning
anticlockwise like some peculiar being
both flesh and ghost, until we came to the O where
those eloquently frantic legs signed their despair.
"Unhappy soul, wedged like a paling," I began,
"tell me who you are. Speak as clearly as you can,
if that upended stance with your taproots higher
hasn't filled your mouth with dirt." There I stood, a friar
hearing last confession from an assassin

buried with his head downward as befits his sin –
he keeps on calling the patient brother back
in hope of delaying the shark-eyed worms' attack –
when these words echoed from the dark. "Boniface," they cried,
"*already*? It's *you*? In that case, the codex lied…
the moment of your reckoning is years away,
or so it's written; are you sated with your prey,
the adorable bride you took by guile and force,
seeking your appointed well before your hour's
come?" I was dumb as a man a gang of youths mock,
who cannot respond since he doesn't get the joke
their flagrant slang conceals. "Tell him," ordered Virgil,

"you're not the man he thinks you are." I did his will,
at which that soul made a double helix of its legs
and replied with the air of a gipsy who begs
in littered streets. "What, then, do you want from me?
If you're so curious as to my identity
that you've dived to this hole to ask it, you should know
I was one that received the immantatio;
but who, being less polar swan than drooling bear,
stashed away earth's wealth as if I was God's banker
and for which I find myself stashed here. Each fissure
below my brow holds in stillness another
of our kind, a depth to which I'll myself descend

when the pope I took you for meets his fated end
and stands unrobed. His time, though, will pass more swiftly –
planted with his feet pointing upward as the tree
of the soul plummets far and spans the seven worlds –
for after him shall come a shepherd from the wilds
whose lawlessness and rancour will outdo us both
in villainy, a pontiff like that priest whose oath
was sworn with three hundred and sixty silver tongues."
"Remind me," I said then. "How many precious things
did Peter have to buy our Lord before the key
to light was granted him? Surely *Walk beside me*
is the sole demand, nor was Peter paid in gold" –

there are some might allege my tone was overbold –
"by the one who took the place of perfidious
Judas. Stay where you are then, there where a righteous
judgement has logged you like a virus in a tube;
only reverence for that celestial Chubb
you once had the authority to open and close
restrains me from using stronger words than those.
The joyful earth is dragged down by such avarice,
trampling what's noble and ennobling those whose vice
chimes with yours. When John the Divine spoke of the whore's
slow fornication with our supposed rulers,
an intoxicating wine that goes to weak heads,

he surely also had in mind the lowborn heads
of a mercenary church… the god you worship
is a golem of gold, for you and the rapt sheep
circling in obeisance to the sleek, flashing calf
are of one kind." I heard at my side a delighted laugh,
and all the while those bright feet moved as if in time –
conscience-stung, perhaps – to the rhythm and the rhyme.
Now my sweet guide takes me in his arms once more,
bearing me up that bank that seemed like a seashore
quivering with eels, and doesn't stop till we reach
the precipitous summit of the next arch
where even the nimblest goat would slip before long.

From there I look out on yet more substance for our song.

20.

New horror and new pain is but fuel for new verse,

the matter of this twentieth section of the first
part of my opus – the path of the descent.
Once set upon that bridge, my brain was wholly bent
on discerning the tear-carved riverbed below…
a solemn procession paced its great curve, as slow
as the prayers that life's grievous congregation drones,
each figure more twisted than those children whose moans
arise from wheelchairs as if anguished by His light;
heads wrenched round, they went in the direction of their sight
with the awkward gait of a film as it rewinds.
O you who weigh this book – *Mystes* – you whose mind's
translucent cells would turn mere dust to liquid gold,

imagine just how difficult it was to hold
my tears back on seeing men whose backs ran with tears
that sped down the cleft where, like stars-scanning builders,
the upper region of their phantom arsecheeks showed –
and indeed I wept, clinging to the fractured road
of adamantine stone. "Only fools," my guide said,
"snivel and sniff at this… true piety is dead
to pangs of compassion for such a warped parade,
and who more reprehensible than him who's made
justice subject to his sentimental notion
of wrong and right? Lift up your brow and see the one
for whom the very soil once gaped its toothy mouth,

Amphiaraus whose catastrophic journey south
ended in Minos's mockery of a court
(*but why in such a rush*, he heard the Thebans shout
as a sudden darkness said the game was over).
Because it was his faithless wish to discover
what time's clemency conceals, his head is reversed
and he goes that way too. There's Tiresias, cursed
with the feminisation of his every part,
who, before he could be man again, had to part
those amorously twining snakes a second time;
the creature whose forward buttocks nudge against him
is Aruns, dweller in a hill-cave where the white

marble awaits the sculptor's penetrating sight,
who could see from that bare room the sea and the stars
enunciate the endlessness of the universe;
as for the woman whose breasts are veiled by hair,
a double modesty as they now swing behind her,
she's one who after searching throughout the earth
came to and settled in the region of my birth...
Manto is her name, and I'll speak of her a while.
After her father's death she roamed far, an exile
from the submissive city of the god of wine,
eventually landing where a rugged line
of snow-quilted mountains separates the Tyrol

of Austria and Italy the beautiful;
at the foot of those heights is a lake called Benaco,
its aqueous body shadowy and slow
yet bathing by means of ten thousand hidden springs
the valleys below, with a chapel (where the blessings
of three bishops go) on an island in its midst.
A fine-proportioned fortress commands the lowest
point of the shore, where level water starts to flow
and in the act of falling forms a blue furrow
charging with succulence the fields it divides –
a river that soon finds a plain and once more spreads
to marshes where the fever flies and no birds sing,

inside which the prophetess as she roved along
discovered space to live alone and wield her arts.
When she died and the soul flew and her mortal parts
lay upon the earth like a puppet with cut string,
men gathered on that spot the bounding fen made strong
and built with those bones the foundations of a town;
this was Mantua's origin, and if some clown
ever tries to sell you a different story
know it's not the truth of myth but mere history."
"Your account, maestro," I replied, "takes hold of me
in such a way that any other voice would be –
by its heat and light – the cold remnants of a fire

the flame has fled. Indulge my one-track mind's desire,
and tell me if amongst those who pass below
are any who are worthy or of whom I should know."
"See the man," he said then, "whose voluminous beard
cloaks his brown back? When Grecian strength had disappeared
to sack Troy – fewer boys were born, it even seemed –
he is the priest who with bird-wise Calchas deemed
it was time for the zealous fleet to cut its cords
and sail… Eurypylus was his name, as the words
of my own sublime tale may have told you before
(a rare edition stored in the depths of a mirror).
Next in this supernal sequence is Michael Scot,

chief astrologer at the second Frederick's court
and accomplished in the magic by which men rule;
behind him's Guido Bonatti, another who'll
allege he is a guide to the upper waters,
and that soul there's the one who renounced a cobbler's
exalted task to squint at the stitching of men's hands;
further back, see hordes of crones like gipsy bands…
the women who left their weaving to work evil
with image and plucked herb. But come, the moon was full
last night – remember how it spared you in the wood –
and now its malevolent presence slides westward
and kisses the ocean of ink beyond Seville."

And so we journeyed on, our talk unstoppable.

21.

We pass from stony bridge to bridge, speaking of things

other than those which my comic opera sings,
and have soon reached a new granite apex from where
we can peer down into the next grim fissure.
You might say what we saw was what we could not see,
being a black seam that absorbed light entirely;
it made me think of the Venetian arsenal
and how, in the sullen depth of winter, men boil
a viscous pitch with which to caulk their unsound ships –
for, the roiling seas unnavigable, one slaps
on pungent tar to seal a voyage-battered hull
as another crafts a fresh boat by sheer force of will,
and yet another hammers at his vessel's prow

whilst hollering to them who labour down below,
and someone turns trees into oars with graceful lines,
and faded sails are patched, and a nut-faced man twines
the dependable rope – except that this pitch
was heated not by human fire but that fire which
burns earthward from above and is art and is divine.
When I say I saw it, then, what I really mean
is that I saw the bubbles that crowed within it,
the mass subsiding and swelling with a surfeit
of poison air; as I gazed in fascination,
my guide gave a sudden cry and I turned like one
who as he flees in terror cannot help but stare

back at the face of the ever-gaining monster
his own dark contrives – turned just to see a devil
come darting up the ridge with a look of evil,
his bat's wings spread wide and his whole demeanour foul.
On the outcrop of his shoulder, a human soul
was pierced through and slung from the tendons of its feet. "A
plaything, Hiddenclaws, an elder of Saint Zita" –
this was the unforeseen horror of his voice –
"to dunk in the sweet water with your other toys…
meanwhile I'll revisit the world's well-stocked cities
where one's marked for high office by proclivities
of the lowest sort, where a No is turned to Yes

and white to black by the injection of such riches
as riches breed, where moneylenders rule the roost
whatever lackey wears the crown." With that, he cursed
and flung his burden down; then, much as a loosed
mastiff pursues a thief, sped off in drooling haste.
The sinner first sank then his rear end reappeared,
at which the demons crowded at the bridge all jeered.
"Be advised not to flash the Holy Face again!
Here it's a distinctly different regimen
from days in the glass of the idling Serchio;
unless you'd like to taste our ire, in fact, don't show
one single hair above the surface of the tar…

now you have to dance, little man, underwater
and pilfer and embezzle out of heaven's sight."
As chefs have sweaty minions prod the broiling meat
in order that each morsel is completely cooked,
so there rained an avid swarm of a hundred hooked
and thrusting spears. "Conceal yourself behind this shard,"
the maestro said, "and wait and do not be afraid
whatever verbal filth they hurl. I know the way
these things work, and how to pass unscathed through a fray
of weaponized words." He leapt onto the far shore,
and the second his toes touched the ground an uproar
as of a pack of stray dogs spotting a vagrant

arose from beneath the arch, and in an instant
they were round him with barbed prongs bristling in his face
(his features serene as one that fear can't menace,
as though there was no place in him for death to strike).
"This," my guide began, "is impressively warlike.
Before you have me flipping like a fish on a fork,
team, somebody needs to step forth and hear me talk…
then you'll decide whether or not to skewer me."
The crowd slunk off slower than it had formed, and he
was alone with the demon I call Baleful Tail.
"Do you really think," he asked, "we've got through all
the ingenious defences hell can devise

without it being willed within the diamond skies
that I show this path to a star pupil of mine?"
You should have seen the speed at which that proud grin
fell, scarcely less fast than his weapon clattered down
at his repulsive feet ("we mustn't poke this one,"
he called to the dense and encircling dark). "Come out
from behind the rocks," said the maestro with a shout,
"where I know you've been watching and shaking like a leaf.
It's safe to come back to my side. I'm still alive" –
this was his idea of a joke, I suppose.
As soon as I revealed myself, countless shadows
crept forward as if night's essence had taken form –

I couldn't help but think of the tentative swarm
of soldiers I once saw emerge from Caprona
under guard – and gazed at me greedily, a lone
wisp of love's breath in death's empire of stone; not once
turning away from that manifold violence,
I drew my body closer to my thin white duke's
upright side. They seemed to impale me on their looks,
and I heard one say "he needs to feel my joystick"
then another voice mutter "indeed… do it quick" –
yet now the demon that my lord had spoken with
spun around and flourished his illustrious teeth
and all were quiet. Turning back to us, Baleful Tail –

his manner of speech now elegant and gentle –
deigned to give us some advice. "The sixth arch," he said,
"is impassable, a ruin, but further ahead
as you tread this chipped spine of rock is another
place you'll get across (yesterday, at the hour
of noon, it was twelve hundred and sixty-six years
since the quake that stunned the gulfs and the topmost stars
wrecked our road). A few of my lads are bound that way,
to ensure we have no furtive gasps or horseplay
in the lanes. Go with them, trust in their innocence.
Come here, Hurler – Carnal Noise – and you there, Dogbonce –
Palescale – Mingewig, you direct the squad – and dear

Robberfly, go too – and good Sir Pig and King Leer –
devout Red Peril – Lovegash – do a quick circuit
of the tar, then guide them safe to the next exit
where the unshattered ridge leads clear across our deeps."
"Look, maestro," I whispered, "at how they lick their lips
and make obscure threats with the twitchings of their brows;
one wary as you are – one who, moreover, knows
the route through the dark – will surely share my instinct
that we should go alone." "Relax," he said, and winked.
"All that's in your head, and those fangs in any case
are saved for those who swim." Like horses in a race,
the fiends were now jostling for the signal to start

(this being, when it came, a sudden thunderous fart).

22.

I have seen in my mind's eye the noble cavaliers

break camp in winter dawn and leave their dying fires
to mount a swift attack on the regicide's men,
and I've seen less than half of them ride back again;
I've known the silent progress of scouts through the land,
the tumult of a raid or a tournament, and
bells and silver bugles outrageous on the air;
faint tattoos have shaken the red drum of my ear
as I watched an astral castle blinking at dusk;
I have witnessed human warships, seen strange ships whisk
defter than thought through the labyrinthine stars,
but never before then a mighty note from an arse
announcing the commencement of a charge. It was,

you could say, peculiar company ("in dive bars
with the boozers and with bluebloods in the palace").
My attention was fully given to the surface
of the light-hoarding tar, for I meant to see
those who kicked within it and understand completely
the nature of this turbulent moat; like dolphins
telling with their leaps of approaching hurricanes,
so every now and then the grossly blistered flesh
of a back would appear and quick as a flash
hide itself once more in that opaque element –
and, as half-submerged frogs vanish the moment
the pond is approached, whole island-chains of faces

slipped down into those black and belching waters
as soon as they saw Mingewig's curled head loom. It still
disturbs me to think of one who waited until
the last second to dive and waited just too long,
for out shot Robberfly's undeviating prong
and lifted him sleek as an otter on a spear.
"Let Red Peril flay him! Cousin, flick him over here" –
that was the baying chorus of the demonic crew
whose preposterous titles I by now knew –
"and he'll catch him on a claw!" "Who," I asked, "is this
wretch who's fallen into the enemy's clutches?"
The good maestro approached him, and, reaching his side,

enquired where he was from. "Navarre," the swimmer sighed,
"sired by a waster and apprenticed to a lord
when my father's lavish means and weak blood conspired
to place him in an early grave; then, in Thibault's
lyric court, I dedicated myself to those
manipulations for which I now pay the price."
This tale was interrupted by a vicious slice
from Sir Pig's spiral tusks, which were sharp as a boar's
(the mouse's guts are strings for the cat's strumming claws!).
Mingewig then grasped him with a single massive arm,
shouting to his comrades to do the soul no harm
so long as it was held. "If there's more you would know,"

he said, turning the slit of his face to the maestro,
"you'd better hurry up, before the dismantling
of this gibbon ends his ability to sing."
"Tell us," resumed my fearless duke, "of your fellow
divers – any Italians here?" "Moments ago,"
he said, "I saw one from that neck of the woods...
ah, would I was submerged and safe from these lizards,
from their unholy stabbing, the talons that grip
and tear!" "Enough!" yelled Lovegash, biting off a strip
of ghost-meat the shade of a foetus in a jar;
Palescale grabbed his legs, at which point a wicked stare
from the general restored some semblance of order.

Not tardy to take this sudden chance, my leader
put another question to the man who now eyed
his grey interior. "Him I saw," he replied,
"was Gomita of Gallura... sly as a submarine,
one of those 'advisors' who are rarely seen
and whose discretion statesmen buy with borrowed cash;
it's people like him who weave the reverent hush
around those who rule. A certain Michael Zanche's
down there too, and harping on Sardinian cheese
is pretty much all those two do. I'm more concerned
with the way that devil's pointed head is turned...
I could tell you more but I sense my poor hide's due

for a scratch." (Here the general turned to King Leer, who
had narrowed his eyes as in readiness to peck.
"Keep back," he snarled, "or I'll wring your filthy neck!")
"If," that trembling thing went on, "you desire to see
a Tuscan or a Lombard, a man such as me
merely has to whistle thrice and nine shall hop ashore…
but this platoon of reptiles needs to stand off, or
no soul will approach us for fear that there'll be blood."
Dogbonce gave an almighty shake where he stood,
and cried – his voice a half-articulate yowl – "how
he plots to work his wiles, to nip back down below!"
"Cunning is my modus operandi," replied

that kings' cold consultant who in his time had tied
so many snares, procuring such unhappiness
for his fellow men (wise solely in the ruses
whereby finance reigns). "Then go," Hurler butted in,
"and I'll be right behind you… not riding the din
of black hooves but skimming, swallow-style, the very
face of the brook. We'll turn our backs and *then* we'll see
whether you're a match for the Hiddenclaws." Reader,
the game was on! Reluctantly, the troop's leader
looked away and the other dragons followed suit;
his timing exquisite, the frogman set his feet
at the ledge and kicked off with a terrific leap

into the tar where the flow is dark and deep
("I *have* you," Hurler roared, yet if we run on fear
what wings can compete?). The spirit had gone under –
his assailant at the last moment banking hard
as an infuriated hawk when the mallard
dives – and, the second that he vanished, Carnal Noise
hit Hurler at full tilt… those fiends locked close as boys
tussling in a blur, then in the pitch with legs kicking
like houseflies on a sticky strip. Wildly barking,
Mingewig sent half his gang to the other shore
and all held out their prongs as sailors reach an oar
to a drowning man. They were by now well-cooked, I think,

and we hastened off and left them in the drink.

23.

Like two itinerant monks we resumed our way,

silent and unaccompanied, the fiends' affray
having turned my mind to Aesop and that tall tale
of frog and mouse (the cases seem identical,
or at least as akin as *This Instant* and *Now*);
then, thought succeeding thought like gremlins in a row,
from this one's open mouth another idea
clambered out and gave new life to my former fear.
The Hiddenclaws, it said, were tricked because of us
and made to look like fools and must be furious
and are more than likely already on our scent
driven by their monstrous will, brutal and intent
as a grinning dog as it closes on a hare –

here I peered over my shoulder, each trembling hair
on my head standing upright and doing the same.
"Maestro," I whispered, resisting the urge to scream,
"dread of the Hiddenclaws has taken hold of me.
Listen… they approach. Let's conceal ourselves, and quickly!"
"I am an insubstantial mirror," he replied,
"imaging within itself the face that would hide
behind your face of flesh; those terrors you just had
grimaced at me too, their appearance as bad
as their gait was strange. If the bank's slope allows it,
we can slip into the next trench and so outwit
the fell pursuers our imagination paints."

Yet no imagined ogre quite slobbers and pants
like the ones I now saw nearing, malign wings spread
and claws all twitching as though hungry for a head
to grip with a grip that bites deep into the bone –
I tried to shout His name but made a stifled moan –
and suddenly the maestro had me in his arms
as a mother roused by the silken throb of flames
bundles up her sleeping child and races through the door
without even pausing to grab a shift to wear,
then launched himself from the ridge on which we stood
onto the next ditch's side. The chill glassy flood
as it accelerates to the watermill's wheel

is less swift than was that descent, as if an eel
carried me on its tense and muscular back...
then all was still again and I could see, looking back,
their silhouettes ranged along the diorite sill
beyond which threshold the inexorable will
of sky-high providence shall never let them pass.
We now found ourselves in yet another rocky pass,
among a crowd whose plucked and painted faces
somehow had the lassitude of one who paces
on like an automaton when his soul is dead;
they wore capacious cloaks and each figure's bowed head
was enveloped by a cowl like those of friars,

and these cloaks were pure gold but their interiors
were leaden as the tailored suit a traitor earns.
I hardly need to mention how our path now turns
leftward with the current of this lachrymose crew,
though because of their speed it happened that we drew
alongside new people with every step we took.
"Why not look around us," I asked my gentle duke,
"and see if there are any here whose deeds or name
we know?" Just then, a familiar accent came
warbling through the merciless twilight of the air.
"Less fast, less fast," it seemed to say. "In fact, wait there...
perhaps I'll satisfy your curiosity."

So we stop and we watch impetuosity
condemned to an excruciating crawl by the crowd,
as if it had been filmed and the footage slowed.
When the man and his companion caught up, they stared
wordlessly a while then conferred. "He's not undead,"
one said, "as can be seen by the pulse at his throat;
that aside, the fact that neither bears a greatcoat
suggests they have the privilege of travelling light."
"The dean of the college of the sad hypocrite" –
now he spoke to me – "requests that you tell him
who you are." "I was born," I answered, "near the stream
they call the Arno and in the eternal town

of Florence. The skin I came in is still my own –
but who are you, cheeks wet with the liquor of tears,
and what gleaming penance is it each spirit wears?"
"Our sunrise-coloured cloaks," one said, "are dusk within,
and so heavy I move less like man than machine.
We were members of the Convivial Brethren,
Loderingo his name and Catalano mine,
chosen by your city to settle the dispute
between Guelph and Ghibelline (the blackened and mute
stones in the Gardingo proclaim our scheme's success)."
I opened my mouth to condemn their wickedness,
yet suddenly caught sight of the prone, crucified

form of one who, as he saw me, flinched and then cried
through the crowning thicket of his beard. "That rapt soul,"
Catalano said, "was he who argued that a whole
people might be saved by a single sacrifice;
both he and his father-in-law, his accomplice,
and the rest of the grasping yet ill-starred council
are staked this way so that their naked limbs will feel –
as all pass over – the dead weight of every step."
The sight of this wise elder had made Virgil stop,
and now I watched him gaze and ponder silently.
"Do you know any gullies," he asked finally,
"by which we can exit the trench to the right

without necessitating angels of the night
to come and pluck us from these depths?" "A ridge," replied
Catalano, "runs straight across but at this side
is a shapeless pile of stones; one you two could climb,
being so singleminded and light of limb."
My noble leader stood a minute with bowed head,
brooding. "Then he gave us dubious advice," he said,
"that beast whose actions ape the true fisher of men."
"Deception is the devil's native acumen,
as I once heard a genuine Christian preach...
there's nowhere his lies and the lies they breed don't reach."
The maestro strode off, a rare anger in his face,

and I followed his footprints at a rapid pace.

24.

At that time you might call the nonage of the year,

when the sun retunes the golden strings of its hair
and the equinox slowly begins to draw near;
when on bare wood and hard field the frailer sister
of the blizzard imagines her kingdom of frost
(a publication which is destined not to last),
the cottager whose stores are running low steps out
and sees the black countryside apparelled in white,
striking his thigh and going back indoors to mope
or shout; but now he looks once more and regains hope
on finding that ghost-world's coloured in an hour,
and grasps a crook and drives his thin sheep to pasture...
so the maestro's pale countenance made me lose heart,

and just as promptly came an ointment for the hurt.
For, the second we reached the bridge's ruin,
he turned around and beamed as once on the mountain
then opened wide his arms like a loving father
and swept me up. Meanwhile, examining whether
the pile of grey and shattered granite could be dared –
to discriminate well is to be well prepared –
he hoisted me bodily towards a steady stone
whilst seeking another and yet another one
that would take my mortal weight. This was no ascent
for those whose outer glamour has them slowed and bent,
Virgil with his light foot and me with his shoving

scarcely able to climb, and it was just owing
to the fact this slope was far shorter than the last –
all ten of Hell's Trenches inclining to the vast
and gaping mouth of the final abyss – that I
was able by and by to clutch the topmost rock, my
lungs on fire and my sole desire to sit and rest.
"Get up... step from this sluggishness," the maestro hissed,
"like a soul from a corpse. A head stuffed with feathers
in the immaculate grave of a bed fathers
no fame, and one without an honourable name
leaves as much trace on earth as smoke in air or foam
on the face of the sea; stand and conquer your

exhaustion with the spirit that relishes war,
that wins every battle as long as a sense
of obscure guilt or of its own preeminence
cannot drag it down. An even longer staircase
waits to be scaled… it doesn't, I'm afraid, suffice
to have left those snakes behind. If you understand,
the time to move is *now*." I rose then, no spectral hand
assisting me, and with a show of more breath
than I truly had. "Go," I said, "I'm strong and death
holds no terrors," as if the words might make it so.
We took our way along the arch, which was narrow
and craggy and steeper than before, and as we went

I chattered like joggers do to prove they're not spent –
hearing which, a clenched and inarticulate moan
came from the trench below. Already on the crown
of the ridge that crossed it, I bent down and scanned the dark
with hungry eyes as though on the bridge of an ark;
the voice had spoken more in rage than grief,
yet no dove flew back into my head with news of life
or any news at all. The gulf was a blacker black
than a crow. "Up here, maestro," I said, "I lack
not just the ability to fathom that yelp
but also the power of sight. Wouldn't it help
if we crossed over to the next ellipse of stone,

then down the wall into the trench itself?" "It's done,"
he replied, preferring to act than idly prate,
and in a trice we stood in gutter number eight
and I was struck afresh by what the night contains.
It appeared that every snake in the vast domains
of Libya's glaring sands had congregated there,
both ones I recognised and ones whose markings were
signs and runes which but to pronounce would be to die…
even now, that strange script appals my memory.
I'd heard tales of the slant, elusive chelydri,
of phareae and chenchres, airborne jaculi
and amphisbaenae that dispute which way to slide,

yet neither Ethiopia nor the lands beside
the Red Sea can boast of a pestilence like this.
Hands tied behind with living ropes that reared to hiss
at their loins where head and tail were knotted tight,
men ran through this vivarium stripped and distraught
and without hope of bolthole or heliotrope
(the stone that's a cloaking device, like Siegfried's cape).
All of a sudden a small serpent sprang towards
one on our side of the trench, biting where the cords
of tendon and muscle fasten shoulder to head,
and never was an *I* or an *O* graffitied
so brisk as he was turned to ash by rampant flame;

then, as soon as it was spread on the ground, the dust came
together in the selfsame form he'd had before –
just as the eternal phoenix, consumed by fire,
reanimates the alien sapphire of its eyes
to rise once more and burn again and once more rise
(this is a bird, recall, that pecks no bread but feeds
on frankincense and healing balsam's tree-wept seeds,
and whose winding-sheet is a shroud or cloud of myrrh).
As a fallen man will leap back up and stare,
not knowing whether some dark force had pulled him down
or an unseen, unsuspected chain of his own,
this newborn miscreant stood and gazed and sighed –

oh the sky's raining blows are always justified! –
then gave this answer to the queries of my lord.
"Not long ago," he said, "I dropped here like a turd
into the gullet of a caked and hairy swine.
The life of a beast and not His image was mine,
half-breed that I was, in recognition of which
they didn't call me Vanni Fucci but 'Old Nick's bitch'.
I lived in Pistoia and made of it my sty."
"Don't let him leave," I murmured, "without saying why
he was filed amongst these thieves, for I remember
him as one who raged." As a grey, heatless ember
brightens at the gentle influence of breath,

that soul turned its face and its mind to me and both
glowed red with the consciousness of what they had done.
"You seeing me here," he said, "hurts me more than when
I was spirited away from the higher life.
I belong at this depth because I am the thief
who robbed a church and kept quiet while a good man hanged;
but rather than gloat, you should hear what our fanged
country has in store if it ever spits you out...
Black will leave an untilled land on foot and by boat,
and your cities will alter their people and their ways;
meanwhile Mars condenses a dark electric haze,
then his lightning pierces every White through the brain.

I tell you this full knowing it'll cause you pain."

25.

Raising his fists in mimicry of two pink rents,

he grunts obscenely at the skies. Now the serpents
seem our allies, for one slips round his throat as though
to say *Enough* while another grips his wrists so
tight that he's unable to gesture any more.
Ah, Cain's cities! If only an atomic war
would reduce the glass ghosts of your towers to ash,
for evil is encoded in their very flesh…
through all the dim orbits of the blaze, no spirit
strutted in defiance of the Holy Spirit
as proud as that one did before he spun and fled.
Then a centaur approached us. "Where *is* he," he said,
in a voice taut with rage, "where's that abortion gone?"

(the number and variety of snakes upon
his twitching hindquarters certainly equalled those
in Maremma's coastal swamps, and a dragon whose
snortings could incinerate draped his human neck).
"This is Cacus," said the maestro, "who dragged that rock
Hercules failed to shift and cowered in his cave.
He enjoys less liberty than his brothers have,
for the crime of making off with another's herd –
and Hercules battered him, and battered him hard,
but I don't suppose he felt a tenth of the blows."
While he was speaking, there'd assembled below us
a trio of souls of which I was unaware

till one called up demanding to know who we were;
the narrative forgotten, we stared down at them
and then one of them referred to a fourth by name
("Cianfa," I heard, "must be mired in funny business").
I laid a finger from my chin to my nose,
a sign that the maestro should prick up his ears –
and a sign for you too, O sceptical readers,
recalling I who *saw* this scarcely think it true.
Now a scuttling snake-thing like a six-legged sinew
darted forward, leapt and latched itself to the face
of the first, locking a pair of slim feet in place
behind his back as wife or goddess might in bed –

then, hind claws on his thighs and its teeth in his head,
it thrust a scaly tail between his trembling limbs
and drew him close. The ivy which sucks as it climbs
never gripped a tree more tight than that creature twined
their flesh together, sinuous as winter wind
nosing in and through the fibres of your clothes; next,
as if each's form had been turned to melted wax,
their separateness seemed to intermix and blend
so all qualities became subsumed in one bland
mass (picture the beige stain which precedes a flame's light,
an army destroying the immaculate white
of the paper before only ashes remain).

Watching this, one of the other souls gave a moan.
"My," he cried, "how you've changed, Agnello, how you've changed!"
By now, man and reptile presented a deranged
countenance wherein each yet neither died or lived;
its mingled face had to be seen to be believed,
the quiddity of both beasts absolutely lost
such that a foul chimera bewildered and cursed
trudged off with a tame and somehow gruesome slowness.
With the speed of a tiny lizard that dashes
so swift across a path it's a flash of green fire –
in the dog days of August, when the blazing star
the wise have called the sun behind the sun holds sway –

there shot toward a second soul the muscled ray
of a flaming snake the black of a peppercorn
which sank its fangs at the spot where, before we're born,
we drink deep from the ever-hidden source. Having
done that, it dropped to the floor like a yard of string
while the one who had been bitten just stood and stared
distractedly like the living do when they're bored –
stood motionless and yawned, as drowsy or transfixed,
not saying a word but with dilating pupils fixed
on the prone creature whose eyes never moved from his.
You who think you've heard odd tales, consider this!
A wisp of curling smoke peered out of his navel,

then shimmied in that way in which sea snakes travel
towards a wisp that coiled from the jaws on the ground.
Lucan with his story of the envenomed wound
that liquefies flesh or inflates it like a blimp
and Ovid with his chaste, subterranean nymph
shall now fall silent, for neither poet quite remade –
and in a mode expressly meant to drive men mad –
not one but two natures transmuting face to face,
merging their matter with the cataclysmic grace
of an exiled angel and an earthly girl.
What happened next is that the cunning reptile's tail
split in half as if in mimicry of its tongue,

while what had been the pins of the man it'd stung
fused from the last whorl of his toeprints to his groin;
skin was changed for scales and scales for counterfeit skin,
his arms folding into the hollows at their base
and the snake's arms growing by a similar ruse;
its back legs, twisting, became the limb which hides
on man's thighs, and his corporeal lance divides
and walks with abhorrent, cold-blooded gait. A pall
of dancing colours contriving a veil, one fell
and the other stood – and neither for a moment,
as hair moulted and grew, broke that gaze so intent
it seemed a beam or conduit for psychic intercourse.

Practically human, no longer on all fours,
the serpent put forth lips and a fine, flaring nose
and at each side of its head there bloomed the weird rose
of an ear (the ears of the one who will now crawl
shrinking to their roots like the eyestalks of a snail,
red tongue bisecting and black tongue becoming whole
and fit for talk). The smoke gone, that born-again soul
fled along the valley hissing as it went
whilst the new man flung after him words violent
as the shots of spit wherewith his speech was interspersed.
Thus, in the seventh channel, I have seen reversed
the poles between which our immortal natures move;

may the strange theme excuse any faults in my weave.

26.

Rejoice, perennial city, for your greatness

is such that even hell's buried blaze witnesses
the questionable flower of your windblown name.
I found five more citizens there and blushed for shame,
staring at the sinister device of my hand
that Love proportioned and whereby these words are penned;
but if as they allege it is the dreams near dawn
that prophecy, those things about which some men warn –
or hunger for – will happen in a blinding flash,
and the sooner the better for this dying flesh
is less able to bear the New with each swift year.
Now the maestro remounted the projecting stair
we'd trod before, turning and stretching out his arm

to where I stood below. Again we began to climb,
taking our solitary way among the stones
and faceted outcrops angular as runes –
our feet without the help of hands hesitant and slow,
and my brain possessed by a dreadful sorrow
that grieves me afresh as I recount what I saw
(though here I must curb, more than usual, this jaw
which has an angel or a devil behind it,
in case it wanders where virtue cannot guide it
and so abuses that divine inheritance
passed down from the hooting stars or some such distance).
As soon as the floor of the eighth trench came in sight,

I perceived it was a tremulous mass of light
much as – in the season when our sun's blessèd face
shines forth, at the hour that wasp and midge change place –
the shepherd who is stretched on a crisp hillside sees
spangle the cypress-spired meadows and valleys,
the loveplay of the fireflies speaking through the dusk;
and, in similar fashion to that whirling disc
within which Elijah was translated to the skies,
Elisha watching until his watery eyes
could just discern a flamelike cloud or cloudlike flame
(I believe *lenticular* is the proper name),
so every airborne glow consumed a thievish soul

just as, each April, the spawn entombs the tadpole.
I'd climbed the bridge and leant right out, straining to look,
and were it not for the fact that I held a rock
I think I should have overbalanced and plunged down.
"Each spirit," said my teacher, "inhabits his own
externalised tongue and is blasted as he goes."
My mind had come to this conclusion, the maestro's
words confirming what I somehow already knew.
"Who is in the blaze," I asked, "whose spire's split in two
like the bifurcated pyre of Eteocles
and his brother?" "That is the house of Ulysses
and Diomedes, joined in pain as once in rage;

within the luminous compound of their cage
they howl at the consciousness of the wily horse
which opened a stargate for Aeneas, the source
of Rome and its skyborn blood, and I'd guess that gem
where Ulysses fumes at the defiled Palladium
feels scarcely more confined a home." "Dearest maestro,"
I said, "can they talk inside those bright cells? If so,
I beg you not to make me move from here until –
and I won't stop this prayer without my iron will
making you relent – the horned craft is blown our way…
see how it has me bend like a girl." "How you pray,"
my guide replied, "is praiseworthy, to a degree,

and I grant your wish on condition that you be
silent for a minute and allow me to speak.
Rein in your mouth, child… the mind of an ancient Greek
may well take fright at its barbaric-seeming noise."
By now the brilliant seed was level with our eyes,
and he addressed them. "You who share the same hot tomb
like twins that wrangle in slow motion in the womb,
if I was anywise deserving when I lived –
when I pulsed and paid my due to the life I loved
in deathless verse – don't steer your ship away before
you tell of where, being lost, you died." Antique fire
swayed and softly muttered like a flame in a breeze,

then, as though it were a mortal tongue, flung forth these
words. "After," it said, "an endless year on the charmed
mountain of Circeo long before it was named,
neither tender feelings for my own darling boy
nor the love of my father or even the joy
I'd have seen in her altered face if I returned
could eclipse or override the fact that I burned
to discover every human virtue and vice,
and so I set out on the deep's embodied voice
with only one ship and the few who had kept faith.
We tasted each isle which that sea's clear currents bathe,
Morocco on our left side and Spain on our right,

and by the time we reached the great pillars the light
in our eyes had faded and we were old and slow
(*BEYOND THIS POINT*, we read, *NONE BUT CORPSES SHALL GO*)
'Brothers,' I said, 'we've endured a hundred thousand
perils and have come to this extreme nub of land,
so why – when something of our life's brief vigilance
lives – should we deny ourselves the experience
of walking in the golden footsteps of the sun,
of breathing airs unfouled by the stale breath of man?
Remember your ancestry, your stellar roots,
and ask yourself whether you were born to die like brutes
or to follow like heroes the wild *connaissance*

of righteousness and love?' Now those fine companions,
fired by my words, turned as one our stern to the east –
no longer withered fools but implacable and fast –
and we took mad flight. Steering ever leftwards,
our nights gazed in silence at the strange-eyed hordes
of the stars near that pole where the high gods once reigned;
the moon had five times swollen and thinned to a rind
when a soaring peak appeared, indistinct and far
and of an immensity no climber would dare,
yet the gladness we all felt was replaced by fear
as from the unknown land a wind began to roar.
It spun us around, our prow went down – this was His will –

then the ocean closed its blue mouth and all was still."

27.

And now the flame itself was quite motionless, quiet,

like the almond of light burning straight in the heart
in the absence of a wind of words. It glided off,
and at the same time we heard a muted cough
issue from another flame that neared us and slowed.
As the empty Sicilian bull – which first bellowed
with the voice of him who'd refined it with his tools,
there being no perils in this life but the holes
we build ourselves – converted to a brazen scream
the death-cries of the soul inside, making it seem
that it was the one that was agonised with pain,
so this attempt at speech was but a lambent moan
as long as it lacked an outlet from the blaze;

then, having struggled through the tip, with the deft buzz
of a human tongue, it produced these sounds. "You talk
in dialect I know" – this meant my Lombard duke –
"for I heard the gentle lilt when you said *Go now*
and saw your touch was light. I, of all men, sense how
late it is, and I hope you won't chafe if I ask
that you wait and converse with me a while (we bask
within the wildfires kindled by our own counsel,
so presumably you can linger a little
if I can manage, too). Since you're freshly fallen
into this unseeing world from that Italian
countryside whose beauty I tainted with my crime,

tell me if my people are at peace or war? I'm
from the mountains between Urbino and the wood
of beeches where the Tiber lets down its blonde flood."
"Speak to him," the maestro said, squeezing my shoulder,
and since I had already composed my answer
I could act without delay. "You, spirit hidden
in your mouth's iniquity, know well that sudden
terror and new outrage is always being brewed
in the famished hearts of tyrants and all those who'd
turn the holy land above to an open jail.
And yet, when I left, the accustomed and banal
details of our lives and days wore the look of peace –

Ravenna's echoing stones still stand, and the fierce
eagle of Polenta still broods in red on gold;
the siege-proof city where the bloodied French were piled
is once more in the death-grip of a green beast's claws;
the mastiffs of Verrucchio still close their jaws
on all they scent, vampires sucking life's sweet marrow,
whilst the blue lion cub now called Maghinardo
holds the cities on the Santerno and Lamone
and changes allegiance with the changing season;
as for the commune whose sides the Savio laves,
her people are as always both free men and slaves
just as she sits between a valley and a peak.

And now that I have spoken it's your turn to speak
and tell us who you are, in order that the world
won't forget your face." The pyre shook itself and snarled
in the way fires do, flickering its phantom tip
lither than a thought. "If I talked with one whose step
could ever return to that bright realm," it then said,
"my flame would tremble no more than a marble head;
yet considering a living man never climbed
from this blackness back to light, or so it is claimed,
I reply without fear of spoiling my good name.
Having been soldier and marauder, I became
a Franciscan in the belief that an outer

habit might make amends for long years of slaughter;
and surely, without the aid of the Antipriest
who returned me to the wrong path (his eyes be cursed),
my faith in my new scheme would not have been misplaced...
how and when and why this devil's evangelist
played me for an idiot child, you shall now hear.
When I sported the flesh-suit dreamed up by my dear
mother, my manner was less like lion than fox;
I knew all the ways whereby men conspire and fix
and I broadcast those arts through the listening globe,
but as it came to the time when mainsail and jib
must be lowered in readiness for that strange port –

we call it death – my proud soul drew itself apart.
What I had once exulted in filled me with grief,
and I thought that in repentance I'd find relief
from the dread I now felt. It would have *worked*, God knows!
At odds with his own kind and not external foes –
a caresser of the strayed feet of Muslim and Jew,
the faux-humble figurehead of the old and new
order of the ages that sculpts a world with war –
that false prophet sought me out as though I could cure
the fever of his abominable pride.
'Don't,' he said, weighing up my silence, 'be afraid…
unclench your wary heart, for we absolve you now.

I hold the master keys to the heights, as you know,
so why not do the clever thing and help me raze
the axe-hung castle of the soul'. It now seemed wise,
talk that only just before struck me as insane.
'Given you forgive me in advance for a sin
I here commit', I said, 'what I suggest is you
promise many things you've no intention to do.
These days, that's the best way to crawl onto a throne'.
When I died and my spirit stood on the ruin
of the form which was once marvellous to behold,
I saw approaching from two distances a gold
dancer and a cherub the colour of this stone –

one of them fair Saint Francis, and the other one
a precocious little shit in a tall silk hat.
'The consultant's mine,' he declared, 'for I have sat
in his hair ever since he started to advise…
do not take what's rightfully ours to the skies,
for his place is amongst the slaves of slaves of slaves;
there can be no congress between ravens and doves,
nor can one live in love and in the same breath yield
to the flawless logic of death'. This said, he yelled
and the sound-wave swept me to the deep atrium
where Minos waits." Its recital complete, the flame
sped off writhing as if disputing with itself

and the pair of us moved on to the next fraught gulf.

28.

Who could ever utter, even in the bleak

disconnected sprawl of newsprint's inched-out block
or by phrasing the same tale countless different ways,
the horror of the abattoir that now met my gaze?
Any known language couldn't help but wholly fail,
for man's power to speak and process and recall
is as nothing next to that symphony of gore;
if all the souls gulped by the stony carnivore
of the fortunate island of earth reappeared,
not spiritual bodies whose wounds are repaired
but dressed in the red and screaming splendour of blood –
squat aboriginals with skin the grey of mud
hacked down by the Trojans when they first stepped ashore,

and those whose severed ring fingers were stacked up, or
contributed a femur to the palaces
which shine as pale as bone in the land's high places
where our warriors are betrayed by their own kind,
and then those felled by weaponry that strikes the mind
and kills by stealth – the grisly crowd would not compare
to the ninth trench's foul and satanic glamour.
No smashed bottle held together by its label
gapes like the man I first laid eyes on, a cruel
slash having unzipped him from farting-hole to chin;
between his legs hung the coils of an intestine,
the crucible where golden wheat is turned to lead

nodding there too as in mockery of a head
below bared ribs through which I saw a beating heart.
Spotting me open-mouthed, he grasped and prised apart
the crimson tent flaps of his skin. "Look," he murmured,
"at the schism in this prophet's flesh. Mohammed
has been sundered and Ali goes ahead in tears,
the factions of his split face at war; the others
you see around you were sowers of division –
divide-and-rulers, theological scission
pitting faith against faith and sect against blind sect –
and right behind them stalks one who loves to dissect
scandalous scandalmongers with his flashing sword…

by the time they've made a circuit of this ring road
their injuries have healed, their lopped limbs have regrown,
and the demon shreds their names and faces again.
But who are you anyway, musing on that rock,
presumably delaying your arrival at the rack
or cross that your accuser's sent you to?"
"He is alive, and, what's more, an innocent too,"
the maestro said, "a neophyte who I conduct
through hell's nine gyrations so that every aspect
of the life of the unliving is seen and known…
I give you the truth." This sudden revelation,
striking the bleeding ears of the walking wounded,

startled them so much that they stood quite still and stared
as though in forgetfulness of their agony.
"Then tell Comrade Dolcino, if you're due to see
the sun once more – since Dolcino must come in turn
to these far hills – to gather all the wood he can
in readiness for the austerities of snow,
or else he and his stinking seraglio
shall be divided limb from limb quicker than they think."
Declaiming this with one foot raised, he gave a wink
and strode off in the pallor of a crescent moon;
gazing about me, I now saw a wretched man
pierced at the gullet like a cancer sufferer

and missing his nose and with a single bloodied ear
still holding out on the high ground of his head.
In front of the astonished crowd, and through the red
orifice of his windpipe, he then spoke aloud.
"So you're somewhat less burdened," he said, "by the load
of guilt that we bear… and if I'm not mistaken
I met you once before my sly soul was taken
from the almost unimaginable domain
up there. Make it known, if you ever view the plain
whose sweet soil slopes from Vercelli to Marcabo,
to those good men Guido and Angiolello –
Fano's best – that unless our precognition lies

they'll be slain on the orders of one whose one eye's
sufficient to survey his spellbound city...
there's never been nor shall be a worse atrocity
committed on the seas by Phoenician or Somali.
I'm Piero da Medicina. Remember me."
He reached and touched the dangling jawbone
of a soul beside him. "This," he said, "is the one
who drowned cautious Caesar's doubts in the Rubicon,
and you'll note" – he yanked it down – "that his glib tongue's gone."
Turning from Curio, the infinite dismay
of whose mute glance will haunt me till my dying day,
I saw a man with both hands missing at the wrist

waving round those horrible stumps so that blood pissed
through the twilit air and then spattered on his face.
"You'll perhaps recall Mosca," he hollered. "My place
in your wicked poem was well earned when I cried
'make an end of it with a blade to the side' –
the only thing I made an end of was life's peace."
"And," I added, sticking the knife in, "your own race."
He staggered off like a person unhinged by grief,
and here I witnessed something that, since there's no proof,
I fear to even mention in case it's thought I lie
(but my conscience reassures me, and with that I
am unassailable as him whose heart is pure).

I can still distinctly picture what we then saw,
a figure with no head pacing with the other
cattle and holding lamp-like a head by the hair;
it turned its eyes on us, this head that seemed to glow
and which – only He understands how this is so –
was one with the body yet a separate thing.
Now just below the bridge, it raised an arm to bring
the face up close enough that it could mouth these words.
"You who bear the flame of your life-breath down the roads
which no breath lights, know me for that Bertran de Born
who opened a rift between king and second-born
and gave my backing to the young and clever prince...

view in me the wages of the lost mind's violence."

29.

All the sad diversity of that charnel-house

had made my bulging eyes lose their mind, like a louse
which having drawn its fill can only slump and stare.
"What are you gawping at? You know that those dead are
as unsubstantial as a battle one has dreamed,
and it's not feasible for shadows to be maimed;
you haven't moped like this before, so get a grip
and consider that the tenth trench of the deep
is twice eleven miles round and seven miles across –
there isn't much more time now remaining to us,
for the moon's beneath our feet yet there's still lots to see."
I had opened my mouth to respond, but he
was already gone so I followed close behind.

"If you realised why I was staring," I complained,
"you would surely have let me linger there a while;
I think in that echoing gallery of hell
was a spirit of my own lineage and blood."
"Don't let yourself be troubled," the maestro said, "or brood
on that man I saw standing at the bridge's foot,
jabbing a white finger while you gazed at the brute
with a lantern head. I believe I heard his name…"
"Geri del Bello," I interjected. "The shame
of his unavenged murder stokes his fury,
and so he went away without speaking to me.
Now I feel more compassion for that vicious soul."

As we walked and talked, we had come to where the whole
expanse of the next vale would be easily seen
if there'd been more light – and then cloister number ten
was right below and I was hit by a thousand
mournful cries, each sound-dart barbed and poisoned
so that like a hunted monkey I curled into a ball.
Were all the sweating bodies from every hospital
in the summer season of malaria's reign
assembled together, the concentrated pain
and stink could not begin to compare to this
(imagine the mingled scent of bile and corpses).
Swerving ever leftward, we descend to the last

shore upon which I can clearly discern that vast
abyss where justice – ministrant of the Most High –
deals with those whose trade was an exalted mimicry.
When, on harsh Aegina, airborne pestilence
compelled the whole island to a rotting silence,
killing not just her inhabitants and her beasts
but even the dreaded worm that cleans as it feasts –
the race replaced, the poets claim, and they should know,
by a population of manlike men who grow
from the translucent eggs of ants – I think the sight
was somehow far less pitiful, less desolate,
than this shadowed valley where diseased spirits lay

horribly entwined, or crawled their retarded way
on stumps that had been shapely limbs. I refrained from speech,
rapt by the spectacle of two lepers that each
made a boulder of the other's weeping back
(and never did a sleepless man stretched on the rack
of an infested mattress scratch as these two scratched,
red scabs like mullet scales cascading while I watched).
"O you," began my guide, "busily preparing
yourselves for the pot with fingers slowly turning
into claws, tell me if any Italians
are near… do as I say if you want your talons
to continue to serve for this execrable chore,

now and forever." "Both of us that you see here,"
one of them replied, a tear finding a path down
the remnants of his nose, "once called that land our own…
and yet who are you to interrogate us so?"
"One that makes the great descent," answered the maestro,
"to death's inner sanctum with a man who still lives,
my intention being to show the ways which love's
betrayal plays out and the places it will lead."
At this both they and some others who'd overheard
those words' echoes turned towards me trembling, and good
Virgil said I should speak with them – and speak I did,
but only to please him. "Who *are* you," I began,

"and where do you hail from and of what class of men?
Your names shall endure in the sempiternal sun
if you come clean now, despite your faces' ruin."
"I'm from Arezzo," one of them replied, "my days
concluding in the pyre which counterfeits this blaze
for the sin of having said, in jest, I possessed
formulae to mount 'unto the sky' like the blest;
he to whom I made the claim, having little wit,
demanded that I demonstrate that royal art,
and, since I couldn't make a Daedalus of him,
had his father commit me to the expert flame.
Though it's not because of lies I'm within our dire

hole, assigned to the tenth groove of putrescent fire,
but due to the fact I once practised alchemy...
it is for *that* crime unerring Minos condemned me."
"A lapse of humour worthy of the French," I said,
turning to my poet, "and just as conceited."
Here the other soul gave a sudden ravaged laugh.
"The ones in question," he said, "are a people who love
nothing quite so much as spending money fast,
and for whom food's cost is the measure of its taste.
Terroir and ancient woodlands are toys in their hands,
yet for all that wealth they have unproductive minds.
Look at my face, boy, and sharpen up your gape –

I am Capocchio, wise Nature's cunning ape."

30.

When Juno was raging at young, slim Semele

(it happened more than once) and cursing her family
and her blood, she sent Athamas so sheer insane
that as he saw his wife approach with their dear sons –
one trotting at each hand – he cried, "a lioness
and her cubs… a blot on this forest's cleanliness!"
and stretched out his claws, for *he* was the lion,
and snatched and whirled high in the air a little one
then dashed on a table his unsuspecting brain;
or when the irremediable winter rain
of misfortune had erased all trace of Troy's name,
the king sunk in the same silence as his kingdom,
and Hecuba sat both an exile and enslaved –

having seen the sacrifice of the girl she loved,
and then found her youngest boy's pale corpse on the shore –
the mind-destroying grief made her yelp like a cur.
But no grave madness, neither Trojan nor Theban,
could parallel or rival that of those who ran
snapping at Capocchio like two rabid pigs
(one lunges at him with a little tusk which digs
deep in the dense meat of his knotted neck, then pulls
him down so his stomach is sliced by the gravel's
granite teeth). "That," announced the first counterfeiter,
his voice like a shaken leaf, "bloodthirsty creature
is Gianni Schicchi… he tears as viciously

at any reprobates he may happen to see."
"And who's the other beast," I demanded. "Tell me
and save yourself, perhaps, from its foaming bite." "She,"
he replied, "is the spectral relic of Myrrha
who came – in another's guise – to lie with her father,
forging, as it were, the cries of blessèd union;
just as, in his greed for a mare, the other one
put on the semblance of a man already dead
and then dictated from his barely-cold deathbed
the favourable terms of a false testament."
All this time my eyes had watched those violent
souls as they were swallowed up by the heinous gloom,

and now I turned to view more creatures who assume –
or who'd endeavoured to – the countenance of gold.
The first I laid eyes on was so grotesquely swelled
that if you sawed his legs off he'd pass for a lute;
a case of the dropsy, when everything we eat
rots in the stomach and can't reach our shrunken limbs –
tiny face and giant gut not on speaking terms –
and one lip yearns earthwards while one lip tries to climb.
 "You," he called, "who breeze unpunished through the mayhem,
consider the misery of Maestro Adam.
I once got all I wanted, whereas here I dream
of a dram or the merest drip of cool water;

those hidden streams and rivulets – whose liquid laughter
descends from the green hills of the Casentino,
freshening its secret ways, into the Arno –
stand before me now like great aqueous trees,
imagination wasting me more than this disease.
Justice's unbending sword, plunging within me
and thus ensuring that 'my sighs are many',
won't let me forget the locations of my sin…
look, there's Romena, where I watered down with tin
that honey-toned coin on which the wild witness shines,
the crime that had me turned to a pile of charred bones.
And yet if I could just glimpse the odious soul

of my former employer in this verdant hole,
I wouldn't trade the sight for a pulsing fountain –
in fact, the creep's already here, or else I've been
fooled by the raging shadows running in our groove
(though it's useless information, since I can't move
for these unmusical strings which bind me tight).
If I were only sufficiently deft and light
that I could crawl a whole inch in a hundred years,
I'd right now be scanning those monsters' retinas
in search of the so-called nobleman – despite the track
being eleven miles around – who made me strike
a currency with grey dross darkening its blood,

who consigned me to this house and its brutal brood."
"Who," I then asked, "are those two wretches over there
that seem to smoke or steam like wet hands in winter,
far beyond the confines of your western border?"
"They were here when I first fell into the ordure,"
he replied, "and in all that time they haven't done
so much as a single lap… one's lying Sinon,
and the other is Joseph's false accuser,
whilst the stink of burning fat is due to the brazier
lit within each red cell by their putrid fever."
Suddenly, one of those miscreants leant over
and punched that taut stomach so it boomed like a drum;

in reply to which, Maestro Adam's rigid arm
shot out like a puppet's and smacked him in the eye
(my pity was *not* kindled, my passion did *not* die!).
"I may be too fat to take a stroll," he puffed, "but this
implement is agile still and does fine service."
"So where was it," the other spat, "when the fire
that you were given quarters in danced with desire
for those graceful limbs? Less ready than when you coined!"
"True," replied the one as round as sails big with wind,
"but were you a good witness outside the city?"
"If I lied then," sneered Sinon, "one falsity
can't compare to the chinking spawn of a demon."

"Remember the horse, and recall that everyone
beyond this burning town remembers it as well!"
"And you recall the lack which cracks your tongue, the vile
waters that rear your own flesh round you like a wall!"
"A mouth gapes and out flies evil, as usual…
though if I am parched yet distended with humours,
you've got an anvil skull struck by fever's hammers
and such thirst that Narcissus's answering glance
would, were you but given the ghost of half a chance,
be lapped up along with the lake in which it played."
"Feast those glassy eyes a little more," the maestro said,
"and soon we'll quarrel too." Hearing this, I span

about with a hot shame that makes me reel again
as I bring it back to mind. Caught in a nightmare,
the conscience, sometimes, dreaming, thinks "I wish this were
just an awful dream," thus hungering for what
actually is the case as though it was not;
in similar fashion, I wanted to excuse
myself and to explain, scarce imagining those
speechless seconds were more contrite than any word.
"Far, far greater failings than yours," declared my lord,
"are washed away by much less shame than you have shown…
cast aside this sorrow and recall that your own
discriminating self matches our every step,

that none but base spirits gloat while beasts fight and weep."

31.

The selfsame tongue that first stung me with shame,

dying both cheeks as if with Syrian rue, came
to me a second time with medicine for the wound
like the light lance of Peleus which can make sound
(or so I've heard) the bodies it has torn apart.
Leaving the trench behind us, we crossed the rampart
in silence to a place on the cusp of day and night –
the dusky indistinctness that baffled sight
now split by a thunder-belittling bugle blast
my eager eyes swam into, countering the vast
resonance all the way back to its single source…
more terrible a sound than when, besieged by Moors,
Roland blew the fatal note on his twisted horn.

After some moments gazing in that direction
I saw or imagined a line of skyscrapers,
as though we neared a fallen city. "The mind errs,"
the maestro said, "due to the tenebrous distance
it strains to look across; when we're closer, your sense
of what is really there will be less blurred by dark…
so come, let us hasten on." Saying this, he took
my hand in his. "It might ease the shock," he added,
"if I tell you those aren't buildings but titans hid
below the navel by the dreadful pit they guard."
As when mist dissipates, the eerie charade
of shapes one had guessed at bit by bit becoming clear,

now vision tunnelled through the gloom-freighted air
and error's ghosts fled and my blood began to chill;
and, as the mossy loop of Montereggione's wall
is measured out and crowned with towers, thus appeared
the giants on that high bank encircling the void –
those for whom the thunder remains a warning voice –
except each tower had a monumental face
and a chest like a hillside and huge dangling arms.
How wise Nature was to deprive impious Mars
of such instruments when she gave up making these,
and if comparable monsters still hymn the seas
it is just because – consider this subtle point,

and you will see her fine discretion – mere bulk can't
threaten sacred order unless equipped with thought,
and what man can resist the combined onslaught
of physical power and a malicious will?
The head I now saw was as big as the pineal
bronze at the Vatican – a sign for those who know –
and his other bones were in like proportion, so
even with his lower half aproned by the wall
three of those brutes that Friesland's butter raises tall
wouldn't nearly reach to where he buckled his cloak,
much less the mouth which suddenly yawned wide and spoke.
Dewina, it bawled, *adin ffog inai amor*,

and I do not think there could have been a more
appropriate psalm for that savage face to sing.
"A fool like you," said my guide, "should stick to blowing
horns when some or other passion needs releasing.
One hangs upon your chest, babbler… follow the string
tied round your thick neck and you'll find it by your heart."
"This is Nimrod," he said to me, "who had the smart
idea of cheating death by means of glass and steel,
a *grand projet* thanks to which humanity's still
divided by innumerable words for 'what?'.
He's his own accuser, and we'll leave him given that
he won't understand us any more than we him

(the tongues he knows have all been reabsorbed in flame)."
We curved broadly to the left – keeping well away –
and came to a second whose ferocity I'd say
was if anything greater than the last, his right
hand pinned behind him and the other hand in sight
but immobile under five turns of a huge chain…
don't ask me what inconceivable suzerain
would have the strength to bind a beast of that size.
"This is what happens," said the maestro, "when one tries
to vie in power with the summit men call Jove.
His name's Ephialtes, and now he cannot move
the arms which once attempted a coup on the stars."

"If it's possible," I said, "I'd like to pit my eyes
against the immense, hundred-handed Briareus."
"For now," he replied, "you can see Antaeus…
his body isn't tied and neither is his tongue,
so he'll do the office of putting us among
the blessèd shapes of error's bitterest dregs.
The other's lower down, his face more warped by rage."
No cloud-scarfed turret ever juddered in a quake
as fiercely as that fiend then shook himself awake,
and but for the chains sheer terror would have killed me.
We proceeded on our way, and soon the swarthy
wrestler of the skull-built house was before us. "You,"

cried the cunning maestro, craning back his neck, "who
once – in the valley where Hannibal turned and fled
and Scipio Africanus inherited
his soul's predestined glory – had as a light snack
a pride of lions, you through whom that brave attack
of depth upon height and the earth against the sky
must surely have ended in total victory,
or so they reckon, set us where the blackest ice
holds Cocytus lifeless. Refuse and you'll make us
have to go to Tityus or Typhus instead,
for this poet here has the means to give the dead
what the dead most crave. Be compliant, don't just stare;

I steer someone who, as he breathes, can restore
name and estimation in the sweet realm above,
God grant that the informing force of grace and love
shan't take him back before he comes into his own."
This oration over, the monolith reached down
and took my dear guide in the hands which Hercules
felt the grip of – and he, in turn, made a *fasces*
of the two of us by hugging me good and close.
As a leaning tower seems to fall when cloud flows
above its pendant edge, so Antaeus appeared
as I saw him bend and wished I'd walked another road;
then, gently placing us at the base of the scarp,

he righted himself like the mast of a gigantic ship.

32.

If I could shape sounds sufficiently brutal, raw

as the singular nothing at matter's inmost core
on which a whole universe of stones rests its feet,
I'd be able to effect a more complete
extraction of the golden juices of my brain;
but, in short, I can't, and consequently the main
focus of this mad errand – creation's black heart –
seems a thing for which to seek a verbal counterpart
is doomed from the very start, as lone a cry
as soldiers shouting for their mothers while they die,
without the mindless loveliness of the Muses
shining through and influencing these dark verses
so that what's seen and what's said are one and the same.

How much better for that crowd of human jetsam,
washed onto a shoreline where my eloquence failed,
to be beasts cropping grass in August's driest field!
Now we stood as though at the bottom of a well,
and I was staring up at the circular wall
and – upon its far brink – the giant's little face
when I heard a voice. "Take good care," it said. "Don't place
your plates of meat on the skulls of our coterie."
Glancing down, I saw what seemed to be the sheeny
surface of a lake that the chill had turned to glass;
the Danube in midwinter, immured in its ice,
or the Don when it's so bitter the swift skies freeze

have not nearly as obdurate a lid as this
(let Ararat fall on it, it wouldn't even creak).
Like frogs which – in the season when their gross, massed croak
fills the gilded evenings and a girl's dreaming mind –
poke slick snouts just above the ripples of a pond,
the sad shadow-folk were all neck-deep in the lake
and clacking cracked teeth to the rhythm of the stork;
each one had his head bowed, a makeshift disguise,
and the rattle of their mouths and their glinting eyes
bore witness to the vast cold and a cold heart's sins.
I noticed two pressed as close as Siamese twins,
hair plaited together, and when they looked at me

their eyes welled up with tears which immediately
froze and locked their lids tighter than a dovetail joint,
at which point they butted brows with knocks violent
as rutting billy-goats. "Such a protracted gaze" –
the soul who spoke had frost-chewed ears and didn't raise
his head – "into this universal mirror...
if you really want to know who that pair are or were,
I can tell you that they're brothers, the onetime heirs
to the landscape which the Bisenzio waters;
you won't find, through hell, two more apt to hang like those
in our sweet jelly like a Turk's pistachios,
not even him whose overshadowed heart was pierced

by Arthur's lance, or crazed Focaccia who first
set cousins at each other's throats, or that boor whose
obstruction of a fat head devised his nephew's
timely death (if you're a Tuscan you'll know the case)."
We went on then and I saw the same doglike face
endlessly reflected, its lips blue-black with cold,
a sight that makes me shiver as it is recalled
and always will do when I cross an icebound ford.
While we were pacing inexorably toward
that centre to which graves and the gravest things tend,
my arteries shaking in the ghost of a wind,
I struck – and who can say if I meant it or not? –

a bowed head directly in the face with my foot.
"Why attack *me*," it shouted, its voice thick with tears.
"Unless it's for my betrayal of empire's cause,
I see no justification for such a kick."
"Maestro," I pleaded, "let me speak with this relic.
I think he can clear up a doubt which grips my brain...
I'll be quick and then we can hurry on again."
That fine soul paused, and I asked the head – still cursing –
who he was. "Who the hell are you more like, crossing
Antenora clumsily as a living man?"
"I am indeed alive," I said, "and one who can
publicise your name with the other tuneful souls."

"You think I crave *celebrity*, you fool? My goal's
oblivion, not the mouths of a halfwit crowd."
I bent down and grasped his fringe and twisted it hard.
"Tell me your filthy name," I said with gritted teeth.
"I refuse," he spat back. "A snarl's my epitaph."
"What's the matter, Bocca," another bowed head cried,
"can it actually be you're not satisfied
with the music of our jaws but have to bark too?
Or does some devil stroke your hair?" "Now I know you,
traitor," I said. "You've earned a certain place in my
immemorial song." "Declaim it to the sky,"
Bocca replied, "for all I care, though don't neglect

to mention the good brethren that you haven't kicked."
Yet we were already out of earshot, my gaze
drawn to a soul which seemed to have a carapace
that, as we got nearer, resolved into a head
biting on the lower one as famished men gnaw bread
(incisors set where the brain and spinal snake meet,
much as when Tydeus took for his final meat
the carnal mirror of his killer's severed skull).
"Who are you," I called to him, "imaging the foul
and inhuman hatred concealed in human veins?
Tell me and I guarantee you that my lines
will – if it transpires your savagery's justified –

defend you so long as their potent sap's not dried."

33.

He raised his face from that barbaric meal, patting

his mouth with the hair of what he had been eating,
and then began to speak. "You ask me to relate –
to put into language, which means to renovate –
a grief and desperation that just to think of
grips my charred heart as the world grips the fire; yet if
speech contained a seed which eventually grew
to a great tree proclaiming how the one I chew
is treacherous, I'd consider both words and tears
well spent. I don't know you, and I don't know what stairs
you have sneaked down to reach our black extremity,
but going by your voice I can guess your city.
I was Count Ugolino, and this creature here" –

he looked at and then dropped the lock of brain-flecked hair –
"is Ruggieri, an alleged man of God,
and now I'll explain why I'm such a very odd
neighbour and the merciless manner of my death;
the fact of it is famous, so I won't waste breath
in describing his sly and predatory mind.
But hear me out and you decide if he has sinned.
The sole window in a stone tower lately called
Famine – in which I am not the last to be walled –
had shown nine moons on the deep, indifferent sky
when I had a disturbing dream, a dream where I
blew aside the light veil that hides what is to come…

I saw this beast spur like a king in his kingdom
across the broad mountain which looms in Pisa's sight,
hunting with muscled mastiffs ravenous to bite
an old wolf and his cubs who ran then seemed to tire.
Oh, the white peaks of a dog's teeth can grip and tear!
I awoke and it was dawn, and I thought I heard
the voices of my sleeping ones whimpering for bread
(you are surely callous if your mind hasn't winced
in thinking on the fate my wise heart had announced,
for if this story cannot make you weep what will?).
And now the four children were awake, and all
had had the same uncanny dream. All were afraid.

It was the time when they used to bring our food,
but there came instead the slow tattoo of nails in the door...
I looked into their faces and neither tears nor
words could frame my grief. My heart had turned to stone.
And the children did cry, but soon the smallest one
said 'what's the matter, daddy? Why do you *stare?*'
and still I didn't utter a single word or tear
and another day and night rolled around our room.
Then a second sun swaggered on the world, a beam
of golden light playing on those faces in which
I saw my bony semblance reflected with such
terrifying clarity I gnawed at my fist.

They thought it was hunger! 'Father,' they said, 'you first
dressed us in these living coats so you take them off.
We'll find that far less painful than watching you starve'.
I kept my anguish close then, as a parent should.
All that day and all the next – ah, the hard earth could
have showed us some compassion and gaped wide open! –
we sat in a terrible silentness, and when
the fourth day dawned my little Gaddo gave a great
cry of *Father!* and died. I had to contemplate,
after two more days went by, the forms of four sons
and for two days after that to repeat the sounds
of their lifeless names. Unseeing, my hands caressed

the braille of a face. Soon starvation did its worst."
He showed the whites of his dead eyes and bit down hard
as a bone-crunching hound on the archbishop's head,
and I felt fresh hate for those cities which destroy
the incomparable world and our innate joy –
your children arrogant, overfed, unconcerned –
and made a solemn promise that if I returned
to light's shores I'd avenge the innocents they've killed.
We now progressed to where patchy snow half-concealed
a people whose mad faces were upraised, heads bent
backwards and their weeping its own impediment –
for the tears, freezing fast, had fashioned knots of ice,

sealing with crystal masks the hollow of the eyes
and forcing their anguish, which could find no release,
to turn on itself and perpetually increase.
Despite the fact the frigid air made my skin numb,
I sensed that what had been a mere breath had become
a mistral which shook the buried tree of my bones.
"Whose power," I asked, "moves this breeze? Without the sun's
animating force aren't all hell's vapours dead?"
"Your eyes will shortly answer that," the maestro said,
"when they view the marvel that manifests the blast."
Just then, a voice arose from in the frozen crust.
"Have pity, spirits cruel enough to be sent

to where He orchestrates the ultimate torment,
and prise these dark glasses from my face so that
I can ease – just a touch – the pain that swells my heart
before the tears clot again and lock it back inside."
"If you want me to do as you ask," I replied,
state who you are – and if I don't assist you then,
may God send me to the ice's core quicker than
a rock dropped from a tower on a windless day."
He looked at me, sizing me up, then spoke. "Okay…
I'm Brother Alberigo whose tartlets taste sharp,
and find myself repaid in this place of worship
at good interest (shall we say)." "You're here *already*?"

"I have no idea," he said, "how my body
is faring in the world where I left it unmanned.
It's the privilege of our level of the damned –
they call it Ptolomea – to receive a soul
when the flesh hasn't had its red thread snipped but still
attends to business, chairs meetings, gossips, frowns, smiles,
and I trust you'll more willingly pluck the grey scales
from my eyes if I tell you something few men know.
When knaves such as I am betray, their spirits go
out of their bodies and a demon takes control;
and, while the heart plummets and winters in this hill,
a charming corpse circulates in soft summer air…

perhaps you recall, if you were recently there,
the dapper husk of the phantom behind me here.
He's been incarcerated many a year,
a certain Branca Doria." "I think you're lying,
for that man yet keeps company with the dying
and eats and drinks and wears fine garments like the rest."
"A vehicle," he said, "for an uninvited guest.
Reach out your hand now, grant me the power to see."
And, of course, I didn't, since it's sheer courtesy
to treat souls like him as the villains that they are –
a cabal whose one guiding passion is to mar
the culture and honour of those of noble birth,

and which should by all rights be expelled from the earth.

34.

"Onward robot soldier, marching as to war...

look up ahead," said the maestro, "and see if your
eyes can discern the liar, the father of lies."
As a distant wind turbine appears when the sky's
obscured with noxious fumes or midnight's inky dark,
so seemed the form toward which we began to walk;
and then, there being no other place to hide,
I took shelter from the blast behind my stalwart guide.
We'd already reached the ring where each submerged shade –
the terror of the sight comes back as it's remade
and recollected in these lines – hung like a piece
of straw in a glassy pond's all-interring ice,
some prone and some erect and several with their feet

pointing right at us, and a few bent in complete
circles like tadpoles which the clotted gel holds fast.
Soon we had advanced far enough that the vast
and once-wondrous face of the idol could be seen,
and my teacher stepped aside and I stood alone.
"This is Dis," he said. "This is the place where man's true
strength must be your armour. Nothing else can help you."
Don't ask, timid bookworm, safe in your library,
how I felt then for palaver failed and fails me;
I was no longer living and yet I was not dead,
and anyone with sufficient wit in his head
shall guess what it is, at that moment, I become.

The unholy emperor of the tragic kingdom
reared half his bulk above the ice's surface,
and to give some idea of his size it will suffice
to say that each finger made those giants seem small
(contemplate this fragment for a sense of the whole).
If he was now ugly as he'd been beautiful
when he set his brilliance against the eternal
breather of the worlds, well might the ogre grieve
and well might that sorrow be the fount of all grief.
Appalling to behold, his single head had three
faces like a bad copy of the Trinity –
the middle one a blood red, the one on the right

a sickly shade you couldn't call yellow or white
and the third as black as Uganda's cannibals.
Beneath each face, bigger than the mightiest sails
any earthly ship ever hoisted up its mast,
a pair of dragonfly-like wings was whirring fast…
source of the cold wind that refrigerates the deep.
Simultaneously, six faceted eyes weep
and a triple maw chews relentless as pistons
three souls who must be the most heinous of felons;
that bite, unendurable though it surely was,
was nothing compared to the swift, spasmodic claws
which had stripped the skin from the central sinner's spine

(I saw thirty-three vertebrae like beads strung on twine).
"That one there," said my hierophant, indicating
him whose head was within the red mouth, legs dangling,
"is Judas. A matchless pain for a matchless sin.
The other two, hanging upside down like Odin,
are Brutus – how eloquent his silence is! –
and burly Cassius. But come, darkness rises…
we've seen what we came to see and now we must go."
I did as he commanded, clasping the maestro
tightly round his neck, and with an unfailing sense
of rhythm he darted forward when the immense
wings were raised and caught hold of shaggy Lucifer;

then, inching down between the walls of ice and fur,
we arrived at the hinge of that tremendous thigh.
With what seemed to be no little difficulty,
and breathing hard, he spun about so that his head
was where his feet had been before. "Hold fast," he said,
"for it is by such stairs you depart from evil."
One moment I thought we were going back to hell,
and the next I was pushed through and sat on the lip
of a gap or fissure in the stone. Looking up,
I didn't see the creature's torso but his legs
and muttered – as a man who dies – "I am perplexed"
(feel free to criticise, morbid crowd, if you don't

appreciate I'd stepped across matter's midmost point).
"Get up," ordered the maestro. "Get onto your feet…
the road is a long one and more hardships await.
The sun will be astir." We stood in no palace
but a gloomy, uneven-floored, dungeonlike space.
"Before I tear myself away from the abyss,"
I said, still confused, "tell me where the black ice is
and by what strange magic the devil's been reversed –
and can it be dawn when so little time has passed?"
"Your mind keeps poor pace with your body," he replied,
"wrongly imagining it's at the other side
of the zero we just entered – back there where

my hands grasped the world-devouring worm's greasy hair,
the hole toward which all sinners and sins converge –
yet we're in a new hemisphere, upon the verge
of the pure antipode chastened by His breath,
right underneath the distant spot that saw the death
of one whose gait was light. Brother, you are treading
a shrunken sphere of lead; on this side is morning,
on that side evening and Judecca's metal face.
The snake we descended up hasn't changed his place,
though you're now on that half of the globe where he fell
and a petrified landmass took the sea's blue veil
then fled to the north where it is cowering still –

and, or so it's fabled, the solitary hill
in the southern ocean is the missing piece which
was chipped from the depths to make hell's exalted ditch."
There begins at the crypt of that pimped, lordly fly
a path that can't be found by the despotic eye
but which you have to listen for, tracing the voice
of the rill that has worn its meandering course
the exact same distance these lines have spiralled down.
And here we take that smooth and hidden track, my own
intellect leading the way back to realms of light;
a shining opening slowly grows in our sight
then suddenly we come forth, small as an umlaut.

It is night once more. The unspeakable stars are out.

BATHE

1.

Thus I put that crude and cruel sea behind me,

trimming the sails to steer my ingenuity
towards calmer waters, and presently I'll sing
of an intermediate realm where the cleansing
without which no one climbs the sky is undergone.
Here poetry's corpse is going to rise again,
for I am yours, slender Muses, soul and body,
so let Calliope stand and accompany
my verse with something of the more than human tone
which made the raucous magpies despair of pardon.
The entire orient now seemed flawless sapphire –
a self-asserting radiance, sweet blue fire
suffusing the serene countenance of the air

as far as the horizon, unutterably clear –
such that the mere fact and nakedness of sight
was a power to marvel at, divine delight,
my lids no longer weighed down by a world of pain.
The beautiful planet who makes all creatures pine
for what they've lost was shining like laughter in the east,
Pisces invisible yet pursuing fast,
and I turned to the right and to the other pole;
four stars were set there, stars the aboriginal
inhabitants of earth knew but never seen since,
and I swear the whole sky rejoiced in their brilliance…
deprived lands of the frozen north, at last we know

why it is you wear the dark clothes of a widow!
As I looked at them I felt they looked *into* me,
a fleeting premonition or a memory
I wrenched my gaze away from to find there'd appeared
at some little distance a man whose white-flecked beard
hung on his chest between his long hair's tresses;
the four sacred orbs lit his face as dawn kisses
the brow of one sitting in the presence of the sun,
and I knew he deserved the reverence a son
should pay to a father for the sake of his years.
"Who *is* this," he asked, the venerable feathers
of his flowing locks faintly swaying as he talked,

"who's swum against the blind tide and seemingly walked
out of the shadow-cage men call Eternity?
Who assisted you in escaping that valley
bathed in unyielding blackness by fathomless night,
for no one could do it with neither guide nor light,
and has the profound abyss's law been broken
or somehow repealed in the wisdom of heaven
to enable a lost soul to land on my coast?"
Then the maestro spoke, though not without having first
made me kneel and lower my head by means of sounds
and signs and, finally, the pressure of his hands.
"I haven't come for my own sake or come alone,

but in immediate obedience to one
who departed the heights in concern for this man…
I am his hurricane lamp and his companion.
You demand to know how it truly goes with us,
so I must oblige. My charge never saw the gorgeous
wrack of fiery cloud that a dying man sees,
yet had progressed so far in his idiocies
that he was close to the point from which none return;
I was sent to rescue him, the ways that burn
being by that late stage the sole alternative
to death. Since he has grasped how the evil dead live,
I intend to show him those penitents who are

mortifying themselves upon your mountain lair.
The story, I fear, would take an age to tell you,
but suffice to say a potency and virtue
which flows down into me has quickened our ascent…
now he can hear your voice, and, no less important,
behold the justice of your face with his eyes.
He's someone who, like you, knows that true liberty's
a thing more precious than bestial existence
and slavish days. He seeks it; you died for it once.
No edict's been transgressed, for this man is alive
and I'm not bound by Minos but one who drifts above
the depths in that circle where Marcia implores –

with a speaking glance – that you consider her yours
in death as in life. Let us pass, for her heart's sake,
through your seven bracing regions and I shall take
word of this kindness to her – if you will allow
your name's sacred syllables to be said below."
"Back then," he replied, "the mere sight of Marcia
left me with no option but to be good to her
however she desired, yet now the unholy
stream runs between us and looks can't bend or touch me…
such is what the new law ordained at my release.
Though we've no need for elaborate flatteries,
if what you say's right and a woman from the sky

guides your every move. Go, although make sure you tie
a reed around his waist and wash his mortal face
(when he stands before His ministrant, any trace
of grime still darkening his eyes will ignite
in a splendour reflecting paradise's light).
The reeds you can find on our island's muddy shore,
down there where the perpetual surf's white thunder
would destroy any plant less able to relent;
don't come back this way, for an easier ascent
shall be shown by the royal disc which now starts to rise."
With that he disappeared, and I stood and drew close
to my guardian's side. "Step where I step," he said,

"and the sloping plain will lead us to the reed bed."
All-conquering dawn was chasing the predawn wind,
the far sea flickering like a Venetian blind,
as we made or improvised our way as a man
who's strayed and doubts he'll ever find his path again.
Soon we arrived where the silver encampment
of the dew survives in shade, and with reverent
touch the maestro laid his open palms on the grass;
then, placing his streaming hands on my grief-lined face,
he restored the vital glow that night had concealed.
On reaching the bleak coast no hero ever sailed
and lived to tell the tale, he girdled me with a thin

reed swiftly replaced by its identical twin.

2.

Already resplendent on the skyline, the sun

was now departing the area whose northern
point is a stony echo called Jerusalem;
adversarial night with her indigo hem
stepped forth from the Ganges to raise the stellar scale
that in October clarity she will let fall,
and what had been the pale, pinkish cheeks of fair dawn
were displaying a tanned and less virginal tone.
We were still standing on that desert coast, like those
who premeditate their path so the wild heart goes
darting up ahead while its body stays behind,
when I saw – as when Mars glimmers red through thickened
mists of an early hour, sullen in the west –

a light approaching over the ocean so fast
it would have outpaced the swiftest bird, more brilliant
and yet closer when I turn back a mere instant
after having turned away to question my guide.
Now there was a luminous whiteness on each side
(what this was, I couldn't think) and next thing a third
indefinite radiance bit by bit appeared
below it; not one word had come from my teacher,
although as soon as he recognised the creature
piloting the craft – each incandescence having
revealed itself as a snowy owl's giant wing –
he cried aloud. "On your knees – join your hands, quickly! –

for this is none other than an emissary
of the Most High, an agent of the All-Aware…
no mechanism drives his ship, or even an oar,
but only those feathered sails whose immortal whirr
propels him from a shore inconceivably far
from here. See, how like music they vibrate the air!"
The divine bird was brightening as it drew near
and I had to turn away as if from a sun,
and then that deft vessel – so light, the water's skin
wasn't even pierced – was right there before us.
His whole form somehow inscribed with blessedness,
the celestial navigator stood on the stern

and more than a thousand souls were seated within.
In exitu Israel de Aegypto, they sang,
the house of life from the house of a deathly tongue,
and *no praise in the noise of the cities of bone*
and each voice was distinct and yet all sang as one.
The angel then made over them a sacred sign,
and they hurled themselves shorewards and the boat was gone.
As when a crowd of Chinese tourists leave their coach,
at first they simply stood bewildered on the beach
and stared as if the ground itself was rare and strange;
the sun, like a madman at a shooting range,
was firing golden beams in every direction

and by now had already driven Capricorn
from his nocturnal seat in the midst of the sky.
Suddenly, they spotted us. "Tell us," came their cry,
"which path we have to take to reach the mountainside."
"We're also foreign to this place," Virgil replied,
"having only just escaped from a maze so dark
that, in comparison, the climb will seem a walk
in a cool and twilit park." Noticing the breath
which marked me down as someone that persuasive death
has not waylaid, the shades grew paler and thronged round –
as a crowd will form where a man bears in his hand
the auspicious olive branch – and fixed those fleshless

eyes on the marvel of my softly pulsing face,
neglecting their ablutions and heedless of the crush.
One of them pushed forward as if to hug me, such
warmth in its demeanour I tried to do the same.
Insubstantial shadows, absent in all but name!
Three times I tried to clasp that semblance, and three
times my searching fingers embraced my own body…
I think I was a picture of comic disbelief
for it drew back and smiled as though stifling a laugh,
then, when I moved towards it, told me to be still.
Here something in the voice identified the soul,
and I implored it to wait and talk with me

a while. "I love you no less," it said, "now I'm free
from my leaded suit than when it weighed me down,
and so of course I'll gladly stop. But what brings one
pinned upon his grinning cross to this distant spot?"
"I go," I replied, "from a place where I was not
in order to return to where I shall be
entirely, a long yet infinitesimal journey.
Tell me, dearest Casella, of yourself and how
it is that you haven't gained these shores until now?"
"If he who pilots the craft which flies at the pace
of an unearthly music denied me a place
month after month, it is not my right to complain;

I spent or endured a whole winter with the rain,
then one day came to where the Tiber tastes the sea
and there the crystal ship was humming hungrily
with a measured, inscrutable will behind it…
he speeds there now, for that river mouth's the exit
for any souls vile Acheron can't claim." "Your voice,"
I said, "is as dear to me as your gentle face;
serenade me like you used to, one of those light
and almost flippant love songs that dance to a height
no scholarship can reach." *Love*, he sang, *gave the wound
which while I breathe will bleed*, with such a wondrous sound
its sweetness has echoed in my heart till this day

and which, as it lasted, seemed to drive away
all shadows of all thought from the circle of our minds;
time was in abeyance, as when a man attends
with his total being to each successive note,
but our reverie was broken by a sudden shout.
"Procrastinating souls, what negligence is this?
Hurry to the mountain," the old man roared, "where His
glory can be fully known when you've shed these skins!"
As a field of feeding doves will scatter at once
if something runs among them, dropping the ears
of shining wheat because gripped by more urgent cares,
so the new arrivals fluttered blindly uphill

towards that absolute antithesis of hell.

3.

Scattered like daytrippers across the gentle plain

that lay between the circling coast and the mountain
where reason probes our depths, the newcomers were gone;
again I drew near to my faithful companion,
without whose stern guidance how would have I followed –
or even have discerned – the long and winding road?
He seemed as if reproaching himself inwardly,
being one of the noble who feel bitterly
the slightest falling from what their strict souls demand,
and it was only when his frantic pace lessened
that my mind could relax and start to take in
the vast peak commanding our whole field of vision
as it rose above the glassy levels of the sea.

The sun's blood-red fire was behind us, and before me
the sole black gash in an unbroken field of light
showed where its shining fingers – strong yet delicate –
rested on my mortal shape and could not cross.
I turned quickly to my right side, fearing the loss
of my guardian when I saw this lone shadow.
"Why are you still so diffident," he sighed, "and so
disinclined to trust that I won't abandon you?
The body I had which heaven couldn't see through
now lies at Naples in the spacious tomb of dusk;
if no manlike dark walks ahead of me, why ask
any more than you'd ask why the celestial

spheres do not obstruct or deviate a single
beam but lets them travel unhindered on Love's track?
The capacity to feel a flame on my back,
and the stroke of a lash and the foul ice's blaze,
is given to me by the supreme force whose ways
are veiled by everything its virtues manifest –
here is the reason frail humanity must rest
content with the fact that things *are* the way they are,
and why he is naive or insane who thinks mere
minds can trace the endless warp and weft of the One.
If our carnal apparatus, working alone,
can see all there is to be seen then why the need

for the Word to be born? Why the dissatisfied
expression on the faces of them whose desire
would've been more than answered, not made the cold fire
inside which each is locked like an Islamic tile
(I speak, of course, of Plato and Aristotle
and many others too)?" At that he fell silent
and paced with a stern and troubled look, forehead bent
towards the ground. Soon we reached the base of the peak,
an almost sheer expanse of such featureless rock
that the nimblest foot could have found no toehold there…
Lerici's ruined cliffs are a smooth, easy stair
in comparison to the immaculate page

we now stood before. "Who can tell," murmured that sage,
coming to a halt, "on which side the mountain slopes,
where someone without feathered heels behind his leaps
can inch his way back to the fundamental tree?"
As he was standing there, pondering inwardly,
and as my eyes played over that mass of bare stone,
I suddenly glimpsed to my left a procession
of souls treading so slow they scarcely seemed to move
at all. "Look up, O maestro," I whispered, "for if
you don't have the answer then here are some who may!"
He gazed where I had pointed. "So we head that way,"
he said, relief clearly audible in his voice,

"rather than wait… see how they walk at a dream's pace,
as though reluctant. Come, my child, and don't lose heart."
When we had gone the distance of a rifle shot
they were still far off, and yet seeing us they shrank
against the unchipped surface of the mighty bank
and stared motionless as a herd of spooked gazelle.
"Elected souls," Virgil called, "you who ended well –
tell us, in the name of the silence that draws you,
where this mountain can be climbed… recall how those who
are most aware sense the loss of time most keenly."
As shy forest creatures will approach – two or three
venturing forth at first while the rest lag behind

united in timidity, nuzzling the ground,
stopping when their leader stops and moving when he moves
as innocent and clear-headed as little waves –
so I saw the bravest of that fortunate flock
come gravely towards us, with something of the look
of girls whose self-consciousness is balanced by grace;
when, however, they spotted the morbid device
of a shadow stretched between my feet and the cliffs,
they froze again like beasts that fear for their lives
and the ones who followed (not knowing why they did)
froze too. "I know that you haven't asked," said my guide,
"but I make this confession to you all the same –

it is a living form which divides the sun's flame
so that light's mournful absence sprawls upon the earth,
and moreover one the empyrean thinks worth
charging with the vigour to scale your precipice."
"Then turn," a spirit said, "and walk ahead of us…
and consider as we go, whoever you may be,
if in the other world you encountered me."
And so I looked back and examined carefully
his blonde hair and that face in which nobility
was everywhere present yet nowhere explicit,
only disfigured where a dagger-swipe had split
an eyebrow's golden line. "I don't know you," I said,

at which he pointed to where a scar's faded red
marked his strong chest. "I am Manfred," he said, and smiled.
"My grandmother was an empress, and my dear child
is now mother of the honour of Aragon
and Sicily. Go to her, I beg you, when you return
and tell her this truth to counteract the lies
that cluster and flicker up there like mongrel flies
around a corpse's mouth. Two deadly blows released
my soul's imprisoned splendour from its vast
panopticon of blood, and towards the sun it flew
and surrendered unconditionally to one who
forgives us with His inviolable will.

In spite of the fact I had thought and done evil,
I was received by that immense benevolence
as are all who come to it; if only Clement's
lackey was more familiar with those words' bright face,
my white bones would still be in their burial-place
beside the bridge at Benevento, under a cairn,
rather than scattered by the black wind and the rain
beyond the kingdom's bounds. No soul cast out like this
is wholly lost to Love when hope's *viriditas*
retains one touch of green, though each miscreant year
will be paid for with thirty years pacing here
beneath these cliffs. Go to my sweet Constance, as her

prayers can diminish the age that I must wander."

4.

When a pleasant or painful thing focuses

the soul's intellectual light, it notices
nothing else but is held by that one potency –
a fact which refutes the error of those who say
the soul is a multiple brilliance within us.
If, then, we hear or see something so marvellous
that the swift ray of our apprehension is bent,
it's not that time stops but its music is silent
(this faculty suspended for as long as a
strange sight or story possesses us entirely).
I speak here of truths which I have known at first hand,
listening to that spirit and wondering and
not even conscious that the rising sun had passed

through fifty full degrees, or that we'd come at last
to a thin hole or cleft in the sheer wall of stone
("be careful what you wish for," they bleated as one).
The passageway we entered was scarcely the size
of a gap in a hedge – one that, when autumn skies
start to flush earth's grapes with night, a farmer might cork
with a head-shaped pile of thorns lifted on a fork –
the herd being gone and the two of us alone.
You can climb to Sanleo by the strength of your own
labouring feet, and I imagine you'd get down
a cliff-cut stairway to some barnacled town
with merely your solid physique for company,

yet here was an ascent where one needed to fly –
to grow plumes of spiritual desire, I mean,
and follow as I did that superlative man
who gave me hope and whose radiance could make all
clear. Up that steep, narrow chink we clambered, each wall
squeezing in on us as we toiled with hands and toes,
and then we emerged and I stood by the maestro's
shoulder at the cliff's top beneath a giant slope.
"Which way now?" "Don't," he replied, "take one backward step
but walk right behind me up the steep mountainside,
never resting until a knowledgeable guide
manifests before us." The summit was so high

that it stood some way beyond my capacity
to see, the gradient greater than the angle
of a line from mid-quadrant to the heart of a circle.
"Father," I cried, wearily, "do not walk so fast…
turn and speak to me or else I shall be lost."
He pointed to where a slender ledge seemed to run
round the mountain's flank. "Drag yourself," he said, "my son,
up there," and somehow those seven syllables spurred
me on and I forced myself to crawl forward
until the circling level was beneath my feet.
Settling ourselves upon it as if on a seat,
we gazed towards the east: zone of the newborn sun,

which is for men both the source of life and a sign
of all that is immortal yet cannot be seen.
I looked down towards the distant shoreline, and then
I raised my eyes to that eminent craft of light
and marvelled at its beams not striking from the right
but from the left where the Hyperboreans are.
Seeing my expression of idiotic awe,
the poet spoke. "If," he laughed, "the celestial
mirror – which moves around its zoological
wheel from pole to pole and back again – was with the Twins,
you'd now be observing its red luminescence
even closer to the white Bears of the north…

assuming, of course, that its customary path
was kept to. Shut your restless eyes and envision
how this lone island-mountain and holy Zion
have their own hemispheres yet share a horizon,
and surely you'll realise the road down which Phaeton
desired to drive his father's astonishing car –
or you will if your mind is unperturbed and clear,
if you're listening well – must run first on one side
of the sky and then on the other." "Teacher and guide,"
I said, "I've never perceived with such clarity,
right here where intelligence seemed to fail me,
that the immense circle they call the Equator –

an invisible wall between warmth and winter –
is as far to the north as it was to the south
when the Hebrews looked back to the Nile's opaque mouth
and all of Africa smoked beyond it. But how
far do we have to climb?" "The going's harder now,"
he replied, "than it'll be as we start to ascend…
you will tell we're approaching our journey's end
when you find those limbs move with miraculous ease
as though the way up was a drift downstream, bowed trees
shading your idle boat. You shall be revived there,
God knows. That's the entirety of my answer."
"Though perhaps," a voice suddenly drawled, "not without

some crises on the way." As if wholly worn out,
the speaker sat hugging his legs in a boulder's
crowded shadow. "Look," I cried, "it's Laziness's
useless brother!" He half-raised his face from his thighs
and examined us, and I realised who it was.
"Go on," he mumbled, "you who are *so* full of life."
I smiled as I approached him, the ghost of a laugh,
for, despite my tiredness, those brief words amused me.
"Did you note," the man continued, a peak-like knee
still hiding his mouth, "how Apollo's battered van
flies on your ill-omened side?" "Belacqua," I began,
"I'll grieve for you no longer. Yet tell me why

you fester here… do you lack a guide, or do I
sense that you've been taken up by your old habits?"
"Climbing's useless, brother, since the angel who sits
at the entrance like a roughneck at a funfair
refused to let me pass into the purging fire;
first the heavens' flashing and many-coloured wheel
must circle round for just as long as my slack will –
when breath still drew me – gave me rein to loaf and sigh,
my only heartfelt moan the one that saw me die.
Unless, that is, the magic of grace-charged prayer
(any other kind the sky simply cannot hear)
comes to my aid." "Quick, let's press on," urged the poet,

"as night already darkens Morocco with her foot."

5.

Having left those shadows in the gloom of their rock,

I was proceeding in the footsteps of the duke
when I heard a voice shout. "Look," it cried, "how that one
forms an impediment to the rays of the sun…
he seems to conduct himself like a living man!"
I turned and glimpsed them gazing in consternation
at me and at the slitted sunshine at my side,
an act which drew a snort of disdain from my guide.
"Why does your spirit so involve itself," he said,
"adjusting its pace to the whispers of the dead?
Let these wasters chatter, and follow after me…
be as a flint-built tower that is completely
unaffected by the boisterous wind's empty threats,

since if one thing's sure it's that thoughts succeeding thoughts –
like interfering wavelengths – sap each other's force
and move all you aim for to a more distant place."
What could I do but do as he ordered, my whole
face glowing with the colour which suggests a soul
is worthy of pardon? A little above us,
we now saw figures intoning verse after verse
of the *Miserere* in a pure, responsive voice;
yet as soon as they perceived that the sweet light's rays
were detained upon my body, the blessèd psalm
metamorphosed into a hoarse cry of alarm
and two of them raced, messenger-like, our way

and demanded to know my condition. "Just say,"
replied the maestro, "that this substance which you see
is authentic flesh and blood; it seems clear to me
you were startled by the darkness he's shadowed by,
so these words should suffice. If you honour him, I
swear the act will profit you." No meteorite
ever blazed its name on the *duomo* of night
as quickly as that pair returned – more lightning-fast
than electrical vapours flicker in the west
in livid August dusks – then wheeled back towards us
with all the rest of the souls, magnificent as
a whole squadron galloping with loosely-held reins.

("This crowd," said the poet, "so eager and so dense,
comes to implore your help... do not, however, pause
but listen as you walk"). "O you," they clamoured, "whose
soul's still apparelled in the garb it was born in,
stop – we beg – and talk a while; if you've ever seen
any of us before, you can take news of him
to the distant north. We were each torn limb from limb,
inveterate sinners until the instant when
the light of another sky broke in to waken
our suddenly repenting and forgiving souls,
both at peace and yet pierced to the very entrails
with a desire to behold the Artificer's

ever-living face." "I don't," I said, "recognise
anybody here... but tell me whether there is
something I can do, and – in the name of that peace
which compelled me to follow the tread of a ghost,
silently summoning a soul thwarted or lost
and thus engineering its own discovery
although whole worlds lay between the treasure and me –
it shall be done as far as I am capable."
"We have faith," one of them began, "in your good will,
provided it's not curbed by deficient powers;
and so, speaking alone before all these others,
I ask that – if you ever visit the country

beside Romagna and Charles's realm – you make a plea
to the people in Fano to pray for me well...
it is only by prayer that lamentable
sins such as mine can be entirely washed away.
It was Fano gave me birth, but the place that I
received three wounds – so deep, I saw my throned life pour
through the breach – was in the lands of Antenor
where I imagined I was safe; being angry
beyond rightful limits, the Marquis of Este
gave the word. If I'd only made my flight toward
Mira when my killers overtook me, I would
still be back where a man is rich in breath. I fled

to the marsh, but the entangling reeds and the mud
dragged me down, and I watched as there spread on the ground
the lake of my voluminous blood." "You who're bound" –
another now spoke – "by your innermost desire
to this ultimate peak, to the tree-shaped fire
that stands upon it and that stands within us all,
take pity on and help my own desiring soul!
I'm Buonconte and I was from Montefeltro…
Giovanna takes no pains for me, therefore I go
in our straggling company with a downcast face."
"Tell me," I said to him, "what happenstance or force
carried you away from Capaldino, so that

the site of your grave was never known?" "At the foot
of the Casentino," he replied, "there crosses
a stream called the Archiano, whose birthplace is
high above the Hermitage in the Appenines.
Running for my life and watering the plain's
soil with the blood which spurted from my punctured throat,
I came to where that stream's last syllable is said;
sight darkening, my long torrent of words ended
on our Holy Mother's name, and only the coat
of flesh my soul had worn now sprawled upon bare earth.
Tell all this to the living since I speak the truth.
As His hawk-faced angel took my spirit's hand, a voice

rose from the inferno's subterranean ice:
Ah why do you defraud me, scoundrel from the sky?
You slink off with his fragment of eternity
which but for the inkling of a tear would be mine,
although rest assured far different laws shall govern
the empty mechanism that sprite leaves behind!
You know how moisture gathers on days of no wind,
rising through the bodiless air to where a chill
grasps it and forms rain, so that malevolent will
conspired with a satanic intellect to move
the vapours and the gloom – such power spirits have –
and to fill the whole valley with low-hanging cloud

and impregnate with liquid grain the greys overhead…
a swollen heaven that then turned into a sea
which hammered down until the earth was completely
saturated and the ditches drank the excess,
whilst from a thousand directions those waters
thronged to the royal river, jabbering in tongues;
encountering my corpse, the Archiano flings
that clod from its mouth into the mighty Arno
and loosens the arms I had crossed when the sorrow
that is death mastered me." "Remember La Pia,"
a third spirit piped up, "composed at Siena,
erased in Maremma. He did the wicked thing,

the one who hooked me with an eternity ring."

6.

A game of dice over, the loser sits alone

and sadly repeats the throws time and time again
as though you could interrogate the face of chance;
the winner, meanwhile, swaggers off in a dense
gaggle of his closest friends – one behind, three ahead
and two alongside, begging to be remembered –
yet steers an unwavering course between their cries,
occasionally holding out a palm so he's
shielded from the needy and importuning throng.
Thus I seemed in that scrum of shadows, borne along
within it whilst turning my head every which way
(at each assurance that is made, the mad melee
diminishes by one and I breathe more freely)

until I was quite clear of the repeated plea
that others plead on their behalf so that they might
not merely come to but *become* divine delight
with far less delay. "I seem to recall," I said,
"having somewhere or other in your opus read –
O guiding star – how the sky's decrees can't be swayed
by prayer, yet such was the desire of that crowd…
does this, then, imply all their wishes are in vain?"
"The inscape," he replied, "of my words should be plain.
Consider things with a steady mind and you'll see
those hopes are not mistaken. Love's fire instantly
accomplishes the work of an age of exile,

though prayer possessed no efficacy until
it found or refound a path to the highest ear…
this was the distinction I was making there.
The peak we call Justice doesn't stoop; man ascends.
Don't adopt the pretence of one who understands,
but stay if you can in these deep uncertainties
till you have it from the shining mouth of her whose
light will be the link between your mind and that which *is*.
Do you realise what I'm saying? I mean Beatrice,
whose joyous face you'll see on this mountain's green top."
"In that case, my lord," I said, "let's quicken our step,
for already I move easier and the shade

of night spreads on the slope above. "We'll go," he said,
"within this radiance as far as it extends,
and then hunker in darkness when the daylight ends.
Again, mere thoughts forge a false image of the fact.
Look how your bladelike fingers no longer dissect
the golden body of the eye the slope now hides…
before we've climbed to where earth's innocence abides,
it will rise once more. But see there, sitting alone
and gazing our way, the fleshless form of one
who'll be able to indicate the most direct route."
What disdainful nobleness, great Lombard spirit,
you embodied and radiated as we neared,

and with what leonine power and poise you stared
from eyes in whose slow regard crouched your lightning wit!
My guide approached you and spoke, and still you did not
respond to his question but asked one of your own.
"Mantua fathered me," the gentle duke began,
at which all that contained force leapt forth suddenly
with a cry of "I'm Sordello, from that city!"
and like long-separated brothers they embraced.
O country of mine – a slave-ship in a tempest
with terror at the wheel, a night shelter loud with
sleepless moans exhaled through diseased and broken teeth,
no princess among nations but a sly, drunk whore!

The life in you is worn down by a silent war
purporting to be peace, whilst inside each calm moat
and sunlit wall is one with his mouth at the throat
of his white-faced friend… ah, look in your heart and see
if there any more than in the venomous sea
the least tenderness or tranquillity endures;
the bridle's in place yet no rider's on the horse,
and that makes for deeper shame. A nation without
its Caesar, a people who do not pay devout
attention to our Father's omnipresent Word –
see what has become of this beast that isn't spurred
by the immutable but led by a common

mob. And you, German Albert, you who abandon
a steed you should be throned upon… the barbed ice
of the stars will pierce your veins to wreak strange justice,
and all shall witness! A holy empire gone to seed,
neglected as a consequence of the vast greed
imprisoning you and your father in its claws –
come and see the noblest men crippled by their fears,
the marble towns lapped by a degenerate tide!
Ah, come and see the widowed city that has cried
night and day for the presence of its emperor…
come and observe how the people treat each other,
and if pity still doesn't warm your veins' live root

then come to feel profound shame for your disrepute!
(High-glittering Jove, is your stern and righteous gaze
turned elsewhere – O you who, the hidden doctrine says,
formed with your downfall the wide world we pace upon –
or is some final good, beyond our perception,
being prepared in that unfathomable mind?)
Every citizen's his own tyrant, and the blind
shouters after justice do the work of darkness
in humanity's name. There's just one city this
digression does not touch, which I'll identify
only as the metropole of those whose sole eye
is as clear as their imagination is quick,

who to embody justice merely have to speak –
unlike those who lurk within their ribs and never loose
the bent bow of the tongue – and who don't refuse
the burden of their blood but wear it joyfully;
surely *you* have more than ample cause to be happy,
wise in what you know so little of and at peace
in each day's new battle, destitute in riches
yet surpassing the law and order of Sparta
and Athens herself with your fine-woven art, a
gesture outshining the most lucid autumn day.
Dreams, dreams! Flick aside the curtain and a ray
of charitable light shows its head, stoops to kiss

the sickbed that you groan on, the fetid mattress.

7.

When they'd embraced several times, the spirit drew

back and scrutinized the maestro. "Yet who *are* you?"
"My dry bones were gathered by Octavian,"
he answered, "before He let loose on this mountain
all whose souls are worthy to undertake the climb…
I am Virgil, who forfeits heaven for no crime
other than that of having little faith or none."
Now Sordello's face was lit with wonder like one
whose eyes behold something he can't believe is there,
and now he bowed his head and neared and clasped him where
a mere man's hands would touch a hero or a god.
"Glory of the spiritual empire's tongue," he said,
"by whom its implicit strength and splendour shone forth –

immortal jewel of the place that gave me birth,
is this visitation due to merit or grace?
Tell me how you came – if I'm fit to hear your voice –
from where they say there are cloisters *in* the fire."
"Not through my own strength," my guide replied. "A higher
power moved me as I progressed from ring to ring
of the kingdom of inconsolable grieving…
what you most long for, the clear vision of the One,
is less for vile or heinous acts than things undone
denied to me forever. There's a zone in hell
or close, a gloomy quarter where perpetual
sighs instead of racked screams lament the shadowed light;

I bide there with the innocents seized by the white
teeth of black-eyed death before a hand could bathe them,
and also they who, unsinning, moved in rhythm
to four virtues though never knew the final three.
Now show, if you can, how we can get more quickly
to where purgatory truly begins." "There is,"
he said, "no dwelling yet no boundary for us,
so I'll accompany you as far as I may…
but before that we must find shelter, since His day
declines and the night is not the time to ascend.
Hard by me to our right is a valley, my friend,
which sequesters several souls; I can shepherd you

there where you'll be safe and, I know, delighted too."
"So," the maestro asked, "one who tried to climb by dark
would struggle or be actively impeded?" "Look,"
replied Sordello, drawing a line in the soil
with his finger. "When the sun has gone down, your will –
both baffled and emasculated by the dense
and thronging shadows – shall consider this a fence
solid as it is high, then decide to turn back
and stagger around the lower slopes in the black
void until the far east unlocks the light once more."
"Convey us to that spot," said my ghost-pale signor,
amazement written on his face, "where you say we

can break our long journey in comfort and safety."
Somewhat further, we arrived at a kind of dip
or valley-like hollow – the peak's maternal lap –
where the tall shade told us we could wait for the dawn,
and I stood on the depression's edge and looked down;
white lead and cochineal, pure silver and gold,
indigo's clear radiance or an emerald
that second split from its sullen matrix of earth –
all these would certainly seem things of little worth
and much dullness next to the verdure we now saw,
inlaid with small flowers of surpassing splendour.
Nature hadn't just deployed her artifice there

in a thousand nameless hues, but the lucid air
was sweet with whole new worlds of undiscovered scents
which harmonised into a note of such intense
yet refreshing beauty that the mind became still;
seated on the greenness of that inverted hill,
spirits the surrounding bank had hidden from sight
were singing *Hail holy Queen, loving Mother of light*.
"Don't ask me to lead you down there," the Mantuan
who'd guided us to that vantage-point began,
"before the sun's last remaining rays go to ground.
It will be easier to observe from this mound
their ways and faces than if we stood among them –

first is he who might have healed the wounds that condemn
our land to a protracted death, a verbose life
which only a rebirth of vision will revive,
seated above the others with the expression
of one who did not do what he ought to have done…
this is Rudolph, and you'll see he doesn't sing.
By him, in an attitude of consoling,
is Ottakar who ruled the region that carries
the Moldau to the Elba and the Elba to the sea's
blue inferno, who even as a speechless child
was superior to his debauched boy that wild
appetite and low ease distend and starve at once.

The small-nosed man beside him is Philip of France –
leaning to confer with the one whose countenance
looks so benign – a king who did great violence
to the fleur-de-lis and who died in headlong flight…
observe how he beats his breast, how the other's right
palm makes a soft couch for his sighing cheek. They know
what now squats on the throne; such knowledge is sorrow.
The soul with shapely limbs, harmonising his voice
with the one whose regal nose commands his whole face,
was belted by the cord of righteousness and faith;
if the youth behind him had ruled after, his worth
had been better passed from warm 'vessel to vessel'

(his living heirs' inheritance is merely soil
and not that light which the blood may happen to bear).
For such vital sap to *ascend* the tree is rare,
this being the will of Him who'd far rather
it has to be sought in the all-bestowing Father;
these words apply equally to his companion
in song, whose wastrel and much inferior son
is the source of Provence's and Puglia's pain.
See also, sat apart, the English king whose reign
was undistinguished yet who grew sturdy branches,
and finally the one looking up at them is
the Marquis of Montferrat… there, throned on the ground

like a man in a sunlit cage, a dog in the pound."

8.

It was the hour when the minds of men at sea

go to those whom they kissed goodbye so recently,
the hour when hearts relent and a pilgrim hears
the distant bell that seems to mourn the day, to pierce
an impervious self with love as sharp as pain;
now Sordello's calm words were at my ears in vain,
transfixed as I was by the shadow who had stood
and declared with a hand he wanted to be heard...
he clasped his palms and lifted them above his head
then stared toward the greying east, a sign which said
I offer this, O Lord, in my entirety,
and sang no less devotedly than tenderly
the hymn beginning *As the sweet light comes to grief*

such that I forgot my lone and ill-conceived life
(the others join in after the first line, all eyes
turned upon the bright mechanism of the skies –
and here, languid reader, you should sharpen your own,
for this cunningly woven veil is right now thin
enough to see through to where the naked truth lies!).
Meanwhile that pale, expectant crowd kept its gaze
fixed silently above it, and suddenly there are
two majestic angels apparent in the air;
each one held a blazing sword with a broken point,
and they wore the selfsame green and flamelike garment
the trees put on in May, trailing out behind them

and billowing in the breeze from their plumed wings' hum.
One of them landed above us, and the other
at the valley's far side; I could discern blonde hair,
but their faces were adazzle with sheer excess
of light. "They come," Sordello said, "from Our Lady's
white breast, watchful for the snake that will soon appear."
(Here I looked around me and suppressed a shiver,
edging a little closer to him as I did.)
"Let's go down among those shadows," he continued,
"who'll surely be delighted by your presence here."
It seemed, if my perceptions were correct, a mere
three steps brought us to the bottom of the valley

where stood a man who was scrutinizing me
as though in recognition; day was almost gone,
but there flashed through the gloom between his eyes and mine
what the bluish distance had impeded before.
O Nino Visconti, with what utter joy I saw
you are not among the doubly dead! We embraced,
and then he asked how long it'd been since I crossed
the vast expanse seething at the peak's jagged foot.
"This very morning," I replied, "we staggered out
of the pass which traverses the night... I am still
in my first life, yet I've faith that by sounding hell
one gains the other." As these words are heard, they both

step backwards like men astonished by the truth –
Sordello turns to Virgil, and dear Nino cries
to a third soul seated nearby. "Look," he said, "arise
and witness what God's mysterious grace has willed!"
"By the thanks you owe to Him whose book is the world" –
he addressed me now – "and whose world's the fathomless
veil and revelation of His primal purpose,
please tell my Giovanna (when you're back beyond
that immensity of waves) to pray... they respond
in highest heaven when innocence calls. As for
my wife, I think she doesn't love me any more
since she cast aside her widowhood's white fillets;

it's plain to see how women's passionate spirits
can only endure so long as their fire is fed
by the stroke of a glance or a hand's warm regard –
although the Milanese viper shall not adorn
her tomb like Gallura's cock, vigilant for dawn"
(all the while that he spoke, his face had the brilliance
of gold stamped with an image of the violence
contained and yet flaming inside a righteous heart).
My hungry eyes were turned toward the sky, the part
where slower stars evoke the axle of a wheel.
"What," the maestro asked, "are you staring at, pupil?"
"At three points of light that illuminate the pole,"

I answered. "Those stars," he said, "command the black hill
that the four you saw this morning have now paced down."
As he was speaking, Sordello made a sudden
grab for my companion's arm and pointed to where
the shining valley lacked a natural barrier.
"Look," he cried, "and see our adversary!" It was
a little snake, a subtle flicker in the grass,
cautiously advancing and then pausing to lick
the uncanny glow of its pixellated back,
perhaps like the beast that once captivated Eve;
I shan't say how because I didn't see them move,
but the next thing I knew the celestial birds

had in a fraction of a moment sprung forwards –
a green blur and outburst in the twilit air
which made the serpent flee, and instantly that pair
of raptors were motionless at their posts again.
The third shade, who as this strange drama had gone on
was observing me minutely, now went to speak.
"Tell me," he said, "since you desire to scale the peak
whose highest garden lights the holy dark, if you've
any news of Val di Magra; I had such love
for my kinsfolk then, love I've heard this place makes finer...
I was known those days as Conrad Malaspina,
not the first to bear that name yet one of his line."

"Where," I exclaimed, "in all of Europe are there men
unacquainted with your noble house, spoken of
not only by knights but by the lowliest serf
so he who hasn't been there feels he knows it well;
I can reassure you that your honest people
are still capable of tender love and clean hate,
and that while a crowned skull contrives to deviate
our world from the sacred path they walk straight and tall."
"Truer than you think," he replied. "The sun's vernal
rest in the golden bed canopied by the ram's
starry legs shall not recur more than seven times
before that opinion is fixed within your head –

by larger nails, though, than what men have merely said."

9.

Tithonus's mistress had slipped from their embrace,

was already sitting marble-white on the sky's
eastern balcony, forehead lit by a jewel
resembling the creature who battles with his tail;
it was the time when night's third watch cedes to the fourth,
and I surrendered to that in me which is earth
and fell asleep on our patterned carpet of grass.
At the hour before dawn, just when the swallows
renew those melancholy cries – and when the mind,
less domineered by thought and no longer confined
by the body it strays from, often prophecies –
I seemed to see an eagle with golden feathers
hang in the upper air as if about to drop

down as Zeus once did on the child who'd hold his cup
(considering myself to be on Mount Ida,
and reasoning while I dream that every other
hunting-ground is disdained by this rapacious bird).
It circled several times then fell with lightning speed
and bore me up, swifter still, as far as the fire
where we were burned indescribably together,
the heat of the imagined blaze more and more fierce
until I suddenly awoke. Like Achilles,
carried by his mother to Scyros as he dozed,
I darted my startled eyes round like one amazed
to find himself in an entirely unknown place;

pure fear made me certain my heart had turned to ice,
yet then I looked and saw my comforter near me
and the glittering immensity of the sea
with the sun already two hours above it.
"There's no need to be afraid," said that wise spirit.
"Rest assured that things go well for us, and don't shrink
within yourself but flourish every strength. This bank
encloses the place where the soul is purified;
see the entrance there, how the wall seems to divide.
While you were stretched out in your flesh, a woman came…
'I am Lucia,' she declared. 'Let me bear him,
let me help this pitiful sleeper on his way.'

So she took you in her arms, and, as soon as day
gave light enough to see by, she carried you here;
Sordello stayed below, while I kept beside her.
Her lovely eyes showed me the portal in the rock,
and then she left and that same second you awoke."
Like one who sees clearly, and in clear sight is free
from all his little woes, this knowledge altered me –
fear turned to confidence, misgivings reassured –
and the maestro simply smiled and walked toward
the barrier above with me pacing right behind.
(Those few intrepid readers who aren't deaf and blind
will perceive at this point that my material

is being raised to the heights, therefore why marvel
if I build the foundations with increasing art?)
What had first resembled a crack in the rampart
revealed itself as we approached to be a door
with three steps beneath, each a different colour;
at the very top an angel sat in silence,
the pellucid brightness of his face so intense
I needed to shade and half-close my widened eyes;
he held in one hand a naked sword, the sun's rays
reflecting with such force we squinted up in vain.
"Keep your distance and state what you want," he began.
"Who's guiding you? For the unwary, the ascent

could be deadly." "We have," said Virgil, "the assent
of a soul well-versed in such affairs, a woman
from heaven. 'There's the gate,' she urged just now. 'Walk on.'"
"Then come toward our stairway, impelled by her grace."
We neared, and in the first step I saw my true face
leering back at me from the marble's glassy white;
next was a thick slab of purplish lava, split right
across its battered length and vertically too;
the third seemed porphyry, that imperial hue
of aristocratic blood spurting from a vein,
and its red mass appeared to weigh the others down.
God's warrior had his feet on this highest step,

throned on a sill so adamant no Imhotep
could carve it. "You must ask him," said the cautious duke
as he drew me up those dreadful stairs, "to unlock
the door." I struck my fist three times upon my chest
then abased myself devotedly and kissed
the blessèd feet, begging that he have the mercy
to admit us. Reaching out his blade, he marked me
seven times with the sign of an *S* on the head –
"be sure and wash those wounds when you're inside," he said –
then took two keys from a robe the shade of ash or dust,
slotting a silver spine into the great gate first
and now doing the same with the one made of gold.

"The mechanism's like a knot too entangled
for less than ingenuity to work it free,
and in this consists the art of the paler key;
proceed, yet bear in mind a single backward glance
will end your journey." The door in the high entrance
gave way at the pressure of his hand, with a raw
dissonant screech of hinges as if even more
loath to be prised than the sanctum at Tarpeia…
a thunderous hum came forth, and I seemed to hear
phrases intermingled with that beguiling tone.
We praise thee, they went, *and all the powers therein*,
the words one moment clear and the next moment drowned

as a hymn's sense in an organ's majestic sound.

10

As soon as we had crossed the threshold of that door

hardly used since true love became a mere amour –
since dull perceptions showed the twisted track as straight –
I heard it slam and the cold steel resonate
and checked myself in the very act of turning back.
We now began to climb a thin, ascending crack,
its granite sides going first that way and then this
like waves' alternate onslaught and retreating hiss,
and the necessary skill made our steps so slow
that by the time we crawled from that needle's eye the hollow
moon had taken to its bed once again.
We surveyed a broad and empty ledge, the mountain
having retreated as a man draws in his breath,

flesh heavy on me and both doubtful of our path
and the silence tremulous as a desert road;
between the high bank's base and the edge of the void
three men could have lain head to head, and that sheer wall
was – I then perceived – formed of dazzling white marble,
carved in such a fashion that Hera's own sculptor
and Nature herself might stare in jealous wonder.
The angel who stepped down to earth with the decree
of peace which century after dark century
had wept for – reopening the deep sky and all
that lies beyond it – was imaged there, so graceful
and so real it was a sight you could somehow *hear*…

his entire demeanour spoke, for also limned here
was she whose inner being is Love's mystic key,
her body expressing her soul as exactly
as melted wax yields to the symbol on a ring.
"Don't let your eyes be transfixed but keep them moving,"
said the gentle maestro, who had me on that side
where the demon-ridden hearts of the living hide –
so I gave my gaze free rein and saw a second
story in the rock on the far side of my friend,
walking past him to have it right in front of me.
There shone the sheepskin-veiled Ark, advancing slowly
towards Jerusalem on an ox-drawn wagon –

the acacia-wood box on account of which men
understand the sacred is a thing that can kill –
and surrounding it were seven choirs who were still
voicing those sweet psalms only the inmost eye hears
(likewise, the unfurling incense made my nose
as envious as my ears of my transported sight).
God's humble lyricist, dancing such that his light
feet barely touched the ground, preceded that pale throng –
in his great ecstasy both less and more than king –
and beyond one saw, framed in a palace window,
Michal glare down with a hate that masked her sorrow.
I moved from where I stood to better examine

yet another tale gleaming ghost-white in the stone,
and now I had before me the haughty glory
of the Roman prince whose worth inspired Gregory
to raise him – I mean the Emperor Trajan,
bending down to speak to a huddled old woman
who stood at his bridle in mourning and in tears,
hemmed by war-bound horses, the golden feathers
of the ensigns above them as though ruffled by the wind;
despite all this clamour, I thought I sensed the sound
of that wretched mother's voice. "My baby is dead
and so's my heart, and blood must pay for blood," she said.
"I'll see what I can do when I return," his lips

snapped back (or appeared to me to say). "Lord, he sleeps
now and now he will never wake again… what if
you *don't* return?" "My successor will hear your grief."
"And how shall another man's kindness help your soul,
if you stint your own?" Every word was visible
yet transparent, wrought of air, placed there by the One
whose wisdom's the sight of the all-renewing sun,
and as I was delightedly gazing at these
embodiments of such profound humilities –
precious for the Mason who hid yet glowed within them –
I heard Virgil murmur. "See, that sluggish stream
of approaching people will sweep us to the stairs…"

My roving eyes, eager for new signs and wonders,
weren't slow to glance that way – and now all you who read
must hear how our Lord ordains man's debt shall be paid,
without letting the blade of your resolve be bent;
you need to look past the *form* of the punishment,
knowing time's last sentence will bring it to a close.
"Maestro," I then began, "I cannot think what those
creatures are but they scarcely seem to be human…
gazing makes no sense of them." "The grave regimen
of their penance," he said, "folds them almost double
and I, much like you, initially had trouble
to interpret what I saw… peer closer and you'll

see each rock-lifting knot is a hunched-over soul,
a tight knot with legs and a fist to beat its chest."
Self-satisfied dupes who abuse the name of Christ,
with your whole outlook skewed and your back-to-front gait –
why can't you recognise that man is a maggot
until the moment his chrysalis splits and he
flies frail and resplendent to the stern sky's mercy,
that your spirits are like larvae sucked into a cloud?
As I now more carefully examined the crowd
I was reminded of those teeth-gritting dwarfs
which hold on stone shoulders entire cathedral-roofs,
and the face of the least laden and least crushed there

said with mute eloquence *this is too much to bear.*

11.

Old artificer who abidest in heaven,

and not just heaven but who illumines even
the lowliest dust-speck the mind can tread upon,
hallowed be your name as it unfolds in each one
of the strange beasts who speak back your spirit and your might;
let silence be established, for man's little wit
can achieve nothing by its meagre light alone,
but rather have us be as those angels who intone
your glories in a wild abeyance of the will.
Give us this day our daily mania, our fill
of soul-crushing burdens without which the soul
shall never find the strength to quit its mortal hole,
and look indulgently on our foolishness

as we laugh at all who manoeuvre against us.
Lead us in and out of temptation, we who stand
unyielding as a dandelion clock, and
deliver us from the broadcasts of the Adversary…
some of this, Lord, isn't strictly necessary
yet is there for the benefit of those left behind.
Thus the burdened shadows drone their weary round
of the mountain's first terrace, purging life's dark mist
with each painful circuit, variously distressed
depending on the size of their nightmare stone –
and, as they pray well for us, much good can be done
by a prayer said by one whose taproot goes deep,

in order that, cleansed, they may eventually step
with light hearts towards the sweet turmoil of the stars.
"Please show us," called the maestro, "how to find the stairs
which a man wearing Adam's carnal vest can climb,
for my companion is eager but makes slow time –
and do it in the name of Him who will remove
your grievous baggage so you can soar above,
each in accordance with the thirst that beats his wings."
This answer then arose, though which one of those things
was speaking I found it impossible to tell.
"Follow us to the right as we skirt this high wall,
and you'll come to a path a still-masked soul may take…

was I not prevented from so doing by this rock
that subdues my proud neck and bends it to the earth,
I'd look at this mystery man who's hung onto his breath
to see if I knew him and if he'd pity me.
I was a Tuscan and an Aldobrandeschi,
the son of the famed Guglielmo no less,
and I exulted in my blood's nobleness
and the centuries of great work to the extent
I forgot our one mother and waxed insolent...
radiating such cold disdain for other men
that I died for it and became (as good children
in Campagnatico know) a cautionary tale.

I am Omberto, and not just me but all
I loved or might have loved were wounded by my pride –
and now, and till such time as God is satisfied,
what I neglected in life I must bear in death."
Leaning down as I listened, I glimpsed underneath
one of those moving boulders a contorted face
calling as if it knew me and twisting its gaze
in the effort to keep my own hunched form in view.
"Hey," I cried in sudden realisation, "aren't you
Oderisi the illuminator, as they term
that devout technique?" "Brother," he replied, "the fame
of Franco of Bologna, he whose pages beam

with brighter premonitions of joyous wisdom,
has eclipsed most of mine and deservedly so;
I can afford to be generous in death, although
when I was alive the whole focus of my heart
was to make every other striver in that art
seem an ape and a fool, a lust for mastery
I am paying for here... here where I wouldn't be
had I not turned to God when I'd still strength to sin.
How vain human genius now looks, less mountain
than a low hill crowned with a momentary May
no sooner seen than it's succeeded by a
slow progression down to winter's age of iron.

Cimabue felt he held painting's fort, yet one
more charged with lucid purpose has made his designs
seem stumbling and unclear, much as the sculpted lines
of a new Guido have surpassed those of the first
(as he'll be outshone in turn by one better versed
in love's holy discipline, its grave mysteries).
The world's self-important sound is merely a breeze
variously named for the wastes through which it blows,
and you're naive if you think that by sporting those
rags of skin and sinew till they're stained and threadbare –
that patchwork inherited from who can tell where –
you give yourself the space and time to found a voice

more considerable than the tentative noise
you lisped when a child, remembering a thousand years
will count you as small as its own span appears
in the light of the Mind men call eternity...
somewhat less enduring than the dream of a flea.
The soul who strolls with tiny steps ahead of me
possessed a name that rang loud throughout Tuscany,
now scarcely ever mentioned where he once raised hell,
and all of your glories are blades of grass that shall
wither in the same force which ignited their green."
"You speak the truth," I answered. "I know I have been
swollen in vanity, my proud heart loath to bow...

but who's the other man you pointed out just now?"
"That," he declared, "is Provenzano Salvani,
and he goes like that with no respite because he
sought to get the whole of Siena in his grasp."
"If souls that wait," I then asked, "until life's thinned cusp
before repenting must spend an epoch down there,
why is he not doing his time but with you here?"
"When he was in possession of his full powers,"
he said, "he trod the streets for as many hours
as it took him to free a dear friend from prison –
relearning to quake along each vein – and this lone
work spelled liberation. My words might be obscure,

yet your own days will gloss them so I'll say no more."

12.

Side by side like a pair of harnessed oxen,

that marvellously-laden soul and I went on
for as long as my gentle teacher would permit.
"Now," he said after a while, "the sail of your wit
and the oars of your will must carry you upward,
as his shall do in time." And so my body stood,
though I was still bent and belittled in my mind.
We'd gone some way ahead, both of us unburdened
and my feet imitating those of the maestro,
when he spoke again. "Turn your mortal eyes below…
it'll ease the path if you watch your bare soles' bed."
As the cold slabs hiding the oblivious dead
are signed as it were with the faces they once wore,

images which cut deep and bring another tear
to the eyes of those who pace there, who remember,
so not only that sheer wall but the very floor
was figured all with forms of far better likeness.
On one side I beheld the noblest of princes,
unequalled in heaven, flashing down from the sky;
on the other, I saw vast Briareus lie
heavy on the earth in a deathly web of frost
with a shard of celestial light in his chest,
and, miniature inside armoured Athena's eyes,
I saw the strewn remnants of immense enterprise.
There was Nimrod by his ill-starred skyscraper's base,

an expression of bewilderment on his face
as he gazed at a city that gibbered and raved;
proud Niobe, your grief-stricken glance was engraved
within the stone walkway with fourteen lidded ones;
I saw you, Saul, and the mountain that hasn't once
been touched by rain or dew since you fell on your sword,
and I saw Arachne half-crawl along a shred
of the subtle masterpiece which wrought her own doom.
What scant menace your true image, Rehoboam,
displayed as it fled pursued solely by its fears,
and how that hard pavement made Alcmaeon's mother's
taste for supernatural trinkets seem to come

at such a cost; it showed Sennacherib succumb
to the knives of his sons as he knelt to Ashur,
and the Scythian queen's icy 'you thirsted for
blood and thus blood is what you get in return'.
There too was shown the severed head of the drunken
Holofernes and the routed Assyrians,
and – how *mean* the relief made them seem – Ilion's
void and ashen ruins through a grey veil of smoke.
What superlative craftsman's brush- or chisel-stroke
could trace the fluent lines and chiaroscuro there,
both death and life depicted as they really are
so that the most ingenious can do no more

but glare, and such too that one who actually saw
each event take place would have seen the same as me
as I paced on the images with stooped body?
Stand tall, sons of Eve, and advance with towering
skulls that disregard the dust in which you're walking!
By now we had done rather more of a circuit
and used more of the day than my eager spirit
had – absorbed in those vivid fictions – been aware,
and suddenly I heard a cry from him whose stare
was ever fixed on the road ahead. "Raise your eyes,"
he said, "and see approaching with a dragonfly's
gleaming precision an angel of the Lord,

the sixth hour's ministrant, and make your regard
and your entire bearing suitably reverent…
we depend upon him for our further ascent,
and this sunlit instant will never dawn again"
(I'd already heard these kinds of admonition
on the right use of time, so his meaning was clear).
Apparelled all in white, that beautiful creature
came towards us with a face like the tremulous
brilliance of the morning star, first spreading wide his
lithe arms and then those fine and iridescent wings.
"Come," he called, "for the way is near and the climbing's
easy, though few have the strength to accept that ease…

O human race, why does the mere breath of a breeze
send you spinning earthwards when you were born to fly?"
He led us to where the wall was split, brushing my
forehead with his wing and saying I'd travel safe.
Like the path to that church above the city rife
with experts and advisors, precipitous rock
riven by steps chipped in the days when record book
and right measure were respected, so here we climbed
to the next circling terrace on a staircase hemmed
close on either side by the mountain's granite mass.
As we turned into it, I heard a blended voice
singing – with a loveliness infinitely more

sweet than man's words can tell – *Blessèd are the poor
in spirit, for they possess the kingdom of God.*
How different these gorges were from those we trod
before, where not hymns but howls had sung our welcome!
Already on the sacred stairs, I felt I'd become
much lighter in limb than when I toiled down below.
"What weight," I asked, "has been lifted from me, maestro,
for this seems to take no effort whatsoever?"
"An *S* is gone," he replied, "and once the other
six – already faded now – have quite disappeared
your pure intent will bear you joyfully upward."
I searched my brow with seeing fingers and marvelled

to find that what he'd said was true, as he quietly smiled.

13.

We finally reached that staircase's topmost step,

where the peak whose slow ascent lessens evil's grip
is cut away a second time; this terrace was bare
and curved sharper than the first, the livid glare
of the stone unrelieved by carving or shadow.
"If we wait here to ask advice," said the maestro,
"I fear our journey will be overly delayed."
Fixing his eyes intently on the sun, he made
a turn with his left side and an axis of his right
whilst addressing it in words like these. *Sweetest light,*
he cried, *trusting whom I enter on this new path,*
conduct us with your shining as we step forth…
the cold-blooded world now basks in your radiance,

and men shall always look to those rays for guidance
unless their cleverness persuades them otherwise.
We'd walked the equivalent of a mile, our pace
brisk as our wills were eager, when suddenly
the sky was filled with ghosts you could hear but not see
as they sped over, clamouring of love's table.
The call of the first was distinctly audible,
a repeated *They've no wine* growing steadily
louder and diminishing once it had hurtled by,
then a second whisked past like an ear-drawn feather
and I heard merely *I am Orestes*. "Father,"
I asked – as I spoke, a third rocketed above

with something on the lines of *All you need is love* –
"what are these voices?" "This circling road," he replied,
"is where the envious are lashed with horsewhips tied
from unbreakable filaments of love. The tone
that constitutes their bridle is the opposite one,
a noise which I think we will hear before too long;
sharpen your gaze and you'll perceive, ranged along
the barren cliff, this second step's inhabitants."
Widening and focusing my eyes, I at once
saw a queue of shadows mantled in cloaks the same
dubious colour as the stone, and as we came
gradually nearer I could hear certain cries

(*O Peter, Michael, Mary, the translucent skies'*
ecstatic multitude of saints, now pray for us!).
I don't believe there's a man on earth so heartless
that pity at this next sight wouldn't pierce him through,
my eyes overflowing with excess of sorrow
when we reached the spot where we could view them up close;
they appeared to me to be covered with a coarse
cloth of knotted horsehair, and each spirit allowed
his neighbour to lean on him (much as the whole crowd
was propped at the sufferance of the peak itself).
They reminded me of beggars moaning for pelf
at the door of a church, their craven attitude

more apt to inspire compassion than any word,
and, as the sightless can take no joy in the sun,
those shades were not granted heaven's light for each one
had its eyelids stitched with wire like a still-wild hawk;
it felt somehow wrong that I was able to walk
ogling at their plight whilst remaining unobserved,
so I turned to speak, yet, before my lips had moved,
that wise guide answered me. "Converse with them," he said,
"but be brief and to the point." He paced at my side
where the spartan terrace presented a sheer drop,
and on my other were the shades that, drip by drip,
forced past the iron sutures the tears which then coursed

down their grimy cheeks. "Say," I began, "you who thirst
solely for that highest, deepest light you're assured
of seeing in the flesh when the grace of the Lord
has removed the dirt from your consciences, your wills –
for as soon as a mind is purified, there falls
and flows within it the clear water of the source –
is anybody here from Italian shores?
If a spirit shows himself, it may do him good."
"O brother," came a voice, though none had come forward,
"there is only one country we care to call home…
did you mean to say is there anyone for whom
that land was a place where the pilgrim soul once stayed?"

Looking to see who'd answered, I noticed a shade
with chin raised expectant in the way of the blind.
"Spirit," I then said, "who in order to ascend
strive to rule yourself… tell me your earthly city's
name, if it was you that spoke." "I was Sienese,"
she replied, "and now I am seeking to repair
the remnants of a wicked life, hoping each tear
that bathes my tattered soul is pleasant to His eyes;
Sapia was my name although I wasn't wise,
finding more happiness in others' misfortune
than in my own warm limbs. Hear of my madness when
those unholy years were in decline, and believe

I tell no lies. I sat and prayed to God above,
desiring on the day that our men went to war
that He would do as He had willed, and as they were
routed and running in ignominious flight
my whole soul shivered with an exquisite delight
I'd never felt before; seeing them hunted down,
I turned to the sky – a bird in a scrap of sun –
and boldly trilled how I no longer feared the Lord.
Finally I sought peace with Him, bared my last word,
yet repentance could not have paid the debt I owe
without the remembrance of hermit Piero…
his pure heart made him grieve for me, and that grief shaped

effective prayer. But wait, who are *you* who've escaped
the blinding needle? I hear life breathe in your speech."
"Envy," I replied, "never bent my eyebeams much,
so if I lose my sight it will be brief. Horror
at what I saw below disturbs my spirit more,
already weighs like lead." "Who guided you up here,
since you mean to come and go as a mountaineer?"
"He who stands next to me in silent hardihood –
and yes, I'm still alive, so ask now if you would
have me move these dancing feet on your behalf."
"This is strange and wondrous," she cried, "a sign of God's love…
just restore my name with my people, who'll be found

among the fools who delve for moonlight underground."

14.

"Who's this strolling around our sacred peak

before his death has set him loose?" "Perhaps he'll speak
with *us* if you address him in a friendly tone…
I don't know who he is, but know he's not alone."
"And his blinking eyes both reveal and hide the light."
Thus two hunched souls, located over to my right,
were quietly conferring; and then, turning to me,
one of them spoke. "Spirit," he said, "which the body
still cages yet that's approaching bliss regardless,
I ask for sweet charity's sake that you confess
who you are and where you're from… this grace you receive
is unprecedented, difficult to believe."
"There's a certain rivulet that goes," I replied,

"through Tuscany's heart from its birthplace on the side
of beechen Falterona, and a hundred miles
of winding cannot stem it… the soft mask which veils
my soul has brought me here from that waterway's brink.
As for my name, it is unknown for now. I think
it would strike your ears as a quite meaningless sound."
"If," said the one who'd addressed me, "I understand
the bare bones of your talk, what you *mean*'s the Arno."
"Why doesn't he say it," hissed the other, "as though
it was one of those words people fear to pronounce?"
"Who knows," he countered, "yet I'd say oblivion's
a fitting place for such a river's name to be –

from its source in the high jaw from which the stony
tooth of Pelorus was once snapped, more teeming there
than at any other point with fertile water,
down to the bay where it replenishes the sea
and pays back the loan of rain, gives itself entirely,
virtue is fled from as if it was a serpent;
that miserable valley's every inhabitant,
whether warped by the land itself or by bad dreams,
is such an offence against Nature that it seems
Circe herself is the owner of the herd.
Its thin course begins amongst brutal folk whose food
is surely acorns as opposed to human fare,

cascading past men like those little dogs that are
far less ferocious than their shrill yaps declare; then,
wrinkling and turning its clear snout as if in scorn,
it continues to fall and as it falls it grows
and soon the wretched and inauspicious furrow's
hemmed by grey streets populous with two-legged wolves
(the more it swells, the more humanity devolves).
Continuing its descent through torrent-carved rocks,
it flows alongside a folk cunning as a fox
and so puffed with fraud it thinks none could detect it –
but I'll not stop there, for the authentic spirit
that touched the prophets is unfurling my each word,

and it would do someone good if he overheard
and kept what I say in mind. I see his nephew
hunt such wolves on the shore of this glassy sinew
of chaotic water, like some beast out of hell;
while the veins still pulse the meat's hung on hooks to sell,
and with their vile lives does his honour ebb away…
he staggers from the forest, black with blood, and a
thousand Aprils will not regreen what he's laid waste."
The other soul, listening, now looked as aghast
as if these events had already taken place,
and the speech of the first and the second one's face
made me so curious I begged to know their names.

"Since," began the spirit who spoke before, "it seems
to be God's will to irradiate you with grace,
I'll be generous and give what you denied us.
I was Guido del Duca, a man who if he
saw a light step or people laughing happily
would flush with bitter envy… thus I reap the straw
I seeded back then. O human race, why *do* your
insatiable hearts crave what other hearts enjoy?
Beside me stands Rinieri, the pride and joy
of a house which no longer produces his like;
and not just that bloodline but many others lack,
between the peaks and the Po and from the seashore

to the Reno, the vigour necessary for
not just a life lived in truth but a bit of fun.
Those lands are a wilderness now, so far gone
no gardener could take their poison thickets to task.
Where are the likes of Lizio now, one might ask,
or Piero Traversaro or Guido di
Carpegna? Where's the good Arrigo Mainardi?
All I see is a shrunken and bastardised race.
When in Bologna will a new Fabbro arise,
and when will Faenza's plain soil put forth as fine
a shoot as Bernadino di Fosco again?
Don't be astonished at my tears, Tuscan, as we

bring to mind the houses of the Traversari
and the Anastagi – both of them lacking heirs –
and as I recall along with many others
the riders and accomplished beauties of those days,
the devout play and playful work that courtesy's
inherent love wished for, the unpolluted hearts.
O Bertinoro, when your family departs
you yourself should vanish so as not to become
sterile heritage rather than a fruitful home;
Bagnacavallo is wise to breed no more men
and the Pagani will prosper once their demon
has been and gone (though the living testimony

of their genes shall bear a dark stain, just as many
more wear suits of ancient guilt), whilst Castrocaro
and Conio are mad to continue to sow
new lords in this defiant and decrepit age...
yet Ugolino de Fantolini, the page
on which *your* name's inscribed is secure from the scrawl
of descendants whose debasement would be total –
though leave me now, Tuscan, for our talk has so stirred
my soul that weeping's far sweeter than any word."
Those shades were attentive to our feet's least move, so
we inferred from their silence as we turned to go
that the direction we had chosen was correct –

and, as soon as we were alone, the air was cracked
by a voice jagged as the bolt which suddenly
shows the night. *Any*, it shrieked, *who find me will slay me*,
then ricocheted away like thunder's dwindling boom.
Our eardrums had just stopped vibrating when there came
a second strike. *I*, this one cried, *am Aglauros
who Hermes petrified!* Hearing this, I drew close
to the poet with a quick step to the right.
All was quiet. "That is the bridle," he said, "as might
keep a man on track, yet you gobble up the thin
worm on Satan's hook and he gently reels you in.
You stumble along looking down at mud and slime,

whilst, high above, His shining lures revolve and call your name."

15.

Between sun and horizon was now the same space

as in early morning when its diurnal course
is just three hours' run, and therefore it was dusk
in Jerusalem and midnight where this desk –
solid as the ecliptic's skittish sphere is light –
awaited my return. Its fatal beams were right
in front of us for we'd circled round to the west,
the vast splendour somehow much graver than at first;
yet even more than that roaring brilliance, the sense
of my own profound and wide-ranging ignorance
put me in such a stupor I had to shade my sight
from excess of both inner dark and outer light.
It appeared that not too far up ahead, in fact,

was a second source which (as glassy lakes reflect
glancing sunrays at the same angle that they strike,
something known by artists and scientists alike)
was mirroring its glory in the smooth stone floor.
"What is it that approaches us, tender signor,
so bright that my shifting hand cannot shield my eyes?"
"Try not to be astonished," he said, "if the sky's
inhabitants still dazzle. This white messenger
has come to invite us to be taken higher…
and soon such sights will no longer be oppressive,
but shall – as much as Nature's enabled you – give
more delight than you'd think it possible to feel."

When we reached that luminous creature, a joyful
voice – less heard by the ear, it seemed, than in the mind –
bade us to enter a portal that we would find
contained a considerably easier stair.
We'd left him behind, and were ascending, when there
came at our backs *Blessèd are the compassionate*
in wondrous harmony, followed by *All create*
a bliss beyond themselves, and man must conquer man!
The sound died away and we were once more alone,
so I thought that I'd question the maestro again.
"What," I asked, "did the spirit from Romagna mean
when he mentioned sharing and the dissatisfied

heart?" "He knows the cost of his worst fault," he replied,
"and seeks with reproaches to lessen others' grief.
If envy makes the bellows of your ribcage puff,
it's because your focus is on what can't be split
several ways without thereby decreasing it –
whereas if consuming love of the farthest sphere
unbent your spine and aimed it at the skies, such fear
wouldn't be the ghost which blows your chest." "In that air,"
he added, "there's not a single joy you can share
without further enriching the star-built cloister,
without compelling love's blaze to burn still faster."
"This has me more brimful of doubt," I said, "and my

mind more greedy for satisfaction than if I
hadn't sounded off my restless mouth. How can one
dissect yet keep the whole, augment through division?"
"Your brain rummages through the ways things are on earth,
and so despite the fact that you're surrounded with
perfect light you conjure up shadowy toys.
An endless, inexpressible Benevolence flies
to love as a sunbeam to a crystalline stone –
giving to all in accordance with their passion,
shining down on each extended tendril with the
virtue and magnetic force of eternity;
the more, you see, that bliss's citizens are drawn

towards one another lovingly – not the porn
of blind desire, but soul surrendering to soul
without restraint – the more love grows, the more the whole
tone of heaven's heightened. This process has no end.
If my explanation is hard to comprehend,
in due course you will encounter Beatrice and she'll
remove that and every other thirst. Strive to heal
those five remaining wounds with the ointment of pain,
making your printed forehead pristine once again."
I was just about to say I was now content
when my bodily eyes told me to be silent,
for we'd come to the next circling step. A sudden

vision of a temple threshold and a woman
then swept me out of myself, and I heard, not loud,
a mother's gentle voice in the noise of a crowd.
My baby, it said, *how could you do this to me…*
to us both? Why would you treat us so thoughtlessly?
As Mary stood there the vision changed, and I saw
one who wept tears born of outrage. *If*, she shrieked, *you're*
in command of the city the very gods seem
to wish to own, and from which shines science's beam,
you'll have the hands which caress our daughter removed!
If that's what we do to him who loves and is loved,
he said, his face mellow as hers was venomous,

what treatment's reserved for the ones that attack us?
The scene changed again and now I witnessed a mob
screaming *Kill, kill, kill!* in white-hot rage, heard the rib
of a young man crack as a flung stone hit its mark;
death was already heavy on him yet his dark
eyes were like portals through which the heavens' splendour
gleamed, and in the midst of that solitary war
he prayed for his tormentors to be pardoned.
The apparition faded, and as I returned
to awareness of the truth of external things
I realised I'd been caught up in mental wanderings
(*alucinari*, to 'meander in the mind')

that were at the same time in error and not false. Kind
Virgil was watching me, observing my eyes wild
and disorientated as a fevered child.
"What's the matter with you? For the past quarter-mile
you've been muttering, stumbling along in the style
of some wine-addled drunk… wake up and get a grip."
"But first let me tell you what I saw in my sleep."
"If," he laughed, "a *hundred* masks overlaid your face,
you'd still be unable to hide the slightest trace
of the thoughts which harry you. This dream-vision
will make you less likely to refuse to open
your heart to the waters of peace, a light that pours

endlessly from an unimaginable source.
I didn't ask what was up in the way of one
who looks without *seeing* at a man who lies prone,
but in order to give new power to your feet –
the likes of you must be prodded, or else the sweet
minutes of fresh vigilance shall have been and gone."
The sun was now sinking and so we journeyed on,
paying attention as much as our minds could see
to that dying radiance, when gradually
there appeared before us a kind of smoke or mist
blacker than a mole's eye when night is at its thickest.
There was nowhere to hide and no time to flee,

and the next instant it engulfed us entirely.

16.

The gloom of hell itself or a night sky veiled

with stygian cloud – no guiding star, no star-bright world
studding Christ's dark but the heavens as if looted –
never made such an evil eiderdown as did
that black and swaddling smoke, like a foul pelt so
rough that it grazed your very eyes. The maestro,
wise as ever, drew near and I clasped his shoulder
as a blind man grasps a friend in order not to stagger
into a pit or under the swift wheels of death;
on we went in what was and is the fiftieth
leg of my rambling journey home, the shaggy air
instinct with voices that each seemed to be a prayer
for peace and for mercy and the disentangling

of sin (*Lamb of God* is the phrase I heard them sing,
a perpetual rebeginning so attuned
in melody and diction that harmony reigned).
"Correct," said my guide, in answer to a question,
"that's the sound of souls endeavouring to loosen
the clenched knot of rage… now keep good hold as we wade
their grim matrix." "Who is this, who, bold as a blade,
comes slicing through our smoke? He computes, if I'm
not mistaken, like one caged in calendrical time."
Thus one of the voices addressed us, the maestro
telling me to answer and ask if we might go
up the mountain on this west face. "Spirit," I cried,

"who'd return in your native beauty, purified,
to humankind's great maker… if you follow us,
I guarantee you'll hear something marvellous."
"I'll come with you as far as I can," it replied,
"and if we can't see, cords of sound will keep us tied
together as we pace." "I make this climb," I began,
"still wrapped in that elaborate, blood-red linen
which only death himself unwinds. I crossed hell's hill
to get here, and since it seems to be divine will
that – cocooned in His sheltering grace – I witness
high heaven's court in a manner that the witless
apes of modern letters couldn't even dream of,

please reveal what they called you when your lungs wheezed life…
and tell us as well if we're approaching a pass
where we might ascend. Your kind words will guide us."
"I was Marco," he said, "and I was a Lombard –
one who knew the eloquent world, who loved that hard
excellence no archer's narrowed eye now aims for.
To go up, go dead ahead." "And," he added, "when you're
finally there, I ask you to say a prayer for me."
"I shall do that for you," I said, "religiously…
yet within me hangs a doubt that's fit to burst
unless I pluck its ripeness here. Tiny at first,
it grew as a pineapple or golden pinecone

spirals its abundance out of 0,1,1 –
and what you have just declared has swelled it further,
whilst confirming something I was told by another.
The world is as barren of virtue as you say,
lidded with noxious cloud, light on its feet as a
full-term mother carrying her rapist's baby…
though please tell me why this is so, for if I see
clearly I can explicate to my fellow men
a cause that some site on earth and some in heaven."
"Brother," he began, after a profound sigh,
"it's plain you're from that myopic world, where the sky
is invariably assumed to be what moves

every sordid detail of your monitored lives;
and yet was this the case, there would be no free will
nor any justice in punishment of evil
or joy that springs from good. The stars initiate
the mechanism of a man, providing light
enough to distinguish maliciousness from love,
but also that freedom which – if it can survive
its first skirmishes with the constellations – shall
ensure victory if he nourishes it well.
Your intellect, however, is not in thrall
to the governing skies but transcends the natural,
subject to a higher power altogether

and in that subjection truly free. If, therefore,
the contemporary world has wandered astray
the cause lies within you… so let me play the spy
and seek it out. Innocent as a toddling child –
when her face lights up, she doesn't smile but is smiled –
the soul comes forth in its all-knowing ignorance
from one who holds us before we take existence,
and, driven by the joy of that supreme artist,
is drawn to what seems like it might be good to taste;
hence the need for stern laws as guides or curbs to love,
for a virtuous king who can discern above
the rubble of the sunset a single tower

of the City of God. Their mouths talk, and yet our
supposed rulers snatch whatever they desire
so the people do the same and seek no higher
embodiment of grace; the degeneracy
of the times is due to misleadership, you see,
not man's immortal self that in essence is pure.
Rome, which carved what's best on earth with the tools of law,
once possessed a double sun displaying the paths
of the *soul* and the *world*… but weakness has quenched wrath's
flame, and the sword is as blunt as the shepherd's crook.
This union bodes ill. If you're sceptical, look
at the wheat's bright ear and consider how every

seed's known by the harvest it unfolds. Courtesy
and valour abounded in the land that the Po
and Adige feed, though any desperado
can swagger there now with little risk of meeting
one whose noble speech or whose mere presence will bring
a deep sense of shame to his innermost mind. Three
gentlemen still endure, old timers for whom the
days which keep them from a better life pass slowly;
the Church, having fused a dual authority,
dirties both itself and its burden where it fell.
But look, these delicate rays show how an angel
approaches through the black smoke. I must turn back, or…

take courage!" With that he was gone and was heard no more.

17.

Deep in the Three Peaks' very heart, does one not find –

perhaps, lone reader, you can summon it to mind –
how a mist so dense the whole body strains to see
slowly starts to lighten and a white disc weakly
glows through the vapours, far more like moon than sun?
Evoke those moments, and your imagination
will effortlessly represent what we then saw,
the day's last gilded minutes dying on the shore
as I stepped from that smoke in the path of the maestro.
Oh how high fantasy can enthral us, and no
sound be heard though ten thousand foghorns blast our ears –
a power which, when the outer world disappears,
is informed by a light that descends from above

at its own or His will. Now flashed a vestige of
she who became the bird which most delights to sing,
the mirage so possessing my brain that nothing
external could creep or thunder in. Next the fierce
and scornful glance of a statesman pinned to a cross
rained into my mind (in the cross's shadow stands
the always blameless Mordecai, clasping his hands),
and as this apparition popped like a bubble
there bloomed in its place the face of a weeping girl.
"Why," she was saying through tears, "would you nullify
your life through *anger*? It is me you cause to die,
for in wanting to keep me you've lost forever

the child who mourns your ruin." As strange dreams waver
when through still-shut lids shines the light of a new day,
so my imagination faded as a ray
much brighter than any earthly beam struck my face…
I was turning blearily towards it when a voice
cried *Here's the place to climb*, and something about
the cadence of those words obliterated thought
and left me with a pure desire to see who spoke.
"This," said the maestro, "concealed in the sunlike cloak
of his excessive joy, is a divine spirit
giving guidance without our having asked for it;
he preempts our request, knowing full well that one

who sees a man in need of help yet offers none
is already meditating his refusal.
But come… now we have to make swift headway while
blue dusk holds the sky, for as soon as night's fallen
you won't be able to accept this invitation."
The second I was on the first step of the stair,
I sensed something like a wing's flicker in the air
and – within that whirr – a voice calling *Blessèd are
the peacemakers, those free of the taint of anger!*
The sun's final, high-lifted rays were vanishing
and faintest stars, at all sides, softly glimmering
when I felt a sudden loss of strength in my limbs;

we'd just reached the point where the narrow staircase climbs
no further, beached like a ship the subsiding sea
has left behind. I listened a moment, to see
if anything could be discerned in this curved street,
and then turned to the maestro and spoke. "Tell me, sweet
father – which sin is purged here? Though our feet are still,
surely your teaching doesn't have to stop as well."
"The love of the good," he replied, "is what's restored
on this fourth terrace, where the sluggish souls who oared
their bones with reluctance must heave and heave again…
cup your intellect and I shall make these things plain,
ensuring that this brief delay bears fruit." "Neither,"

he began, "the Creator nor any creature
was ever driven other than by love, my son,
either natural love or the complex passion
that stems not from the heart but from the mind. This much
you know. Love never errs, yet mental love finds such
paltry objects for its brilliance to transfigure
or goes astray through excess or lack of vigour;
so long as it is directed to the primal
good and restrains its taste for base ones, sensual
elations and habits cannot trap it – but when
it's bent to active malice, or else will hasten
after some holy or unholy goal with less

or more than a suitable singlemindedness,
one conspires against and works counter to our Lord.
Understand from this that the love in you's the seed
of every virtuous and every heinous act,
a love that cannot wish mischief on its subject
any more than it could hate the cardinal bliss
which, at the deepest level, is what it *is* –
no creature being wholly divided from the One.
That remaining, then, is delight at evil done
to the man next door, a grave sickness which can rise
from your soul's internal Styx in a triple guise:
first there is someone who assumes he'll feel less small

in proportion to his neighbour's abasement, all
his proud will determined that rivals be suppressed;
then there's the one who feels belittled by the best,
as if another's soaring erased his own name;
and lastly you have they who take vindictive aim
at those who originate real or dreamt-up slights.
These false loves are lamented on the lower heights,
the terraces we've passed, whilst in this fourth circuit
are they who love but lack the verve to *act* on it;
we each confusedly desire, you see, the peace
of soul that's the only way to make sorrow cease,
yet so many seek it in mere inessentials…

such warped love is bewailed in the next three circles."

18.

"In just what way perverse affection splits in three,"

he added, "you'll have to find out presently
on your own behalf." His exposition over,
he regarded me closely as if to discover
whether I was satisfied – I whose parched brain
was already dying to question him again,
a question I was at first loath to ask for fear
I would tire or irritate my truthful father.
Seeing the wish within me, timid as a bird,
he emboldened it with a single well-chosen word.
"Wise maestro," I then began, "your discourse's light
so invigorates my intellectual sight
that I clearly perceive whatever it lays out;

therefore I only ask you to expound, devout
and gentle teacher, the love you discern behind
each person who works marvels and all who have sinned."
"Direct on me your comprehension's piercing gaze,"
he said, "and I shall show you the error of those
who, despite their blindness, presume to pose as guides.
The human mind, made so quick to love, darts towards
whatever pleases it for simple pleasure's sake,
and in this act your powers of perception take
an impression of the truth to which the soul turns
when it's unfolded within you; if it then yearns
for this shining copy, that inclination's love

and Nature's way of binding. Then – as fire will move
upward in accordance with its form, born to rise
to where its spectral matter endures in the skies –
the mind thus bewitched is seized by a desire
that shall never let you rest until the entire
possession of the thing loved allows it to rejoice,
a pallid foretaste of our being face to face.
Perhaps it's now apparent to you how the true
state of things is hidden from those sybarites who
declare any passion is inherently good,
thinking that bad carving is redeemed by fine wood
or that the soul's wax can receive a demon's seal

and still be divine." "Parsed by my wit, your words reveal
love," I said, "and yet make me more great with doubt –
for if love comes to us from outside, the spirit
proceeding on that single foot, then what merit
is there in its not being warped but walking straight?"
"I can only," he replied, "describe what reason
knows and sees. Profounder knowledge must come from one
faith illuminates… you'll recall whose face I mean.
Distinct from the matter they incarnate within,
all substantial forms have a specific virtue
we cannot see or demonstrate other than through
what it *does* – as, say, the shade and shape of a leaf

speak of how a certain plant can take or give life.
It follows that no one really knows where our sense
of primary notions comes from, or that intense
nostalgia for things which embody true beauty;
it's in us as the knack for honey's in a bee,
an archaic lust wanting neither praise nor blame.
In order that all other passions may conform
to this one's innocence, you possess an innate
and watchful faculty like a guard at a gate –
here is the principle that determines your worth,
in accordance to the degree to which it both
lets good desires enter and intercepts the bad…

a native freedom once perceived by those who had
gone in their inspired thought to the very depth of things,
bequeathing us the fruit of fearless voyagings.
Even supposing, then, the inevitable
blazing of some or other thirst, you're capable
of restraining it as well. This nobility
is what Beatrice means by free will… make sure and see
you keep it in mind if and when she speaks of it."
The moon now resembled a dented brass bucket
filled with glowing embers, diminishing the stars
as – delayed until nearly midnight – it rose
and swam against the tide of the turning heavens,

taking the channels the sun flames when the Romans
see it slide between Sardinia and Corsica.
That noble shade because of whom Pietola
is more renowned than any other Mantuan town
had set the burden I had laid upon him down,
whilst I – who'd reaped from questions such limpid harvest –
sat drowsy as a sated epicure. My rest
was suddenly, however, disturbed by a throng
approaching from behind, thunderous along
the circling shelf like the crazed mob the Ismenus
and Asopus saw dance on their banks when Bacchus
had a hunger for the Thebans and they for him.

It seemed pure will and righteous love were spurring them,
since the whole crowd was galloping and I heard one's
voice crying *Mary hastened into the mountains*
and another sob *Caesar hurtled into Spain,*
and then *the art of the good makes grace green again*
if time's not lost due to enthusiasm's lack
came as though in answer from the horde at their back.
"People," said Virgil, "whose great fervour now, perhaps,
begins to compensate for your lukewarm works' lapse
from proper mastery, a loveless negligence,
this man is alive and wants in his innocence –
truly, I don't lie – to continue climbing when

the light resumes the sky. Can you direct us, then,
to the nearest aperture or slit in the rock?"
"Come," replied a spirit, "and we'll show you a crack...
we're filled with the compulsion to be on the move
and cannot take even a moment's rest, so you've
got to forgive us if that makes us seem like boors.
In the reign of the one whose salutary wars
Milan won't forget – by which of course I mean
the mighty Barbarossa, more god than mere man –
I was abbot of San Zeno at Verona. He
who shall before long weep for that monastery,
regretting he ever had power over it,

already has the grave's black crumbs upon his feet
from forcing the appointment of his changeling son."
I don't know if he ended there, but now he'd run
so far ahead that this was the last thing I heard.
Two more came puffing past us, stragglers of the herd
pursued by the hyena teeth we call remorse,
one shouting out *the holy land will not be yours*
until death's drowned all who once wandered through the seas
and the second *those indulgent of their ease*
choose a degenerate life, days void of glory.
When they'd vanished too, an idea came to me
and another and another in a branching stream

until, imperceptibly, thought turned into dream.

19.

At the hour when the day's subsided heat

no longer tempers the ice of our satellite,
siphoned off by earth or by Saturn's crystal ring,
and geomancers see Greater Fortune rising
with bright oriental meaning up a track
that in that predawn silence is absolutely black,
a stammering woman came to me as I dreamed.
Her sight was squint, her gait bent, and her gnarled hands seemed
more hideously pale than an albino snake –
and, much as the sun's resurgent rays warm and wake
limbs chilled to stillness by the giant crypt of night,
so my gaze thawed her voice and made her stand upright
and, before too long, gave an animated glow

to her dead face (those shining cheeks young lovers know).
Her tongue set free, she started singing with a lilt
against which my will was powerless to revolt.
I am She, the song went, *the suave and serene
siren of the ocean's heart, a harmony seen
by sailors who're filled with disbelief to the brim.
He who stops with me, so wholly do I please him,
tends to stay forever… the avid Ulysses
altered for my strange psalm his path across the seas.*
Before her swollen lips had quite closed, a lady
quick and devout as a little bird suddenly
appeared at my side. "Virgil, Virgil," she cried, "who's *this*?"

The question was urgent, and he neared her with his
eyes looking nowhere but upon her cleanliness;
then, lunging for the siren, he tore her red dress
to reveal a grey and tumour-eaten stomach
the stench of which was so grotesque that I woke.
"At least *three times* I've called you," the maestro was saying.
"Arise and shine, my boy… let's find the opening
that you may enter by." And now I rose and saw
how all the terraces of the holy peak were
bathed in newborn light, the sun's fingers on our backs,
then went pensively ahead like a man who makes
half a bridge's arch with his curved, brain-laden spine

when suddenly I heard, more gracious and benign
than any tone that ever moved this mortal air,
a voice saying *Come, the passage you seek is there.*
With outspread wings as dazzlingly white as a swan's,
the one who'd spoken gestured to where the mountain's
volcanic hardness was divided by a cleft;
then, our faces fanned by his vast feathers, a soft
cry of *Blessèd are all those that mourn for they
shall know what consolation is* sent us on our way.
After we'd ascended some small distance, my guide
asked why my gaze was fixed earthwards. "I," I replied,
"have had a vision the obscenity of which

distorts my very thinking, filling me with such
misgivings I cannot let it go." "You were shown,"
he said, "in the form of that ancient witch the one
defect we mourn on the remaining terraces;
you were also shown how authentic freedom is
to be accomplished... let that knowledge suffice.
Strike your heels upon the ground, child! Raise your wild eyes
to where the eternal king wheels His glassy lure!"
Just as a falcon glances past its feet before
turning bodily to the voice, desirous of meat,
I thrust my way up through that mass of split granite
and then stepped forward onto circle number five.

Outstretched and facedown, as though spying on a grave,
each figure I now saw sighed a long, muffled sigh
(*my soul kisses bare cement*, I think I heard them say,
albeit so unclearly that I can't be sure).
"God's elect," implored the poet, "you who suffer
less severely due to justice and blessèd hope,
can someone direct us to the ascending slope?"
"If you're both exempt from lying down," one answered,
"simply keep your right hands on the ocean's side
and you'll find the quickest way." "Spirit," I then said,
"whose tears sweeten what reorients man to God –
tell me who you were, why you weep with upturned backs,

and whether you'd have me intercede for your sakes
when I return in the flesh to the house of life."
"Your second question will be answered, yet first I've
got to say I was a successor of Peter.
Between Sestri and Chiavari, fair water
falls and gives both name and distinction to my blood;
as for the mantle which to bear above the mud
is a burden making all others seem feather-light,
I wore it for scarce a month. I converted late,
and, when I became the mighty shepherd of Rome,
understood that life was a seductive dream.
Perceiving how my famished heart still had no peace

even in the broad earth's most exalted office,
the love of the spirit was lit within me.
Until that moment I was wretched, completely
severed from the source and consequently greedy...
for which I am now paying the price, as you can see.
Our postures illustrate what avarice will attain,
the bitterest agony of this whole mountain.
Our eyes were not raised but scanning the pavement's grease,
so now they are sown in the ground by His justice;
our greed extinguished love and coloured all we did,
so now retribution has these ghost-limbs knotted.
For as long as it pleases Him, we shall lie

immobile." Having knelt down as I listened, my
muscles miraculously following the thought,
I started to speak but he interrupted me. "What,"
he cried, observing my stance by hearing alone,
"makes you think that you should bend your proud frame down?
Straighten your legs and stand tall, brother, or you err –
we're fellow servants of that single dreadful power,
and in the resurrection mere worldly honours end
(as scripture intimates with thrice-sacred sound).
Yet please go on your way now, for this lingering
distracts me from the shower that is ripening
the seed of which you spoke. All I have's a niece...

a good soul, unless my kind have swayed her into vice."

20.

Against a strong will a weak one shall always fail,

so I lifted the sponge which I had meant to fill
with satiating water. On we went, my guide
keeping to the empty spaces on the cliff-side
(the far edge thronged with those who, tear by molten tear,
distil the evil that darkens earth's atmosphere
as if the world was occupied by hell itself).
Be forever cursed, immemorial wolf
whose black bowel thirsts for men like no other creature's…
O planets and stars, whose stupendous dance alters
life down here, when will her destined predator come?
As we paced slowly onward, I heard a phantom
raise its voice above those pitiful moans and cries

like a woman who, bringing forth life, almost dies.
"Blessèd Mary," it called, "we know that you were poor
by the shed or hovel in which you sought shelter!"
"O good Fabricius," it said next, "you wisely chose
a righteous poverty over vice in fine clothes!"
These sounds were so pleasing to me that I strode on,
eager to meet with the spirit that had spoken –
which, as I got to it, was discoursing of how
the saint dropped three purses through a broken window,
an act of largesse that saved three daughters' honour.
"You who descant of much good… tell me who you were,"
I said, "and why just you reanimate such words –

phrases that will not be without their due rewards,
when I go to complete the transitory stroll
of our deathbound life." "I'll do so," replied the soul,
"less for any help I expect from that quarter
than for the sake of the grace your whole demeanour
radiates, despite the fact you're still cased in flesh.
I was the root of the poisonous tree whose lush
foliage overshadows all of Christendom,
causing its fruit to be bitter and unwholesome;
and yet if strength is with Bruges, Douay, Ghent and Lille –
I pray for this to One whose judgement we must feel –
vengeance soon will strike. I was called Hugh Capet then,

the seed of the branch of kings known as Capetian…
every Philip and Louis, both now and to be.
Born a slaughterman's boy in a Paris alley,
I found myself with the kingdom's reins in my hands
when Charlemagne's line died out; so rich in new friends,
as if by magic, and so mighty that my son's
head was blessed by the widowed crown. Those sainted bones
begin with him. Our blood was insignificant
but did no harm, becoming fierce and fraudulent
only when the dowry of Provence took its shame;
and then – as though it were making up for lost time –
it started its foul spree by seizing Normandy,

Poitou and Gascony. Entering Italy,
Charles decapitated Conradino and sent
Thomas back to God. I foresee, not too distant,
a time when a fresh Charles comes prowling out of France
unarmed except for Judas's venom-tipped lance;
with this he'll tear open fair Florence's stomach,
an act of purest perfidy that shall not make
him wealthier in lands but in mortal error
(the more casually he regards these sins, the more
they will weigh him down). I see yet another Charles
price his own daughter as corsairs with their slave-girls…
what *else* can you destroy, what else, O avarice,

possessing my line such that it no longer cares
for its own flesh and blood? To make them appear less,
crimes done and to come, I see how the fleur-de-lis
will enter Anagni and capture Christ again;
I see Him mocked once more, I see Him slain between
two living thieves; I see the elixir reborn,
and a brand new Pilate advance with greed-swollen
sails against the Temple of the authentic rite.
O Lord, when shall I at long last have the delight
of seeing your hidden rage's sweetness blaze down?"
"As for what I was saying," he went on, his tone
calmer now, "of the Holy Spirit's sole true spouse –

the phrases which made you turn to me for a gloss –
such is our responsive prayer while it is day.
When night falls, however, we take an entirely
contrary strain, remembering Pygmalion
whose traitorous gold-lust transformed him into one
capable not only of theft but parricide;
we recall Midas, whose desire was satisfied
in a manner simply priceless for all save him,
and how Achan fingered the auream regulam
and still feels the kiss of those stones to this hour;
we accuse both Ananias and Sapphira,
then hymn the hooves that kicked Heliodorus;

we circle the entire peak with the infamous
name of him who murdered the child Polydorus,
and then finally we cry *Crassus, pray tell us,*
as one who knows the answer, what's the taste of gold?
Our voices are sometimes resonant, sometimes mild,
in accordance with the force by which they are spurred;
when you overheard me earlier, praising the good
as we do by day, I wasn't speaking alone
but just more hotly than any other person."
We'd already left him, though, and were struggling to
move on fast as it was in our power to do,
when I felt the whole mountain jolt like a thing

possessed; a chill seized me then, colder than death's sting,
for surely even Delos didn't shake and sway
this wildly before Leto's twins adorned the sky.
Now on every side there arose a shout so loud
the good maestro drew near, saying he was my guide
and while that was the case I'd no reason to fear.
Glory to God, the words went, *in the highest fire*,
and – like the shepherds who were the first to witness
that song – we stood with breath suspended, motionless
until it was through and the immense tremor passed.
We rebegan our sacred way, and, it seemed, vast
ignorance plagued my mind with the longing to *know*;

onwards I trudged below a timid, pensive brow.

21.

The natural thirst that natural things never

quench but which needs an everlasting water
assailed me as we walked, the thought *we must be quick*
snapping at my heels while I pursued my pale duke
and grieved in compassion for justified torment.
It's written in Luke that as two disciples went
reasoning down their bleak road Christ appeared to them,
fresh from the invigorating dark of the tomb,
and so in likewise fashion there now reared a shade
behind us as we tiptoed through the prone, weeping crowd.
"O my brothers," he cried out, "may God grant you peace,"
at which we both spun quickly round. "And may the bliss,"
the maestro replied, having made a certain sign,

"of truth's court and council be yours and be yours soon,
despite that it condemns me to endless exile."
"Who has guided you," he demanded of us while
we all paced swiftly together, "up His staircase
if, as you say, you can't ascend to where there is
only our Lord's face?" "Look," my wise instructor said,
"at the marks the angel scored on this man's forehead
and you'll clearly see he must reign with the devout...
yet since the twine of his days and nights has not played out,
his soul – which is sister to yours and to mine –
sees in other ways than us and can't climb alone.
I was called from the fire's wide throat to be his eyes,

and his eyes I'll be as far as my expertise
can take me. Though divulge, if you know, why sudden
quakes just shook the ground, and why the whole mountain
from peak to sea-washed foot seemed to shout in unison?"
"Nothing," the spirit answered, the maestro's question
having threaded the needle of my thirst so that
I already felt less dry, "happens here without
being sanctioned by the island's reverend law...
nothing that is contrary to Tradition or
a higher order. Above all alteration,
our crag only traffics in such gleams as heaven
receives from its scattered self. This is the reason

no frost or dew or snow or biting hail or rain
trespasses beyond the little three-stepped stair;
neither heavy nor web-frail clouds ever appear,
nor thunder nor Thaumas's elusive daughter
who conjures Eden's gate by crossing light and water;
arid vapours never rise above the highest
of those steps, where the toes of Peter's vicar rest.
Subterranean breeze sometimes rocks the foothills,
but these heights only shudder when a spirit feels
sudden cleanliness and starts its climb towards the sky
to the accompaniment of that vast cry.
We know that we are pure again by the will's own

rediscovered freedom, no longer weighing down
the soul with base desires but making it rejoice;
at long last, it's liberated from evil ways
and what it wants and what the heart requires are one
and the same (the latter having tasted divine
justice to the precise degree it wished to sin).
I have been stretched in contemplation of my pain
half a millennium and more, yet felt just now
entirely free to stand and pass to where sorrow
has no place – and so you sensed that tremor and heard
each pious soul returning praises to the Lord
from across the whole peak, the sooner to ascend."

This account was such a sweet draught to my parched mind
that I was lost for words, and thus the maestro spoke.
"Now I understand what force made the mountain shake,"
he said, "and see the net you're tangled in, and why
a single soul's release is cause of all souls' joy –
but now, if it pleases you, tell us who you were
and the reason five centuries have kept you here."
"At the time when glorious Titus, fortified
by the universal king," the spirit replied,
"avenged the wounds which gushed with the blood Judas sold,
I was famed as poet – that title can't grow old
and is mankind's greatest honour – and yet lacked faith;

Rome heard me and called me, I was so honeyed with
the spirit of holy song, and there I became
fit to wear the myrtle. Statius was my name,
and for men it still is. I sang of the seven
at Thebes, and of the mighty Achilles, but then
whilst bearing this second burden stumbled in the way.
My desire was set alight by the sparks that fly
like incandescent pollen from that divine pyre's
brilliance, the starter of more than a thousand fires –
I mean the *Aeneid*, which in the art of verse
wasn't just my beloved mother but my nurse
and without which my entire corpus would be

tenuous, inadequately nourished, sickly;
to have lived then, when Virgil's mind was drawing breath,
I'd happily undergo this ritual death
years more than I owe to regain my soul's balance."
At this, my guide shot me a look that meant *Silence* –
yet the strength of the will is not infallible
and, in all honesty, is least reliable
in those who are guileless, hence quick to laugh or weep.
I smiled the slightest smile, at which the ghost peered deep
into that place where our joy is exhibited.
"I saw a flash of laughter in your face," he said.
"For the sake of your long labour, now tell me why

that was." Caught between contrary demands, I sigh
and the maestro understands. ("Don't be afraid," he says,
"but grant him what he asks for with such eagerness").
"You wonder, old soul, at the half-smile I let slip
though *you* are the one I would have amazement grip...
the shade who has conducted me to this great peak
is the very Virgil who gave you strength to speak
of both men and of gods, illuminating earth
and embodying the light. That trace of mirth
was for no other reason." He'd bent to embrace
my dear teacher's feet but Virgil made him rise.
"Brother, we're wraiths." "My love," replied Statius, "is such

it seems our emptiness is something I could touch."

22.

The angel who had led us to the sixth terrace

stayed behind, first blessing those who thirst for justice
and erasing one scar in the shape of an *S*;
my limbs now moved with extraordinary ease,
and to follow those souls cost no effort at all.
"It is," Virgil then began, "only natural
that love lit by virtue inspires the same affection
once its flame is visible. From the second when
Juvenal braved the grey brink of the inferno
to reveal your devotion, I've felt for you so
much warmth that, at your side, I hardly notice
these steps. But tell me, and forgive my recklessness
like the beloved friend you are, how avarice

found a home in a breast deep studies had made wise?"
"Everything you say testifies to what you feel,"
said Statius, suggesting with a subtle smile
how the poet's words had moved him. "How true it is,
though, that matters can deceive us when their real cause
lies hidden. Your question shows me you believe
I was avaricious in my initial life,
a consequence perhaps of the place where we met;
if this is the case, you should know and not forget
that greed was so remote from me it's taken thousands
of lunar cycles to correct my lack of bounds
and give back a sense of measure. Had it not been

that I changed my path when I understood the line
where – almost as though raging at the fallen world –
you cry *O sacred hunger of pernicious gold*,
I'd now be jousting with a boulder down below.
Discerning that the hands' clenched wings can also go
as far the other way in mad expenditure,
I repented of this vice too. How many more
will – through their ignorance – rise with priestlike tonsure,
having rejected neither in life or at death's door
a wanton lavishness? Just perceive, wise father,
that failings which stand opposed to one another –
like two rutting goats – must cure their green together…

my presence among the avaricious, therefore,
is because the contrary disorder was mine."
"When you sang about the savage war that gave twin
sorrows to Jocasta," my tender bard replied,
"it appears from your exchange with the lucid-eyed
Clio that you didn't yet possess that faith
without which all effort's vain. If I speak the truth,
tell me what sun or lesser radiance dispelled
your mental darkness so that latterly you sailed
in the snow-white wake of Him whose words can hook men's souls."
"It was you who first sent me to drink where there wells,"
came the response, "a clear source over craggy stone,

you who first illumined my path to the Alone.
You were like somebody that, breasting blackest night,
gives no thought for his own salvation but shines light
behind him to assist the people who pursue
when you said *the solar age commences, a new*
race of tall primordials steps down from the skies;
righteousness is reestablished, and now justice
shall annihilate those thieves who have dressed as kings.
Yet let me add some colour to these mere inkings,
to show more vividly how I became through you
not just fellow poet but a Christian too.
The true faith was already stirring deep within

the world, seeded by the messengers of heaven,
when I was drawn to visit and revisit those
whose vision and whose utterances echoed yours;
they grew to seem so touched with holiness that when
they were hacked and brutalised under Domitian
every agony was accompanied by mine,
and I helped them and began to look in disdain
at such cults or sects as lacked their luminous ways.
Before I took the Greeks to where fine water flows,
I was baptised though played the pagan out of fear…
a tepidness which earned me a four-hundred-year
tour around the terrace of cupidity.

But tell me where our cunning Terence is, tell me
of Varro, Plautus, Caecilius… do you know
in what evil district their faint remnants now go,
you who uncovered all the good of which I speak?
We've still some way to climb." "They're with that peerless Greek,"
replied the maestro, "him to whom the Nine gave more
sweet milk than any other, just inside the door
of the blind dungeon. Both Persius and I are there,
and how often we converse of the twin peaks where
our lovely nursemaids live! With us are Antiphon
and Euripides, Simonides, Agathon,
plus many more whose brows were crowned by laurel's

noble green." Here the poet stopped short, as the walls
we'd gone between suddenly opened out and we
had reached the next ledge and could look around freely;
hour five was gunning the sun, her dazzling engine
already halfway up the sky's blue mountain.
"I believe," observed my guide, "we're to keep the sea
on our right side." And so we did, less uneasy
for that spirit's quiet assent, the makers ahead
and me behind noting what their discourse hinted
concerning the royal art of rhythm and rhyme.
Like the inverse of a cypress a boy can climb
with ease, since the branches taper to its summit,

the great tree we now encounter is laden with sweet-
scented apples on its spreading upper boughs;
from the cliff at our left, crystalline water flows
silently down and wets each bright and nodding frond.
As the two poets near the trunk, there comes the sound
of a voice inside the foliage. *You shall not,*
it cried, *eat this fruit!* And then: *Mary gave more thought
to the holy nuptials than to her own mouth;
the Roman noblewomen kept to water, both
they and Daniel setting wisdom above greed;
the first time was a golden time, when devotion made
streams nectarous, when even acorns tasted good…*

locusts and wild honey were the Baptist's sole food.

23.

While I'm peering fixedly up into the leaves

like some idler who squanders life because he loves
the pursuit of little birds, my ancient father
is calling me. "Come, my child," he says. "We've other,
more useful things to do in the time that's ours."
So I turn my face towards those two grave seers
and my steps no less swiftly, and as they talk
I listen with such interest I seem to glide not walk.
Suddenly we heard low cries lamenting *O Lord,*
open thou my lips in a way that made each word
bring forth both joy and pain. "Gentle teacher," I said,
"what sound's this?" "That of the shadows we are when dead,
bent on unravelling the knot of what all owe."

Like pilgrims overtaking people they don't know,
then turning and looking round at them while they pace
on and ever on, now huge crowds pass us and gaze
wonderingly back through the black holes of their eyes –
and, as in that story where vast addiction dries
Erysichthon to the merest rind of a man,
the face of every soul was so shrunken and wan
it was more like a skull papered over with skin.
("Behold the people penned in Jerusalem when
that girl," I thought, "got her teeth into her baby.")
They were thin enough, in fact, one could read quite clearly
the lost word spelled by our articulate bones,

void eye-sockets like rings divested of their stones.
Who'd *believe* the smell of fruit could work such wonders?
As I walked whilst racking my brain as to the cause
of such awful hunger, such emaciation,
I saw – a bear looking from its winter cavern –
one fix me with a stare. "This," he cried, "is God's grace!"
I would never have recognised him by his face,
but in his voice still shone the person he had been;
my power of sight rekindled, I looked again
and saw Forese. "Ah," he implored, "ignore these
scales discolouring my skin – it's only scabies –
and my fleshlessness as well, and explain to me

your presence on the mountain. What's this company
you keep? Don't torture me with silence... quickly, speak!"
"The face," I answered, "that I wept for at your wake
I now weep for again, finding it so hollowed.
One can't express oneself when the tongue bears the load
of a contrary wish, sluggish with amazement –
tell me first, in the name of God, what violent
wind has stripped the leafage from your spine's every branch?"
"All these tearful singers," he replied, "lived for lunch,
the slaves of their wide-open throats, and hence famine
and raging thirst provide a spirit-medicine.
That clear stream, saturated by divine power,

calls such scent from the fruit with its spray that our
appetites grow to an unbearable degree,
a pain that is repeated perpetually
as we go the rounds... I say pain yet mean solace,
for it's by this one desire we are drawn to pace
towards the trees which drew Christ to triumph in death."
"From the day, Forese, when you rode your last breath
to a better life barely five years have passed.
If your capacity to sin," I went on, "was lost
long before that awakening whereby good men
know the sacred grief through which we wed God again,
why are you already beyond the seventh stair?

I'd have thought to meet you on the lower slopes, where
time's remedied by time." "I've been brought so swiftly,"
he said, "to drink the sweet wormwood of this agony
because of my Nella and the tears she has shed;
her heartfelt prayers and deep sighs liberated
my soul from that coast and the other circles too.
My widow, my darling wife, is one of those who
is the more loved by God for labouring alone,
since to tell the truth some barbarian crone
is almost vestal in comparison to those
whores in that stone forest where I last kissed her face.
What can I say? Dear brother, I foresee a day

in the near future when the brazen display
of nipple and breast beneath the thinnest silk shift
will be met by a calamity that the swift
skies are preparing (if they knew *what*, they'd open
rouged mouths and howl). No Hottentot, no Saracen
ever seemed to need dire threats or prohibitions
not to pout like a tart – and, if my prevision's
right, they'll grieve before one now softly sung to sleep
has the soft beginnings of a beard on his lip.
I have spoken… conceal yourself no longer, brother,
for you can see that both I and every other
spirit here stares at how your substance veils the sun."

"If you're able to recall," I said to him then,
"the nights we used to rage together and to what
we were reduced, the memory will seem a blot
like oil upon a page. I was turned from that life
by this one who walks ahead, the pale sister-wife
of the sun being full, and subsequently led
through the absolute blackness of the wholly dead
still clothed in my holy flesh. From there, with his aid,
I've climbed the winding track that unwinds the twisted…
he'll come with me, he says, till I'm where Beatrice is.
It's the great Virgil who has accomplished all this" –
here I point at the maestro – "and the other shade

is the weight of which your kingdom was just now freed."

24.

Our journey isn't slowed by our jaws nor our jaws

by our journeying, but – as when a good wind roars
and swells a clipper's sails – we travel swiftly on
and talk as we pace. The shades, meanwhile, so far gone
in thinness they seem to have died a second time,
stare in astonishment when they realise I'm
a man and not a ghost, each eye a collapsed star
sucking in life. "Tell me if you can," I asked, "where
"your Piccarda is, if there are amongst these dead
any spirits I should note." "My sister," he said,
"whose visage was as lovely as her soul was pure,
rejoices even now… a victor in that war
whose heroes and heroines feast on Olympus."

"Here," he then added, "it's not forbidden to us
to identify a soul, long diet having
turned each fat face into some desiccated thing.
This," he said, pointing with his finger, "is and was
Bonagiunta of Lucca, and that man whose
bones almost pierce his cheeks once held the Bride of Christ;
he was originally from Tours, and our fast
purges all those eels of their night of costly wine."
So he showed a multitude of souls, one by one,
and nobody scowled to have their name said aloud.
I saw how Ubaldino de la Pila chewed
the frugal air for hunger, and glimpsed the marquess

who used to drink more leisurely and with far less
thirst. As when we look and discriminate between
an array of objects, I was most of all keen
to know the man from Lucca; he was murmuring
a name – was it, perhaps, *Alice?* – just where the sting
of justice had withered his ripe lips to the stalk.
"You," I called, "who seem like me to want to talk,
speak with a clarity which satisfies us both."
"Have this insight," he began, "from the site of my mouth…
a woman has been born and raised, as yet unwed,
who'll make you fond of my city despite what's said
by them that reproach it. If you chanced to mishear

my mutters, be assured events shall make all clear.
But tell me if I'm right in presuming the man
who wrote the unprecedented lines which began
O ladies lit with the intelligence of love
stands before me now." "I am one," I said, "who when Love
breathes within him listens well, and to its own
imperious measure sets his dark symbols down."
"Brother poet," he replied, "I'm aware of what
it was that held us versifiers back, the knot
which tied us to the ground whilst the sweet new style flew;
your songs are less wrought than received, I see that too,
and how this one thing differentiates our schools" –

he ended with a nod, as to say only fools
would pursue the matter further. Like those white, Nile-
wintering birds whose squadrons shift to single file
if they need to fly more swiftly, so now that crowd –
made light by His austerities – quickened and flowed
forwards together in their grave eyes' direction,
while (like a runner who might in mid-marathon
walk for a minute to let his heaving chest subside)
dear Forese eased his pace, strolling at my side
as the sacred herd straggled quietly past. "When,"
he demanded, "will we see each other again?"
"I've no idea," I answered, "how long I'll live,

yet my death can't be so soon that I won't have
already reached my homeland many times in dreams;
the city where birth placed me, you understand, seems
hellbent on ruin and sheer degeneracy."
"Best believe," he exclaimed, "and in fact I foresee –
dangling at a beast's tail – the one to blame for this
dragged to the black valley which knows no forgiveness,
that steed racing faster and ever faster till
his battered features are unrecognisable…
though now I must get on, since time is precious here."
As a knight will spur his horse and come at a canter
from amongst a troop of riders, eager to be

glamoured by the first skirmish with the enemy,
he lengthens his stride and is soon so far ahead
my eyes strain after him as everything he'd said
seems to dwindle in my mind. Here I turn and see
the living, laden branches of another tree
and under it a crowd, shouting with lifted hands
like brainless little children begging one who stands
and holds a toy or cream bun just beyond their reach.
Pass on by, something says, *and do not dare approach
this scion of the tree that was bitten by Eve,*
and thus the three of us skirt the base of the cliff.
Recall, it went on, *how the centaurs, crazed by wine,*

*battled Theseus with torsos where the divine
and demonic meet, and also think on those whose
bodies bent to drink like animals, not Hebrews.*
Hearing such instances of greed repaid amply,
we came to a deserted road and silently
paced, deep in thought, for a thousand steps or more.
Now imagine, if you can, a voice like a roar
and yet somehow gentler than a mother's lullaby.
"How meditatively these voyagers go by,"
it said, making me leap like a startled young hare –
I raised my brow to see who had spoken, and there
a creature stood as clear and bright as red-hot glass.

"This is the path," it went on, "which leads to the peace
all errant souls desire… take this turning here
if you wish to climb to the precincts of the fire."
So I followed those wise scholars' footfalls, being
dazzled by the light to the extent my hearing
had to be my eyes. Like a predawn breeze in May,
the soft annunciation of an untouched day
bearing the holy scent of lilac and mown grass,
I felt my forehead blown upon and then white feathers
made the air fragrant with memory of her face.
"Blessèd," I heard, "are they so luminous with grace
their hearts don't smoke through too much greed for meat and bread,

coveting spiritual sustenance instead."

25.

It was no time for uncertain, stumbling feet,

Taurus now at the meridian and night
having been given over to the scorpion's sway,
so one by one we entered the narrow passageway
like men dire necessity won't permit to rest.
As the fledgling stork, safe inside a treetop nest,
keeps raising its wings then thinking better of it,
my wish to ask questions was lit and doused and lit
while my lips kept silently lining up the words;
despite the speed with which we were striding skywards,
Virgil seemed to sense the discord in my thought.
("Let loose the bow," he said, "whose string you've pulled so taut
the arrow's iron cheek is trembling at the wood".)

"How's it possible," I demanded, reassured,
"for wraiths which need no nourishment to get this shrunken?"
"If you brought to mind Meleager, the one who, when
the log was at last consumed, became ashes too,
it wouldn't be half such a conundrum for you;
or if you merely thought of how a reflected
image counterfeits one's smallest feint, your head
wouldn't be fretting over what should be quite clear.
Yet so that your desires can rest easier, hear
from him who'll cleanse and heal that mutilated brain.
I ask you to treat him, brother... the boy's not sane."
"If I unfold the viewpoint of eternity,"

Statius replied, "let the inability
to refuse be my excuse." "Child," he then began,
these words will illumine like holy medicine
if you listen well and preserve them in your mind.
Perfected blood, not circulating but retained
inside the heart – like food prepared though uneaten –
takes on the power to devise a new human
as blood carried by the veins nurtures each organ;
digested still further, it descends, within men,
to a region that silence suits better than speech,
from where it can hurl itself through the blessèd breach
and there mingle with the essence of another...

one parent providing matter and the other
form, due to the great place that oil of oils was pressed,
the latter working by coagulating first
and then quickening the substance thus made firm.
The actifying virtue, having now become
a kind of plant-soul – yet different from a plant's
which is at its journey's end, whereas our advance
through the kingdoms has only just begun – next contrives
a body that, like a sea sponge, senses and moves
in archaic innocence, gradually starts
to shape the organs for those faculties the heart's
chalice held as liquid seed. How, my son, does this

mere animal become the noblest thing there is,
a creature capable of speech? I shall explain.
At the completion of the labyrinthine brain,
the prime Mover turns to it – delighting to see
the accomplishment of Nature's art – and gently
breathes in a novel soul, replete with wondrous force;
all that it finds active there that spirit now draws
into its own essence... self-conscious, live, entire,
like grape juice changed to wine by the sun's divine fire.
Its days then play out, and when their thread has unspooled
the soul is set loose from the flesh, whilst keeping hold
of both the higher and the lower faculties –

will, intelligence and countless memories
far keener than before, the other senses dulled –
and instantly finds itself on this or that wild
coastline where it sees it's still travelling, still mad.
Now the same informing power, as it once had
dreamt meat into awareness, radiates a figure
resembling that carnal ghost in voice and measure
(much as when the atmosphere, charged with drops of rain,
is transpierced by sudden sunrays whose refraction
paints a spectral miracle on the darkened sky),
nubile air yielding to the spirit's potency
and then dancing to its tune as a flame obeys

the fire. By means of this body, our tears and sighs –
the cries you may have heard around the mountain – are made;
it colours in the soul and hence is called a *shade*,
possessing glands and organs fully like your own
and altering its form in accordance with one
or other sensation or desire… this explains
the thinness that you marvelled at." But fresh concerns
now gripped us, for the steps ended and we swerved right
onto the last ledge where the whole cliff was alight;
from under the brink beside the terrace, wind blew
back a raging wall of flame, just enough that you
could pace – as on a tightrope – between the blaze

and the sheer drop below. "As we pass through this place,"
my guide said, "we must keep a close rein on our eyes…
to stray would be too easy." *Lord of clemencies*
I then hear sung from that furnace, and turn and see
spirits walking unburned within the brilliancy;
it was such an incredible sight that I kept
darting my downward gaze back to them as we stepped
cautiously upon the razor's edge, as they praised
Holy Mary Mother of God who was so chaste.
And now they sing the hymn again, softly at first,
and now they name every loving couple whose thirst
was only for each other, and on their canto

goes as long as fire refines and there's a wound to sew.

26.

We went along that slender path in single file,

the maestro repeating his warning all the while
and the hot sun striking my shoulder from the right;
its rays had now turned the whole west from blue to white,
and where my shadow lay on the flame-wall it made
an even ruddier glow. "Look," exclaimed a shade,
noticing this clue, "does that figure there not seem
a living man rather than a simulacrum?"
Then some approached as close as they could, taking care
to remain inside their aquarium of fire,
the foremost addressing me like this. "You who go
in apparent reverence as opposed to woe,
speak to one gnawed by love's inferno and vast thirst…

how is it your substance won't let the sunbeams past,
as if death hadn't yet entrapped you in its mesh?
A parched Ethiopian never longed for fresh
water as we long to receive a swift reply."
I'd have made myself known with no delay, but my
eyes had encountered still another strange new thing:
a second line of spirits was now approaching
through the blaze, and much as two ants will pause and touch
antennae then scurry darkly by (as though each
second not devoted to their cause was time lost),
so when the armies meet they merely kiss in haste
and pace on without breaking step. As faces part,

each strives to surpass the other with a shout –
Sodom and Gomorrha! from those whose eyes I can see,
and *Into the mimic cow clambers Pasiphae!*
from the others in response – after which they turn
back to their sad songs and the justice where they burn,
hurrying in opposite directions as cranes
wheel off to warm sands or the Riphean mountains.
Now I addressed the ones who had first questioned me,
pronouncing these words as they listened eagerly.
"O souls guaranteed, sooner or later, to be
received into His raging peace, my limbs' every
hinge and cell has accompanied me here. No old

or youthful corpse lies coffined, clothed in fur of mould,
but this body traverses your realm by the grace
of a woman from above; when I see her face,
I'll be blind no more. In order that your deepest
desire may soon be satisfied, and the highest
heaven enclose you in a vastness charged with love –
and in order, too, that my busy hand can move
unimpeded, ruling the virgin page with lines –
please tell me who you are, and also of those ones
whose backs are receding behind you through the flames."
Like some hill-dwelling woodman who falls quiet and seems
both awed and troubled in the glow of the city,

the shadows were speechless with incredulity;
then, his astonishment and stupor laid aside
at the speed of one with a noble heart, the shade
who had first questioned me once again drew near.
"You are blessed," he said, "and will embark from this frontier
with rich store of things endured so as to die well.
The others sinned the sin for which a triumphal
Caesar was taunted with a cry of *Hail the queen*,
and by shouting those words they ease this bonfire's pain;
our sin wasn't contrary to nature, but for
chasing our appetites like beasts outside the law
we reproach ourselves with the name of her who made

such bestial noises in the heifer-styled hide.
Now you know what we did and what we failed to do –
as for who we are, there's not the time to tell you
even if I could. I will, however, gladly
give my own name… I'm Guido Guinizelli,
and I bathe here because I turned my back on hell
when there was still life to live." You've perhaps heard tell
of Lycurgus's grief and how Hypsipyle
was embraced by her two sons, and now that I see
our father name himself – the father of all those,
my superiors among them, who've used and shall use
the music of sweet partial rhymes to utter love –

I become as they became and pace, dumb and deaf,
looking at him deep in thought, and but for the blaze
I'd have done the same as they. When my humbled eyes
are sated, I declare myself at his service
with the firmness of speech that gives faith. "These words trace,"
he said, "such a clear shape within me as Lethe
herself won't ever make fade. If you spoke truly,
say why there's such affection in your voice and gaze."
"So long," I answered, "as our fallen world endures,
your work exalts the very ink it's written in."
"O brother, *he* was a far finer artisan
of his mother tongue" – I look where his finger points –

"surpassing every amorous verse or prose romance,
despite what certain idiots say who prefer
the one from near Limoges… all those, in short, who err
in allowing mere repute to decide their minds,
the weathervanes of their faces spun in the winds
and blind to art and intellect and the way
things really are (thus it was with old Guittone,
acclaimed by whoop after critical whoop until
time and timeless truth tipped him from his pedestal).
Yet if you really have such ample privilege
as to be permitted to enter the college
where Christ is abbot, please say a Paternoster

to Him for us… as much of one as we require
in this world where the power to sin's not ours."
He turned and, with a deft flick, vanished in the fire's
depths like a catfish to the bottom of a lake,
and I sped up and said I was eager to make
a shrine inside my heart for that other soul's name.
"Your words", he replied, "are so ingenuous that shame
cannot and will not make me shy. I am Arnaut
who reviews his vast follies and sings in sorrow,
who foresees, rejoicing, the joy he would attain…
I beg you – when the time comes – to think of my pain,
by the selfsame force that conducts you up this stair."

Then he withdrew into the flame which makes men pure.

27.

The sun now reaches out his reborn rays to light

the place where his Maker bled, and it is midnight
where Libra balances high above the Ebro;
a white noon blazes down where Ganga's currents flow,
and so the southern sky is bathed in deep blue dusk
when His lucent messenger appears before us.
He was standing outside that barrier of flame,
and – with a voice which made our human art seem tame –
was intoning *Blessèd are they whose hearts are pure!*
"You go no further," he then said, as we drew near,
"without first feeling the incisors of this fire…
step within, hallowed souls, and do not fail to hear
a second blissful chant." Now I became like one

nailed while he lives inside a tailor-made coffin,
my hands clutching at each other and my eyes
almost popping out as I recollect bodies
whose fat I'd once seen melt on the exacting pyre.
"My son," said my tender guide, turning to me, "here
there'll be severe agony but there won't be death.
Remember, now, *remember*! If I steered us both
safely on the flying snake, do you think this close
to Him I'd let you down? A hundred thousand years
in the flame's crimson womb couldn't singe a single hair,
and if you still doubt then approach and reassure
yourself with a finger or the fringe of your gown…

come, turn and enter – *confidently* – and lay down
your brain's endless qualms and fears." I stood there rigid,
for all that my heart knew the truth of what he'd said.
"Put it this way," he added, a mere suggestion
of impatience in his voice, "this wall stands between
you and Beatrice." As when, at the name of Thisbe,
Pyramus opened his dying eyes and briefly
beheld her face as the mulberry flushed blood-red,
so – hearing the sound which ever blooms in my head –
my rigor mortis eased and I looked at my guide.
"So then," he laughed, "we aren't remaining on this side?"
Smiling as upon a fretful child you can calm

with a shiny apple, he stepped into the flame
before me and called to him who'd gone between us
to walk behind. Truly a lake of molten glass
would be a frigidarium, wondrous refreshment,
after one bare instant of that fire. As we went,
my gentle father kept talking of Beatrice
and saying how he could already see her eyes;
a distantly singing voice was our guiding star,
and, gazing ever at it, we soon emerged where
we could once more climb. *Blessèd of my Father, come!*
sounded from within a light whose prodigious beam
was far too bright to look upon. *The sun descends,*

it added, *and darkness waits. Hasten while dusk blends
night and day in the glowing crime scene of the west.*
The path rose ahead of us and my body sliced
the now-level rays, made a shadow pointing on,
and then that finger faded and the sun had gone.
We each choose a step for a bed, as an immense
horizon shows shreds of blue and green-gold brilliance
and before the stars succeed to their thrones again,
the nature of the peak having caused a sudden
loss of our strength and any joy in the ascent;
like goats which mildly ruminate, still and silent
as they'd been ravenous and haggard on the heights,

sitting in a holm oak's shade when the midday heat's
most fierce, the goatherd leaning on his crook close by –
or as the idler whose roof is the written sky
reclines beside his sheep to guard them from the wolf –
so all three of us were protected by a shelf
of overhanging granite, I the breathing meat
and they the watchful herdsmen. The stars are more bright
than usual and larger too, and as I gaze
in deep thought I'm seized by sleep (one who knows the news,
on certain strange occasions, before it is done).
At the hour when Cytherea's lantern shone
down upon the mountain – those rays that always seem

love's silver light itself – there came to me in dream
the likeness of a girl both beautiful and young,
gathering meadow flowers as she breezed along.
Whoever asks my name, she said, in words less speech
than song, *should know I'm Leah whose slim fingers reach
for blooms that will adorn my beauty in the glass,
whereas my sister Rachel is as desirous
as I to weave garlands to simply* see *her eyes…
my nature lies in action, while she satisfies
her soul through contemplation.* I stood then and saw
the sky already lucent with predawn splendour,
more welcome to the pilgrim as he nears his home,

scattering the shadows and my slumber with them.
The poets were already up. "That sweet apple,
which mortal men seek as far as they are able
along ten thousand branching paths, shall bestow peace
on your famished heart today." The maestro used these
plain words, yet no gift ever gave so much delight;
at each step I felt feathers grow as if for flight,
such hunger upon hunger did I have to be
above. The last staircase is ascended swiftly,
and when we reach the top he turns and looks at me.
"We've seen, dear child, the cold blaze of eternity
and a transient fire… you here attain the place

where my discernment ceases, where the cunning ways
of art and ingenuity can't go further;
your cleansed perceptions must take you to the Father,
now that the tortuous and narrow tracks all end.
See your golden forehead, sunlit, reawakened,
and round us see the flowers and green spires of grass
this sacred earth yields with unutterable grace;
sit or pace amongst them until those beautiful
eyes arrive, joyous, whose tears brought me to you. Your
discrimination's now free – upright, whole and pure –
and it would be an error not to do its will.
Expect no more from me in either word or sign…

you're a sovereign soul, wearing mitre and crown."

28.

Eager to delve deep within, to roam the divine

forest that veiled with its dense roof of living green
the pristine day, I wandered forth without delay
and began to stroll – soft-footed, soundless, slowly –
through a realm which breathed subtle scents at every side;
around my temples the gentlest of breezes played,
suave and unvarying, bending each tremulous
tendril towards the peak's shadow on the waters,
although not so much that a multitude of birds
was distracted from its task of putting in words
witty yet unearthly the joy of light's return;
beneath this spoken song the small leaves made their drone,
like the giant hush passed from pine to swaying pine

in the natural cathedral north of Classe when
triple Aeolus sets the wild scirocco loose.
I'd gone quite far into His ancient grove – the place
where we had entered being wholly lost to sight –
when I was stopped by a stream which flowed from the right,
bowing with little ripples the half-submerged grass
embroidering the verge (beside that restless glass,
our blear world's purest spring would seem somehow unclean –
for though it moves where sun and moon are never seen,
its darkness is a darkness whose depths are crystal
clear). My gaze crossed the water as I stood stock-still,
reflecting in my own night the profusion

earth once knew, when I caught sight or had a vision –
thus, sometimes, marvels unexpectedly appear
and scare thought as at a clap, leaving the brain bare –
of a lone figure walking and singing whilst she
chose from the blooms that grew in such variety.
"Slender beauty," I called, "basking in love's radiance,
or at least if I'm to trust that your fair semblance
bears true witness to the heart, let it be your will
to come nearer to this river so the tranquil
melody I hear can make its meaning plain…
it has me recollect where and what Proserpine
was when we lost her and she forfeited the spring."

As a lady must spin within the dance – pressing
close-set toes closer to the ground, one lithe foot just
a shade in advance of the other – this modest
woman turns in my direction on the yellow
and vermilion petals, then approaches so
near that what had been mere sound could be understood.
Reaching where the grasses bathe in the lucid flood,
she gives the sudden gift of her unlowered glance;
Venus's own face never shone with such brilliance,
not even when, by chance, she was scratched by her son's
narcotic dart and strange havoc coursed down her veins.
Now she is laughing on the bank, straight-backed, both hands

busy with the manifold colours these highlands
pronounce without a single seed. Just three paces
divide us, yet the Hellespont – crossed by Xerxes,
thoughts of what happened next still curbing all our pride –
was no more hated by Leander when the tide
and December squalls kept him from love's ecstasy
than I blamed that stream for not parting like a sea.
"You're newcomers here," she then began, "and maybe
the fact of my delight in our sanctuary,
this elected forest, human nature's eyrie,
is what makes you marvel as though suspiciously.
The psalm *O Lord, how I rejoice in your great work*

will illuminate those whose inner eye's still dark.
But say if you'd hear more, you who walk ahead…
I'll answer your questions until you are contented."
"Flowing water," I said, "and the forest's vast hum
conflict with some new knowledge I've been given. I'm
torn, as it were, between these wonders and my mind."
"I shall purge the mist that's made intuition blind,
and explain how what you sense proceeds from its source.
This place was given as a pledge of timeless peace
to you who were created good and *for* the good
by that solitary excellence men call God;
you didn't stay here long, sweet play and clean laughter

changed through error into weeping and hard labour,
yet nonetheless our heaven-nearing outcrop still
climbs far beyond the chaos earth and wave exhale
and – above the guarded gate – is serene and free.
The whole zone of living air turns circularly,
in accordance with the primal sphere, this motion
imparting to our sylvan height a vibration
within which each plant prints the wind with unseen seed...
seed that, once it falls, sows your variously-treed
world wherever soil is rich and skies pour and gleam
(armed with this higher knowledge, it shouldn't now seem
bizarre that species occasionally appear

as if born of light, that the demesne where you are
displays such plenitude, such peculiar fruit).
The water between us issues steadily out
of an imperishable spring – not from some vein
forever sucked dry and then fattened up by rain,
feeding rivers that brawl or limp with the seasons –
which His will sustains as it takes two directions.
One branch is able to erase the remembrance
of your failings and crimes, man's abject violence,
whilst the other makes you realise what you were worth;
but in order for them to be effective, both
dark Lethe and Eunoè must be *tasted*... this

stream before you has a tang above all others.
Having surely satisfied your thirst even though
I reveal nothing else, I will however now
give you a corollary by way of sheer grace –
nobody's debased through exceeding what they promise.
The pagan poet-seers whose words sing a time
of archaic virtue just glimpse this place in dream,
their lines transcribed on Parnassus as they snore.
Up here the human root was absolutely pure,
here where April's resurrection is eternal...
this is the nectar of which golden verses tell."
I glanced behind and saw those visionaries smile,

and then I returned my attention to the girl.

29.

Now she sang again like a woman in love,

and when the song had finished she added a brief
line from a psalm without bridle or bit; then,
as nymphs used to flit through the primal woods, alone –
some searching for the sun and some for deeper shade –
she set off against the current on the stream's far side
and I did the same on mine, matching step with step.
We'd done fifty paces when the banks made a sharp
bend to the left so that I faced the east once more,
and now she turned around and softly spoke. "Brother,"
she said, "listen and look!" That second, a shining
tremor swept across the whole forest, like lightning
not instantly gone but increasing in splendour;

wild melodies ran through the luminous air,
at which I couldn't help but curse the fault of Eve,
who – all Nature obedient, and her just-made –
tore aside the veil underneath which if she'd stayed
man had been bequeathed these ineffable delights.
As I walked amongst the first-fruits of the infinite's
overflowing love, suspenseful and desirous
of an intenser joy, the dusk ahead of us
blazed fierce as a forest fire below the green boughs
and the swooping notes were revealed to be voices.
*O sacrosanct and virginal Muses, if I've
endured cold and pain and sleepless nights for your sake,*

*now come to my aid as I endeavour to make
sounds to embody what the brain can scarce conceive…
I call on Urania's stars to help me weave
a prayer mat of words, and let high Helicon's
water flow down so that this withered tongue might dance!*
We continued on and I thought I glimpsed seven
golden trees in the distance, a false impression
fostered by the long tract of gloom that lay between,
for, as we neared, they grew distinct and could be seen
as candelabra, and the voices could be heard –
Blessèd is he who comes in the name of the Lord!
Above them, light's apparatus flamed far more bright

than a full moon's unveiled radiance at midnight,
and when I turned in sheer amazement to my guide
there was more wonder still in the look that replied…
I gave back my gaze to those grave, exalted things,
which approached so slow a bride in all her trappings
would have left them far behind. "Why," the lady said,
with a note of reproach, "you seem more affected
by the living lights than by what comes in their wake!"
Then I peered and saw, as if trailing some great duke,
people clothed in whiteness the world has never seen;
on my left side, meanwhile, the stream's resplendent sheen
imaged my body as though in a looking glass

whenever I glanced down. Now the wondrous army was
directly opposite me on the other shore,
and I stopped walking in my hunger to see more.
The sevenfold flames were still advancing, and their
featherlike forms seemed to paint the very air
and left on it a trace of the rainbow's bright chord;
those imperial banners extended backward
far enough I couldn't see their ends, and I'd guess
the outer two were divided by ten paces;
twenty four elders marched beneath that panoply,
paired and every one of them crowned with a lily
and intoning *Blessèd be the fruit of your womb!*

and then *Blessèd is the beauty on which no tomb
will ever close!* After these chosen spirits pass,
having not even bent one single blade of grass,
there came – as star follows strange star in southern skies –
four mighty animals whose wings were filled with eyes
such as once studded Argus's all-seeing head.
I won't waste rhymes on them, but anyone who's read
Ezekiel's first-hand account of their descent
from the hyperborean zone with violent
glimmers and dark rumblings will see them clear enough;
these animals would be the same as his ones, if
only they had had four wings instead of twice three…

on this point, let it be said, John and I agree.
The space between the creatures contained a two-wheeled
chariot or juggernaut which a griffon pulled,
his golden eagle's gold wings stretching up so far
their tips were lost to sight, whilst his lion flanks are
vermilion and white; Caesar or Africanus
never rode through Rome on a car as glorious,
and beside it the sun's own craft would seem a poor
counterfeited thing like a face in a mirror
(that craft which, when it strayed, was downed at the request
of the devout earth and Jove was obscurely just).
At the right wheel, dancing in a circle, came three

maidens, the first of whom flamed so red you'd hardly
distinguish her limbs in the centre of a fire;
the next had the countenance of one whose entire
body has been carved from a single emerald,
and the third girl shone like snow. First their lithe forms coiled
as if led by the white one and then by the red,
and in time with the latter's song they slowed or sped.
Beside the left wheel stepped four figures in garments
of a regal purple, attempering their dance
to the sweet voice of her who possessed a third eye,
then two solemn elders with features equally
resolute and pure although differently dressed –

one of them appeared a familiar of highest
Hippocrates, who life made for those it most loves,
and the other whirred a sword deft as wings of doves...
even from the far shore this made me thrill with fear.
Then I saw four of humble bearing, and then there
paced a solitary figure as though wakeful
in his sleep; these seven true witnesses were all
crowned not with pale lilies but with crimson roses,
each flower as dazzling as the fire that blazes
and yet never burns. Now love's chariot stood right
opposite me, and the tremulous peal of light
was followed by a flash of almighty thunder

at which they froze as if forbidden to go further.

30.

When the septentrion of the highest heaven

came to a halt – never clouded except by sin,
seven stars that haven't ever set or risen
but which unalterably tell what must be done
just as the lower ones direct the helmsman home –
the people who radiated truth and wisdom
turned towards the chariot as though towards peace
itself; like a holy messenger from the skies,
one of them then cried *Come with me from Lebanon,
my sister-child, my bride,* and three times everyone
sang those nine words in response – and, as all the blest
will step swiftly from their catacombs at the last
fated trumpet-blast, intoning hallelujah

with voices dressed in undying flesh forever,
so on the juggernaut a thousand ministers
of eternal life replied in praise of that verse
(*Hosanna,* they were crying, while they threw lilies
all around as if obedient to Anchises).
I have sometimes witnessed the eastern sky, at dawn,
flush with a roselike tint while the heights adorn
themselves with the blue of an immutable peace,
Helios rising mist-trailed so his golden face
doesn't dazzle but can be endured for a time;
so now, invested in the shade of living flame
beneath a green cape, her white veil edged with olive

and through clouds of flowers descending from above,
there appears before me the woman that I love.
It's not my eyes that tell me, but she seems to have
mysterious power in her presence… it pours
across the space between us such that the force
which once made me tremble is felt and known again;
transfixed as I had been when I wasn't yet ten,
I turned to my left as a little child might go
for solace from his mother. "There is," I murmured, "no
blood cell in me that doesn't shudder as it flies…
the ancient flame's rekindled, how I recognise
the signs!" But Virgil, gentlest of fathers, to whom

I had given myself to deliver me from
the grim wood and hectic wolf, was no longer there –
and not even all our primordial mother
once lost could stop the hot tears darkening my face.
"Don't cry just now, Dante… don't cry because he goes,
for first you must be pierced by a yet sharper sword."
Like an admiral who strides backward and forward
on the deck of his warship, inspecting the fleet,
so – spinning round at the sound of the name I set
down here only since necessity compels me –
I saw on the chariot's left side the lady
who'd been indistinct, viewed within a lily-blur,

directing her gaze at me across the river
though veiled still and wreathed with Minerva's silver leaves.
"*Look* at me," she said, haughty, like one who reserves
the full heat of her anger, regal in restraint.
"I am Beatrice, indeed… I am she you'll not paint
in mere *words* unless your ink also fades to white.
Don't you know that man's happiness dwells on this height?
To what do we owe the honour of your visit?"
My glance fell to the crystalline stream, but as it
reflected back my doleful face I turned to the grass…
the taste of unripened compassion is harsh.
In the silence that succeeded Beatrice's words,

a cry of *the sole house of refuge is the Lord's*
rose from the angels – and, as snow turns to ice
on trees that, like living columns, line Italy's
igneous spine, compressed and chilled by Slavic winds,
then melts like wax in fire when the shadowless lands
send vast lion-scented exhalations from the south,
so in tears and violent sobs from eyes and mouth
there pours the glacier that had long gripped my heart
(and all this due to the supernatural art
of those whose music is concordant with the spheres,
in which I heard the compassion of One who fears
nothing yet cares more than sinful tongues can express

and that seemed to say *Lady, why unstring him like this?*).
Still statuesque on the destroyer's port side,
she now turned and spoke these words to that mild-eyed horde.
"You are ever vigilant in an endless day,
and hence, as the world goes or staggers on its way,
neither night nor sleep makes you miss the slightest thing;
my response, understand, is geared to this weeping
figure, so that guilt may be counterpoised by grief;
he was one who showed such promise in his new life
that every nurtured virtue couldn't fail to be
bodied forth in fine invention, for not only
the immense wheels whose movements guide each mortal seed

to its own end – inasmuch as it's accompanied
by some or other stars – but a divine largesse
showered blessings on his birth (I must call it grace,
since it comes from a height even *our* keen gaze can't
reach). Thistles and weeds are all the more malignant,
though, when the gardener is absent and where
the soil's good. For a while I fed him with my fair
countenance and my shining glance, leading his feet
down righteous paths, yet when I rose from flesh to spirit –
hugely augmenting that fleeting potency –
he gave his attentions to a painted beauty,
turning onto a way of deceit and unease

and pursuing those bright and empty sophistries
which mimic goodness yet are ashen in the mouth.
I tried to call him back, but it appeared that both
dreams and secret signs were unable to touch him;
he'd fallen, and the sight of the black seraphim
was the last remaining chance of salvation now,
and thus I carried my prayers and my sorrow
to the very brim of the empire of the lost
and the soul who brought him here. If Lethe was crossed,
and he tasted the clear waters of remembrance
without having paid his fee through such repentance
as can't be uttered other than in agony,

he would be breaking our Lord's exalted decree."

31.

"You who stand across the sacred stream," she resumed,

indicating me with the point of what had seemed
lethal when I just saw its edge, "are these charges
true? After such accusations, you must confess...
say, *say* if they are true!" I attempted to speak
yet my voice expired in my throat, for I was weak
from sheer confusion. She endured this but briefly,
then spoke again. "What are you thinking? *Answer* me,
while you retain the awareness of your errors."
As when a crossbow cracks and the shot has no force –
both the cord and bow having been drawn back too far –
so in mingled disorientation and fear
I gasped a *Yes* that one needed sharp eyes to hear

then snapped under the burden, disgorging mere air
like a hooked fish that stares as it flaps on the shore.
"When you longed for me," she said, "and by your desire
were being led to the love of that beyond which
there is no greater joy, what chain-link fence or ditch
across your way so entirely stripped you of hope;
what did you think to gain elsewhere, why did you mope
half the time and strut about the other?" A sigh
escaped my lips, and, with an immense effort, I
got sufficient mastery of myself to talk.
"Present things," I mumbled between tears, "made me walk
in unreasonable pride or despondency...

false pleasure bent my path when you were gone from me,
once your face was hidden." "Had you remained silent,
or simply lied, your guilt would be as evident
as this confession has just made it... such a beak
knows you!" "Yet if," she went on, "the sinner's smooth cheek
yields and he becomes his own accuser, our court
sets the whetstone back against the blade of the sword;
now listen to me and stop scattering your tears
as peasants their seed, and perhaps in later years
you'll be more able to resist the sirens' call...
listen now, and hear how my body's burial
should've turned you not to the mud but to the sky,

and learn to bear your shame with equanimity.
Neither nature nor human art has ever wrought
such beauty as the limbs wherein my soul was caught,
yet whose fate was to sprawl in fragments under earth –
and if this apotheosis failed you with my death,
what scrap of flesh could subsequently catch your eye?
Having received that first blow from things which lie,
your instinct might have made you fly to a woman
no longer richly apparelled in deception;
your wings should not have been weighed down, vulnerable
to further missiles from the glance of some slim girl
or another novelty of like duration,

for nets are spread and swarms of arrows shot in vain
at a keen-eyed, fully-fledged eagle." As children
being reprimanded will silently listen,
standing still and studying a certain pebble
and coming to recognise themselves in the tale,
so I stood and so I hung my penitent head.
"If hearing this causes you such pain," she then said,
"why not lift your beard and observe and suffer more?"
An oak is easier to uproot, its huge claw
prised out of the ground by winds from Iarbas' land
or northern gale, than it was to heed that command –
and the trope through which my man's chin evoked my face

had been, I knew well, venomed like an adder's kiss.
Now I raise my brow and see those primal creatures
have ceased their rain of flowers, and I see Beatrice
turn to the beast whose one person has two natures;
still veiled, across the stream, she appears to surpass
her old self more than she'd eclipsed other women
when she was young. Remorse's nettle stung me then,
and all that ever tempted me with apparent
love I now loathed with a passion as violent…
self-knowledge's teeth tore my heart to the degree
I fell entirely unconscious, and only she
who caused that profound swoon knows where or what I was.

When my depths relinquished my perceptive powers,
I saw her I'd met picking flowers above me
and commanding *hold onto me tightly, tightly;*
I was submerged in the stream right up to my throat
and she was pulling me through whilst, deft as a boat,
she skimmed across the water's skin. As we drew near
the shore, I heard what I cannot reproduce here
or even remember, too ineffably sweet
are the words that sing of purified hearts, light feet.
Now she grasped my bone-dry head, pushing me under
so quickly I swallowed a mouthful of water,
and then up and straight into the midst of the dance

of four beauties. "We are," they sang, "her handmaidens,
ordained before she took on flesh, and we are stars;
we'll conduct you to her eyes, but a joy not ours
shall shine all the brighter once you go past the three
waiting beyond us… they see and know more deeply."
"Don't spare your vision," they then said, having guided
my steps to the gryphon's great breast where Beatrice stood.
"We've placed you in front of the emeralds whence true
love, and not its cold inversion, made war on you."
A thousand longings fiercer than the fiercest blaze
drew my gaze towards her illuminated gaze,
that aspect seemingly transfixed by the gryphon

and in which, a mirrored sun, alternately shone
the plumage of an eagle and a lion's fur
(consider my astonishment, pensive reader,
when I saw that the beast was absolutely still
yet transfiguring as if at its own wild will –
one instant divine and the next instant human –
where within her clear eyes there played His eidolon).
While, equally amazed and delighted, I first
taste that bread which both satisfies and makes one thirst
for more and always more, the three they'd spoken of –
showing by their movements how far they are above
the merely natural – dance forward, keeping time

to the angelic carol, their least motion rhyme.
"Turn round, Beatrice, turn your holy eyes," went their song,
"to one who for sight of you has voyaged this long…
be gracious in the name of His grace, and reveal
your mouth that he may see the second wonder you conceal."
O splendour of the living, everlasting light –
what unafraid poet, labouring in the night
which Parnassus's vast shadow lays on the world,
could drink so deeply or become so pale and chilled
that his mind would not be powerless to portray
you as you now appeared, veiled only by
the wheeling heavens' invisible harmonies

and showing your face in that atrium of trees?

32.

My gaze was so wholly enthralled, so attentive,

imbibing at the countenance I'd had to live
ten withered years without, that every other sense
was as good as dead; jet walls of indifference
hemmed in my swimming eyes on this side and on that,
her divine smile so caught them in its timeless net,
and in the end those goddesses physically
wrench my head to the left ("he stares too fixedly,"
I heard them say). I was briefly blinded – like one
who has looked for some moments straight into the sun –
yet when my eyes adapted to that which only
paled in comparison to the supreme beauty
they'd had to tear me from, I saw the majestic

army once again. It was slowly circling back,
wheeling about with the seven flames at its front –
as, encased in shields, a retreating regiment
turns its bright banners before the troops can follow;
the holy militia of the skies, white as snow,
passed us once more before the carriage turned its poles
and the dancers went to their places by the wheels
(the gryphon drawing the wonderful burden, his
plumes so unruffled they were like granite feathers
on an Egyptian god). I walked with Statius
and the beauty who had dipped me in the waters,
just behind the wheel whose track made a smaller arc,

and thus we advance through the original park –
emptied by her who took a reptile at his word –
tempering our steps to the melodies we heard.
We'd gone perhaps the distance of three successive
flights of an arrow when that descendent of Eve
climbed down from the car, at which a universal
murmur of *Adam* went round; a dry tree so tall
it would dwarf Kerala's most venerable teak
now arose right before us, surpassingly bleak
with its dark and spreading crown completely despoiled.
"Blessèd are you, gryphon," the circling army yelled,
"for not tearing with your beak that fruit sweet to taste

yet far harder than any other to digest."
"Thus," said the double animal, speaking at last,
"is preserved the seed of the righteous and the just."
Then, having removed the great cross-pole of the car,
he tied it to the widowed trunk and left it there
where in another age it grew. As earth's plants swell,
renewing their unearthly tones when the martial
quality of Aries filters heaven's great light,
now the orchard tree that had appeared desolate
was entirely covered in flaming flowers whose
shade was between that of a violet and rose;
the hymn that those people then sang has never been

framed by mortal mouths, to discern what it might mean
as impossible as its notes were to endure.
If I could sketch the eyes whose vigil cost so dear,
eyes the charming story of Syrinx lulled to sleep,
I would like one *sur le motif* depict the deep
slumber which possessed me then (though you'd have to be
steeped in unconsciousness to paint it faithfully).
And yet, failing that, I'll pass on to the moment
when – as by a sudden splendour – sleep's veil was rent
and a voice cried *Child, arise... what are you doing?*
Confronted with the luminously blossoming
limbs of the apple tree whose fruit each angel craves,

celebrating endless nuptials in crystal naves,
John and James and Peter hid in oblivion –
only returning to themselves at the spoken
word that once broke an altogether deeper doze,
both Moses and Elijah gone and the Maestro's
dazzling raiment too; so I hid and so I stirred
to see, standing over me, her who'd been my guide
beside the sacred stream. "Where's Beatrice," I murmured,
momentarily in doubt. "Sitting there," she said,
"beneath the new foliage and on the gnarled root...
the elect now reascend, in joyous pursuit
of the gryphon and singing with that easy lilt

which is of known and unknown things the most difficult
(a song both lighter yet less frivolous than yours)."
If she said more I didn't hear it, for my eyes
were already on the one who had made me blind
to everything else. Throned upon veracious ground,
she was surrounded by the seven nymphs; they held
those flames that would not so much as tremble when wild
Boreas or the hot sirocco blows. "Here,"
she said, "you'll be but briefly a forest-dweller,
whereas with me you will for all eternity
abide in the moment of true Rome... Christ's city.
Pay attention to the juggernaut, for the sake

of the hospital that you call the world, and make
sure – when you get back there – to record what you see."
No shining bolt ever dropped from clouds so swiftly
as Jove's eagle now crashed through the tree, metal claws
ripping its bark and the immaculate flowers
and striking the ship like a tropical cyclone;
a fox which long famine had turned to skin and bone
leapt on the chariot as though into a cot,
my lady putting its scrawny form to flight,
and then I saw the bright raptor descend once more
and leave the ark embellished with the feathers it wore
(*little bark of mine*, a voice laments from the sky,

what a burden you bear!). Next the earth suddenly
gaped just beneath the wheels, a dragon injecting
the base with its tail before withdrawing the sting –
quick as a wasp – and, in doing so, destroying
a whole section of the car. As meadows in spring
renew their grassy fur, the strange battleship now
flourished with an eagle's plumage from stern to prow
in the time that a yawn makes an O of the mouth.
Thus transfigured, the sacred edifice put forth
heads at its compass points and three along its spine;
these central ones had the curving horns of oxen,
and each of the others was like a unicorn...

truly, such a hybrid has never yet been seen!
Sitting on it with her wrinkled breasts bared, secure
as a fortress on a mountain, an ancient whore
was staring around as if looking for 'business'.
From time to time she exchanged an odious kiss
with a fair-haired giant standing at her side,
who, when he saw how she turned her dissatisfied
eyes towards my body, whipped her from head to foot;
then, twisted with suspicion and fury, the brute
untied the beast and led it off into the wood
and out of sight so that suddenly whole leagues stood –
leagues of trees like temple columns, of dim forest air –

between me and the gloating crone on the monster.

33.

Lord, the seven cried, *the infidels are come,*

passing the phrases back and forth so that the psalm
sounded less old lament than dirge for future things;
and now – sighing, grievous, fierce as flame – Beatrice sings
a little while, sisters, and you shall not see me
and *the time approaches… I will show you plainly.*
We hadn't gone ten steps, the dancers up ahead
and the girl, the sage and I behind, when she said –
her bright eyes dazzling mine, yet an absolute peace
pervading the features of that beautiful face –
"quicken your pace so you can hear me when I talk."
I did as I'd been told (a goddess turns men meek),
and, once I was by her, she addressed me once more.

"Don't you want to question me, profligate brother?"
"Lady," I replied, my voice faltering and weak
as those who, crippled by their awe, attempt to make
sense at the feet of a master, "you know me best."
"The shame and fear," she said, "born of self-interest
is what I require you to detach yourself from,
so you'll no longer moan as if caught in a dream.
The vessel the gleaming snake wrecked 'was, and is not',
but the culprit must believe that such a zealot
can't escape the Lord's wrath with the customary
crust; the eagle who feathered the ark will not be
without an heir for long, and the stars already

come into position – I can see them clearly –
the unstoppable influence of which shall give
man the divine agent whose sign is five-one-five…
it's he who'll slay the giant and the thieving whore.
Perhaps my dark saying would persuade somewhat more
if it wasn't – like those of Themis and the Sphinx –
resistant to the little teeth of one who *thinks*,
although soon time herself will play the prophetess
and solve this obdurate enigma with no loss
of cattle or of corn; mark these precise words
for the sake of those whose days are a mad rush deathwards,
the pursuit of dust, and recall as you compose

everything you've witnessed of this tree whose branches
have now been desecrated not just once but twice.
It was created holy for a holy use,
and all who plunder fruit or tear a single leaf
blaspheme against the author of the book of life
(having bitten it, the first soul had to endure
the unendurable privation of those four
thousand and three hundred years exiled from the light).
Your wits surely slumber if you can't estimate
the true reason it's so vast, and, moreover, made
as though rooted in the sky; had vain thoughts not played
through your mind like Elsa's petrifying waters,

darkening the brain as the blood of Pyramus
stained the mulberry, it would have been apparent
that the tree's nothing less than the embodiment
of His justice upon Earth. But it's plain to see
your God-given intellect's become completely
fossilized, and is therefore blinded by my speech;
for this reason I'd have you carry home, as each
returning pilgrim's staff is twined round with a frond –
visible reminders of the Holy Land –
an emblem of that radiance if not the full sense."
"As wax beneath a royal seal," I said, "my brain's
obedient substance bears the trace of your talk…

yet why does its import, a disappearing hawk,
get increasingly remote the more that I squint?"
"So," she replied, "you may see your path was distant
from the sacred way as the soil is from the spheres."
"I recall no estrangement. No sharp remorse gnaws
at my spirit like a token of betrayal."
"If your conscience fails you," she countered with a smile,
"try to remember you have just tasted Lethe…
as smoke denotes a fire, this lapse of memory
suggests your desire possessed a wandering eye.
Henceforth my words shall go unclothed, as much as I
reckon callow sight can endure their nakedness."

Brighter yet with slower pace, a white sun blazes
at that aerial summit whose location veers
here and there relative to where a person peers,
and the seven ladies halt – as a jungle guide
freezes if he sees a spoor, his head to one side –
at the very edge of a shadow such as those
thrown on mountain streams by verdant leaves and black boughs;
in front of their toes I seem to glimpse, issuing
together from a single unpolluted spring,
then – reluctant as lovers – taking separate ways,
Tigris and Euphrates. "Crown of the human race,
what water is this whose solitary source

falls into multiplicity as its light pours
down and out into the world?" "Matilda's the one,"
came the reply, "to whom you should put that question."
"But I have told him this, and other things besides,"
she said. "It can't be the draught of Lethe which hides
such knowledge from him now." "Perhaps," answered Beatrice,
"greater concerns obscure these fresh discoveries
or loot recollection like robbers in a tomb.
See where Eunoè is welling forth… conduct him
to its joyous anamnesis and thus restore,
as is your custom, the capacities that snore
in his delinquent soul." Proffering no excuse

but – like the truly noble spirit she is –
submitting to divine will at the slightest sign,
that lithe and graceful girl clasps her hand round mine
and indicates to Statius that he come too.
If, *semblable*, I had sufficient space to tell you
so much as a hundredth of the sweetness of a drink
in which all Love has ever thought and shall ever think
is realised and surpassed, I'd make the attempt;
yet I've reached this second book's border, neatly kempt
as the page of a scribe or an Englishman's lawn
and art's liberating bit won't let me go on.
Unbending from the river like saplings, we are

pure and new and fit to climb beyond the morning star.

BLISS

Are holy leaves the Echo then of blisse?
                              Echo.   Yes.

George Herbert, *Heaven*

1.

The glory of the One through whom each thing stirs

is a splendour that permeates the universe,
salient in some places and at others less;
I have been to the heaven in which His darkness
shines more than anywhere else, and there I saw
such things as a fallen tongue cannot mention for
lack of both the science and strength it would require –
as the intellect, understand, nears our heart's desire
it goes so deep that no recollection follows –
and yet, despite all this, the ensuing cantos
will strive to embody as much of that sacred
realm as I could store in the castle of my head.
Benevolent Apollo, for this last labour

make me into a mere vessel for your power
such as you ask of those who'd wear the laurel wreath;
ability's sufficed to get this far, but both
the twin peaks of Parnassus will be needed now
that I step into the final ring. Blow, ah, blow
an air within my lungs as you once blew when
you drew Marsyas like a sword from his red-lipped skin!
If, divine omnipotence, you grant the barest
trace of yourself so these poor words might manifest
the shadow of the royal land branded on my brain,
you will see me come to your tree's foot, weave a crown
of the leaves of eloquence and inspiration.

They are gathered too rarely (human volition
being just a ghost of what it was and shall be)
for a genuine king or poet's victory,
and any who thirst for the Peneian leaf
must make you, joyful god, throw back your head and laugh
with laughter fed by joy. One spark can seed a blaze…
perhaps lither voices will speak in later days,
praying with such grace that the oracle replies.
The world's great lamp has many gates through which to rise
to those destined to die, yet its brilliance appears
on truer course and synchronised with better stars –
tempering and stamping the matter of the earth

with its incandescent emblem – when it sails forth
where four rings and three crosses join. Such an entrance,
or near enough, had bathed one hemisphere in dense
blackness and the other in a dazzling white,
creating morning there and dusk where I now write,
when I saw her turned left towards the source of light:
eagles couldn't gaze with that fixity of sight.
As a ray reflected in a marble pavement
mounts back towards the heavens like a pilgrim bent
on his dear home city, so Beatrice's action –
transposed by my eyes into this imagination –
became the pattern for my own, and now I stared

at the sun as no carnal soul has ever dared...
things we're not equipped for here are done in paradise,
being mankind's native and most propitious place.
My look was a brief one, but not so brief that I
didn't see it scintillating as fire-motes fly
off a hammered ingot fresh from the forge's flame,
and then suddenly – *light upon light* – a selfsame
sun was as if added to the first, doubling day.
Her eyes are still locked on the ceaseless roundelay
of the spheres when I glance down and rest my eyes on her;
gazing at that countenance, my human thoughts were
transformed like Glaucus was when he was made

mad and sane as Neptune by the virtue of a weed
(words gesture towards though cannot express this change
that is death and yet death's end, so let the strange
illustration serve for those who'll *see* for themselves).
You know, almighty Love – whose governance revolves
the whole artifice of night – if I was then just
that part of myself you enunciated last,
for it was your radiance that raised me on high.
My gaze was now drawn to the immense harmony,
explicit but restrained, of the heavens' rotation,
and the sky seemed filled by a conflagration
broader than floodplains silver with rain; beheld sound

and heard light pierced me with longing like a knife-wound,
a thirst to know their cause, yet the woman who sees
me as I see myself spoke first. "Fantasies
and imaginings," she smiled, "inflate yet weigh your mind;
a man who has discarded them isn't so blind.
You're not on Earth, where you suppose yourself to be…
no bright bolt ever shot from its birthplace swiftly
as you have just returned to yours." "B-b-but how,"
I asked, free of my initial doubt though caught now
in a second, "can a body rise through these light
bodies? Amazement follows wonder with no respite."
"There exists," she then began, regarding me

as a mother her sick child, "a hierarchy
amongst created beings, a sacred order
whereby the universe resembles our Father;
the finer the intelligence, the more it divines
that the world is an array of symbols or signs
of eternity… to lead to this perception
was the sole reason for such order's foundation.
Within the hierarchy, every creature
is positioned according to how its nature
departs from or cleaves to the primal unity;
they head for different ports across Becoming's sea,
steered by that which some term *instinct* and some *love*.

This is what impels the billowing flame to move
upwards to the moon; this force drives each mortal heart;
this is what prevents Earth's dust from flying apart
and holds it in a glowing singularity;
this obscure potential like tensed yew not only
fires those who have just grunt and howl for dialect,
but also those ignited by the intellect
which – in turn – a higher passion lights. Providence
measures all this out, quietens with its luminescence
that heaven within which, unutterably fast,
the furthermost crystal rotates so that the vast
silentness beyond can touch it everywhere

at once… the healer's bow shall now propel us there,
the string which effortlessly hits the sweetest mark.
Sometimes – as when what an artist sets out to make
does not accord in the end with his intent,
the material recalcitrant – a creature's bent
from this track because it has the *will* to be so,
diverted by counterfeit bliss and diving low
like celestial fire crackling headlong from on high.
You should no more marvel at your rise than ask why
a mountain stream descends and doesn't flow uphill;
for if, unimpeded, you stood on earth still
it would be as strange a thing as a motionless blaze."

With that, she turned her clear gaze back to the shining skies.

2.

O frail flotilla in my wake, all those who long

to eavesdrop on the craft whose engine is this song,
return to your familiar shores. Do not set out
on depths where, losing me, you'll lose yourselves. Wheel about!
No man ever dared these waters... the task is mine.
Minerva blows, Apollo pilots, and the nine
Muses show the stars. Yet the few, you happy ones
who've stretched forth your beaks for angelic sustenance –
that bread which both gives life and makes appetite new –
are welcome to sail behind me, to pursue
my white trace across the salt gulfs before it fades...
the glorious Argonauts weren't half so amazed,
when they saw Jason turn ploughman, than you will be

presently. Now we rose at the velocity
of stormblown skies, propelled by the spirit's inborn
and unkillable thirst for its rightful kingdom;
Beatrice was gazing up and I gazed at her eyes,
and then – faster than a bolt strikes its target, flies
and is shot by the bow – I saw we'd reached a place
where wonders drew my sight. Turning to me, her face
joyous in sheer beauty, she spoke. "Direct your mind
in gratitude," she said, "to Him who has conjoined
our souls with the first of the stars." It seemed to me
a smooth cloud enclosed us, solid but absolutely
clear, dazzling as a diamond hosting the sun;

like waters pierced by a ray and yet unbroken,
the eternal pearl received us within its sphere.
If I was flesh then – and we can't conceive, down here,
how one body and another could coincide –
the result would simply be an intensified
thirst to see that essence where man and God are one...
to know at first hand, not via demonstration
but in the presence by which mere belief's annulled.
"Lady," I answered, "He who plucked me from the world
I thank with deep devotion. But tell me of these
blemishes on this structure, the source of stories
concerning Cain." "If," she said, smiling just briefly,

"opinion errs without a perceptual key,
surely there is no need for stupefaction now
you see its wings flail even with a stare to follow...
what, though, do *you* think?" "I expect," I replied,
"that bodies variously dense or rarefied
explain those different shades." "Listen to me closely,
and you'll see how entirely sunk in falsity
your ideas are. The eighth sphere displays numberless
lights, like faces of diverse aspect and brightness;
if this was but a case of varied density,
then one sole power would glisten in every
star – here strong and there weak, and some places the same –

which would be identical, in its inner form,
with its massed neighbours. If, similarly, those brown
shapes you ask about were due to variation
of dense and rare, this would require the moon to be
riddled with absences, or, alternatively,
marbled with lean and fat like a pendent slab of meat –
or a book, if you prefer, where motley leaves meet
at the fore-edge, giving the impression of stripes;
in the first case one would see, during an eclipse,
the sun wink through as through all translucent things...
this clearly isn't so, hence your imaginings
cringe into ashes like a crisp leaf in a blaze.

And now let us consider the latter case:
that in which the rarer matter does not extend
throughout, but is combined with solid parts which bend
the swift rays as they strike (like colours reflected
off glass backed with lead). Predictably, men have said
each dim zone's caused by a more remote reflection;
the following can free you from this objection,
for experience is the source of true science
and art. Place two mirrors at a single distance,
and a third between them but further off... a light
behind you will shine in triplicate, equally bright
in three images although smaller in one. So,

as midday sun's relentless throb divests the snow
of its whiteness and its cold, I am now inclined
to imbue a soul likewise frozen in his mind
with a vital brilliance that trembles to the sight.
Inside the outer sky whose peace is infinite,
there speeds a body from whose vigour we're given
our fundamental being; the stellar heaven,
so wondrous to the eye, distributes that being
through manifold existences, each lucent thing
united by the sombre shell; the lower spheres,
downwardly directing their various powers,
attain their ends in well-sown seed... thus, as you see,

the world's instruments descend degree by degree,
receptive to the heights and creative below.
Pay close attention here and observe how I go
from this point to the insight you desire, for then
you'll be able to wade the flood alone. Motion
and force are transmitted to the holy gyres
by the blessèd movers' breath, much as the hammer's
art flows from the smith, and a darkness wild with stars
is the impress of the mind – unfathomable, vast –
which rotates the heaven that is its sign and seal;
and just as, within your body's dust, the soul
differentiates itself into organs that all

incarnate a function, the intellectual
light proclaims its goodness... dazzlingly multiplied,
yet spinning on the Self by which it's unified.
Diverse powers produce diverse alloys – binding
themselves to each planet's precious flesh, entangling
radiance with substance like the life inside you –
and this makes those bodies shine as delight shines through
the pupil of a living eye, epiphanies
of joy. Such, then, is the true origin of these
differences of shade, not matter rare and dense...
a formal cause that produces in accordance
with its inherent nature the obscure or bright,

this perplexing blend of lucidity and night."

3.

That sun who first flamed my caged heart, who made it sing,

had revealed to me – in proving and refuting –
the lovely face of truth, and here I raised my head
in order to confess how I was corrected;
yet this very moment there appeared a vision
so compelling that certitude and confession
both vanished from my mind. As through sheer, transparent
glass or clear waters with no trace of a current
though not deep enough that the bottom's lost to sight,
we see ourselves imaged in spectral white-on-white
less vivid than a pale pearl on a pallid brow,
I glimpsed an array of eager faces and now
fell into a grave error that you might well call

the reverse of what made the boy dote on a pool.
Instantly, I turned aside in expectation
of viewing the crowd I'd seen in dim reflection –
but then, finding nothing there, looked once more ahead
and directly into the illuminated
features of my guide, her eyes shining with a smile.
"Don't be too surprised," she said, "if your still-puerile
notions cause amusement, not trusting as they do
to stand firm on the truth but rather wheeling you –
as usual – vainly around. These are substantial
figures that you see, who through failing to fulfil
an undertaken vow are lodged or exiled here;

feel free to talk with them, and credit what you hear,
for the true light – by which they have been made complete –
permits no sly steps, no devious-minded feet."
"O happily-created spirit," I began,
almost hampered by an excess of volition
and addressing the shade that seemed keenest to speak,
"who in eternity's living beam know the sweet
and incommunicable taste of the divine,
be so kind as to say your name and condition."
"Our charity," she replied, laughter in her glance
and her response immediate, "allows entrance
to any pure desire, like the love of that king

who desires his whole court to be just as loving.
In the world I was a virgin sister, and my
augmented beauty – search now with your inner eye –
should disclose and not conceal my identity...
I am Piccarda, located in this slowly-
turning sphere, blessèd with these other blessèd ones;
lit only by the Holy Ghost, our affections
rejoice to be conformed to its ordering force,
and this lot – which may seem humble – was perforce
granted us for vows somehow neglected, unfulfilled."
"Yet your radiant faces," I replied, "are filled
with unearthly resplendence, to such an extent

my mind didn't know you. You claim to be content –
don't you long to *see* more, to burn with those above?"
A smile swiftly flashed through them all – as vast shoals move
in unison – and then she addressed me again
with a joy like that of first love, leavened with pain.
"Brother," she said, "our will is calmed by charity,
by virtue of which we don't yearn to have or be
anything else than what we are, what we possess;
to want to stand higher would be to do no less
than go against the will of Him who's placed us here,
as if one could smash open one's allotted sphere
instead of obeying the wild necessity

of abidance in love (ponder my words carefully).
The very quality of this state of being,
you might say, consists in our not contravening
the supernal will; and hence our wills breathe as one,
and so the whole hierarchy of this nation
is as pleasing to each rank as it is to the king.
His breast's the ocean toward which all is moving,
both what He creates and what His worlds compose...
every soul is restless until it knows that peace."
It was suddenly clear to me how everywhere
in these skies is paradise itself, although there
descends in an unequal measure the rain

of total grace. But as at times there can remain,
when one dish has filled us, the yen for another,
now I gave thanks and enquired – with speech and gesture –
what weave she hadn't drawn the shuttle wholly through.
"Perfection situates in higher, deeper blue
a spirit by whose sanction women take the veil,
so that – whilst still on earth – they may keep sweet vigil
entwined with the groom who accepts their loving vows;
I fled the blind world when young, determined to house
my soul in her habit and walk her sacred way,
though men whose tongues were more used to curse God than pray
tore me from those cloisters… only the Father knows

what becomes of me in the hard life that follows.
This other spirit on my right, blazing with all
the splendour of our sphere, views herself in my tale –
the holy band was ripped off her forehead, and yet
she never stopped wearing the veil upon her heart…
the radiance is the noble Constance, who bore
to Swabia's second blast its last emperor."
Thus she spoke to me, and then she began to sing
Ave Maria, whilst like some heavy thing
slipping into water, she slowly disappeared;
I turn around to someone that much more desired,
to Beatrice, who is at first so dazzling to the sight

the question on my lips is silenced by her light.

4.

A free man placed at the precise midpoint

between, let's say, a steamed trout and a spit-roast joint
will starve before deciding which one to devour –
like a lamb between two wolves, paralysed with fear,
or a mastiff hungering at deer to left and right –
so if, poised between twin doubts, my lips were sealed tight,
I think myself worthy of neither blame nor praise...
I was silent, although to tell the truth my face
was a canvas where the attendant desire
and the questions themselves were depicted as clear –
even clearer, perhaps – than in articulate
speech; and, as Daniel with the unjustly irate
Nebuchadnezzar, she somehow soothed me. "I see,"

Beatrice said, "two wishes simultaneously
pulling you separate ways, your very eagerness
hobbling itself, your snorting psyche breathless.
If – you reason with yourself – a pure intent
endures, on what possible grounds can the violent
actions of another affect what we receive?
The second cause of consternation, I believe,
is that the fact that these souls have appeared to go
back to their sphere would seem to justify Plato;
these are the doubts which divide your will, your spirit...
first I'll address the one with the poison in it.
The most God-intoxicated of the seraphim,

Moses himself, whatever John you care to name,
or Samuel – *none* of them, not even Mary –
is situated any more exaltedly
or owns an iota more of time's storied round
than those you've just encountered... everyone is crowned
in the first sphere, *la dolce vita*, different
solely in that not each feels to the same extent –
though all comprise its beauty – the breath of eternity.
These souls aren't exactly there, but you're made to see
bliss's lowlands via their resemblances;
what has to be conveyed in terms of the senses
you'll in due course intuit by mind alone,

and this is why the Church represents as human
Gabriel and Michael and that other one
who made Tobias sane or, rather, sane again,
and why scripture as it were condescends to your
faculties and gives 'hands' and 'feet' to the Creator...
always saying something else, speaking in disguise.
When the great pagan, in his *Timaeus*, argues
that our souls return to their native stars at death
he presumably holds that for literal truth,
yet perhaps even his meaning is other than
what he seems to declare (maybe the intention,
not to be despised, was through a tale to express

the source of malign and benign influences
in these lofty wheels – although, ill-interpreted,
the principle once had the ancient world misled).
The other doubt disturbing you is venomed less,
since it couldn't lure you from me with its malice;
that divine justice looks unjust to mortal eyes
attests more to live faith than evil heresies,
but this is a point that your mind can grasp, and so
I shall do as you desire. Spirits that had no
part in some violence undergone are not excused,
for true will – in subjection – isn't thereby doused
but like a natural blaze darts up a thousand times

almost as if animated by the beaten flames;
if, therefore, the will of those souls had been entire,
like that which kept Saint Lawrence grilling on the fire
and made Mucius treat his right hand so coolly,
they'd have leapt back to Christ as soon as they were free...
such inner fortitude, however, is rare.
These words, if you've properly received them, will cure
the mind of thoughts that might've given much trouble.
Yet now your eyes confront another obstacle,
too daunting to get past without an accomplice;
I have planted in you the certainty that bliss
makes a soul incapable of telling a lie,

so close to the primordial truth does it lie,
but you heard that Constance's heart remained a shrine
and this seems to contradict me. Yet often men
do something they shouldn't do, with huge reluctance,
if in peril – like Alcmaeon who was at once
dutiful and savage when he killed his mother –
though think how brute force and will mix with each other
in cases such as these, which cannot be forgiven.
Absolute will won't consent to be thus driven,
but the conditioned will relents to the degree
it thinks resistance could cause more difficulty…
what Piccarda said of Constance earlier

referred to the higher will and not the lower,
hence we both speak truly." This pellucid rippling
overflowed from the sacred source, that crystal spring
where all truth has its origin, and the one
and the other desire was granted peace. "Divine
creature," I said, "beloved of the first lover –
the sweet inundation of whose speech plays over
consciousness and thaws it, gifting ever greater life –
the deepest of my feelings isn't deep enough
to recompense you grace for grace, but I trust He
who has *virtù* and vision will answer for me;
I can see how the mind is never satisfied

unless illuminated by that truth outside
of which no truth exists, the light that once possessed
gives such sanctuary one knows the perfect rest
of a beast softly breathing in its inmost nest
(and next to which nothing is of real interest).
So doubt blooms at truth's foot, our nature driving us
towards the white peak through ranges that seem endless…
yet tell me, and I ask this with due reverence,
if other goods are ever placed in your balance –
in an instance of lapsed vows, I mean – and not found
wanting?" Now she gazes at me with such profound
love, such sparkling eyes, that my powers turned and fled

and left me standing – almost wholly lost – with downcast head.

5.

"Do not be astonished if love's heat ignites me

in a manner surpassing anything earthly
and to such an extent that your sight is thrown down,
for what it proceeds from is perfected vision –
which, in the light of apprehension, moves light feet
toward the apprehended good. The infinite
already gleams in your higher mind, a brilliance
that, once seen, cannot but spark the one true romance...
whatever else seduces you can only be
due to some trace or vestige of eternity
shining through it, albeit poorly understood.
You want to know whether some other service could
replace an unfulfilled vow, sufficiently so

to save a soul from accusation?" The canto
thus begun, Beatrice continued her pure discourse
like one immune to interruption. "God's largesse,"
she said, "gave no gift more aligned with His goodness,
created nothing that He accounts more precious,
than the free will which only the intelligent
creatures possess. You will see – as the argument
follows from this premise – that when you make a vow
both you and He consent together, and therefore how
much value that vow has; by means of such a pact,
a priceless treasure's sacrificed by its own act...
what, then, could you ever offer in its place,

for to put what you've given to another use
would be like some robber baron's feigned charity,
as if one could heal with demonic energy.
Regarding the main point you should now be certain,
but as the Holy Church gives dispensations
in such matters – which would seem in contravention
of our sacred law – you must, for your digestion's
sake, stay seated at the board a moment longer...
this is not milk but dark meat to make you stronger.
Fix in your dilating mind what I've made explicit,
since he who hears something without retaining it
keeps as witless as before. The essence of this

sacrifice consists of two things… the one which is
laid on the altar, and the actual covenant;
the latter can only be cancelled in fulfilment,
whilst to change what's placed in the flames – as the Bible
clearly demonstrates – is at times permissible…
this being the wax, the other the signet ring.
But that burden can't be altered without turning
the silver and the golden keys, and unless
the replacement contains what it replaces –
as four is held in six – the alteration's folly.
That which is of such value that it easily
tips any scale… what could you ever change it for?

Take no vow lightly and be neither faithless nor
perverse like Jephthah who kept that idle promise
as opposed to acknowledging his foolishness,
or like the Greek king due to whose idiocy
Iphigenia wept for her innocent beauty
and made both wise old men and simpletons weep too
at the news of such a rite. Christian souls, you
should be immovable instead of fluttering
like pennants in the breeze… don't assume every spring
will wash the heart clean. You have the New and Old
Testaments to guide you, the Church to guard the fold;
that's plenty enough for your salvation, and when

greed hollers otherwise do not be sheep but *men*
in order that the Jew shan't snigger in your homes.
Don't carry on like wayward and scatterbrained lambs,
self-divided from the very day they leave the teat."
Thus, or more or less, Beatrice lectures as I write,
then turns back with immaculate desire towards
the place the world's most full of life. Her unsaid words
and transfigured face reduce my mind to silence,
despite the thoughts that throng it, and then at once –
like an arrow that strikes while the string still quivers –
we are sped into the second realm. So joyous
is her countenance upon entering the white

lustre of that sphere it appears to shine more bright…
and if a planet pulsed and laughed, think what became
of one such as I who in my mortal nature am
unending transmutation! As in a pond with no
breath of wind the sleek carp surface, the zero
of each round mouth jostling any speck that lands,
now I saw drawing near us, in their thousands,
eager brilliances that we could tell were joyful
by the light with which they glowed; imagine how you'd feel,
reader, if I stopped here, how hungry to know more,
and you'll surely understand my longing to hear
of their situation the instant I saw them

and caught, as though said or sung by each resplendent flame,
a chorus of *here's one who will deepen our love!*
"Well-conceived poet, destined by the skies above
to lay eyes on the thrones of victory before
concluding your campaign – whilst the holy war
of life on earth endures – the radiance we are
ablaze with is the self-same cry which flashes far
through every hell and heaven… if, then, you desire
to be enlightened by and about that fire,
question at your pleasure." So one of them addressed me,
Beatrice urging me to converse with them freely
and to take them for gods. "I can well see," I said,

"how the luminescence within which you're nested
is drawn from your eyes, for it shines out when you smile,
but still I do not know who you are, blessèd soul,
or why you haunt the sphere that with another's beams
veils itself from human sight." Suddenly it seems
the glow that first spoke is more dazzling than it was;
as when midday heat has burned away dawn's vapours
and Helios is hidden in his own excess,
so that sainted form through still greater happiness
is swallowed by its rays… and now, as if doubly
clothed in sanctity, the spirit answers me
with a voice like the vibration of a snow-white wing…

the mode in which the following canto will sing.

6.

"When the eagle's flight was reversed by Constantine –

counter to the sun and the way it had once been
led by the forefather who took Lavinia –
the bird of the Lord sojourned on Europe's border
two centuries or more, close to the mountainous
place it first emerged, waxing imperious
with the sacred shadow of its feathers' vast span
and passed from grasp to grasp until it came into mine.
I was Caesar and I am Justinian,
who pruned from the law the superfluous and vain
in obedience to the primal love that breathes me;
before that great work, I had thought there was only –
restricted by this creed – the one nature in Christ...

yet the blessèd Agapetus, the lordliest
of shepherds, brought me to the pure faith with wise speech.
I trusted him, and now it's as plain as that each
contradiction marries a falsehood and a truth.
As soon as I was set upon that righteous path,
God's grace inspired me to start the high endeavour
to which I gave myself entirely, handing over
the command of my troops to Belisarius –
he whose arm was joined with the sword arm of the skies,
a clear enough sign I should rest from warfare;
my reply to your initial question ends there,
but I need to add a few words to help you see

the motives of those who would oppose the holy
emblem, and also those who claim it for their cause...
see how reverence is due to its unearthly force,
from the moment Pallas died to let it rule.
You know it was three hundred years in Alba, till
the two sets of triplets fought for its possession,
and what it accomplished in the reign of seven –
from Lucretia's sorrow to the Sabine women –
as it subdued the mindless tribes. You know that then
it hovered above the illustrious Roman
legions as they battled Brennus's blue-eyed men
and Pyrrhus and every other barbarous prince,

where the true renown that my willing mouth anoints
was earned by the Decii and the Fabii;
it crushed the hordes Hannibal led though the high
crags where, dear Po, you initiate your journey,
saw Scipio and Pompey's precocious glory
and proved bitter to the hill beneath which *you* were born.
When the hour neared that the desire of heaven
was to lead the world back to her immanent peace,
Caesar took it by Rome's will; and what it did was
seen by the Isere and the Loire, the Rhone, the Seine,
and every hamlet from the Var up to the Rhine,
and what it accomplished beyond the Rubicon

was a flight such as neither human tongue nor pen
could keep up with or pursue... first the serried host
turned towards Spain and then the Adriatic coast
and then it struck Pharsalia, that grievous
cry heard far as where the black Nile sweats. Antandros
and Simois followed, where it first flew, and the grave
where Hector lies; Ptolemy's downfall was its next move,
and now it hit Juba like the kiss of lightning
and rounded on your west while the diminishing
note of Pompey's trumpet could yet be heard. As for
its actions in concert with the next emperor,
Brutus and Cassius slaver and snarl in hell

just as Modena and Perugia wailed (lustful
Cleopatra laments it still, still fleeing
but to reencounter the inevitable sting
of gaudy death). With Augustus, it then coursed
as far as the Red Sea's coraled shore to the east,
announcing such silence the double shrine was shut;
two renowned rulers over mortal realms, and yet
how diminished it all seems when you view the bird –
that living archetype – on the hand of the third
Caesar, if you watch with a lucid heart and eye,
for the same divine balance these lines are spoken by
now granted it the glory of exultant

revenge. Contemplate, child, what these word-mosaics chant…
later on it was Titus who settled the feud,
and, when the Holy Church was mauled by the Lombard,
Charlemagne came conquering underneath its wing.
Now you're fit to judge those I was accusing
and from whose machinations your miseries stem,
one who opposes gilt lilies to Rome's emblem
versus one who'd use it for political gain
such that – if anything – it is quite uncertain
who is most to blame. The Ghibellines' royal art
must adopt a different sign, since to pull apart
eagle and principle negates its very self,

and let not the new Charles or any other Guelph
strike but fear the talons that tore a greater lion!
This minor star's adorned with those whose work was done
for love of fame, and when desire is thus inclined –
straggling sideways like a bonfire in a crosswind –
caritas's flame rises less vivaciously;
our state and merits correspond, and that we see
the precision of this is part of our delight,
immortal justice modulating every bright
soul so it could never *think* to turn aside. Different
voices produce the finest chords, and the blent
sounds of the whole hierarchy of His life

harmonise the skies. This pearl's lambent with the love
of one whose work had scant reward… a Romeo,
although those who manoeuvred against him have no
smiles upon their faces any more (truth be told,
he walks a crooked path whose arteries run cold
at the sight of another's blessedness). Raymond
Berenger had four daughters, and each one was crowned,
and all of this was achieved for him by that lone
spirit; but when low guile, lizard talk, made it known
his loyalties weren't exactly where they should be,
he was treated in ways that live in infamy…
yet if the blind world saw his nobleness of soul

his reputation would be unassailable."

7.

Hosanna holy lord of hosts, illuminating

from afar these sweet realms of fire! Thus seemed to sing,
spinning on a silent note, that twice-bright substance,
both he and the others reinvolved in the dance
then veiled in sudden distance at the pace of starlight.
"Speak to her," urge my restless thoughts, transfixed by doubt –
craving that voice, for a drop of the elixir
to slake its raging thirst – yet so do I revere
the merest trace of the first letter of her name
that I bow my head like one burdened with a dream.
Beatrice endures this spectacle briefly, and then,
with a smile inside whose rays you'd forgo heaven,
commences. "My infallible awareness,"

she says, "tells me you're confused as to how justice
could rightly strike back against a rightful vengeance…
listen and I'll undo your brain's bedevilments,
whilst elucidating a fine point of doctrine.
He who was never born, who would endure no rein
nor curb his will, condemned his children with himself;
in consequence of this, an enfeebled race spent
millennia in error until the descent –
like a headlong diver entering a storm-lashed gulf –
of the Word into the flesh, joining strayed nature
with its great Maker in the one mortal creature…
a single act of His eternal love. Now

focus your attention on the words that follow;
man's being, as originally made, is pure,
yet was blinded to its own blissful nature for
bending from the sacred way, the authentic life.
No punishment was ever more justified, if
measured by the nature being taken on,
than that of Christ upon the Cross; equally, no one
ever suffered so unjustly, considering
who it was who suffered there… hence it was pleasing
not only to God but to the Jews, a sole death
shaking earth and hewing a celestial path.
But I can see your head caught up again, leaping

from self-important thought to thought, imagining
the mind doesn't tighten the knot it would untie.
I understand all that, I see you reason, yet why
this mode of salvation over another?
That decree is a mystery concealed, brother,
from the sight of those not brought to maturity
in the furnace men call love... the merely witty
could never even hope to put it into words,
though since it's a target so many aim towards
I will tell you how that path was the most worthwhile.
The divine glances forth, limning the eternal
beauties that blaze within itself, and a jealous

thought has no place there; each drop of it is boundless,
for eternity's watermark can never be
erased; each drop is also wholly free, as *we*
aren't subject to the force that warps each mutating thing.
That which flows down without any mediating
influence resembles Him the most, and therefore
causes Him most delight... for the holy fire
that God is, and which irradiates the cosmos,
is clearest in those created in His likeness;
the loss of just one of these treasures, equally,
constitutes a fall from the innate nobility
of the human soul. In fact, it's only sin

which separates man from the Good, from origin,
such that its light scarcely shines in him at all,
and the sole way back to paradise is to fill
that pleasure-gouged void, is to redress the balance.
Your nature, sinning in its very seed, erred once
and for everyone, thus making itself remote
both from the Garden and its own proper state;
neither could be regained – consider this subtlety –
without either God in His sublime courtesy
granting pardon, or man atoning for his madness
unaided. Now turn your eyes onto the abyss
of the deathless counsel, fixedly as your mind

is fixed upon my words. Man could hardly descend
in obedience and humility as far
as, disobeying, he had meant to rise before,
and so he couldn't compensate for it alone;
what was necessary was for one of God's own
ways to restore mankind to an integral life,
and – since art pleases more the more it shows the love
shining in the artist's heart – the divine goodness
that prints each thing and every world with its device
consents to use both, makes you raise yourself again.
From the last night to the first dawn, there's never been
nor ever will there be so dazzling an advance

on either of those paths... use your intelligence
and you'll know the gift of Himself was generous
far in excess of merely granting forgiveness,
and at the same time that anything less
than the bleeding body of His son on the Cross
would have fallen short of justice. Now two or three
points need returning to, in order that you see
with full clarity. Earth, air, fire and water – you think –
briefly mingle only to wind up in the stink
of soft corruption... yet they were created too,
so should be exempt from death if what's been said is true.
Brother, the angels and this unalloyed country

were made as they are now, in their entirety,
and the elements and everything they comprise
are both formed and informed by virtue of the sky's
native creatures; just their *matter* was created,
as were the vital and wisdom-saturated
stars that wheel around them. A plant- or animal-
soul is drawn out of some compound's dim potential
by those hallowed lights – their rotation and their beams –
but your life is breathed into you by the Supreme's
benevolence with no intermediary,
making you love and long for Him eternally...
to have confidence in man's resurrection, just

recall Adam's flesh was conjured from the dust."

8.

The world once subscribed to the dangerous belief

that the lovely Cyprian radiates the love
which runs to madness, in antiquated error
sacrificing to her with pious terror
and honouring Dione and Cupid for her sake;
and they named a great body after her I take
my new departure from, the star that woos the sun
now at this and now at that deep blue horizon.
I was not aware of our ascent, but that we
were suddenly inside it the increased beauty
of my darling furnished proof; and as you might see
sparks in a blaze, or, as in plainsong, a barely-
discernible second voice calls within the first,

coming and going more elusive than a ghost,
now I beheld other circling lights in the light
move swift or slow to the measure of each soul's sight.
No squalls ever swooped from icy cirrostratus
so fast that they wouldn't seem almost languorous
compared to the approach – leaving the dance begun
amongst the exalted seraphim in heaven –
of those divine luminescences, such a cry
of *Hosanna* rising from the closest that I
have hungered ever since to taste its sound again.
"We are here," commenced one of them, speaking alone
and drawing near, "with no thought other than to please,

than to make our joy yours. We revolve at the pace –
and in a sole orbit and with an equal thirst –
of those same celestial princes you addressed
with the words *You who move the third sphere with your minds…*
although writing, back then, as one the world half-blinds.
We're replete with His love, and, to work your delight,
this silence is endurable and even sweet."
My eyes going to Beatrice with due reverence,
and having been given fresh strength and assurance,
they turned back to the light that had promised so much.
"Who, then, *are* you," I said, my voice imbued with such
affection that that radiance visibly grew,

as if somehow this one small joy made all joy new.
"The world below," it replied, "confined me only
a little while, and much evil that's still to be
would not have been had I lived longer. Happiness
hides me from you, for, like the creature that stitches
a silken tomb, I'm veiled by the encircling rays
of our pure delight. You loved me well, and had good cause,
since in time my own love would have surely shown
you more than just its leaves. The land east of the Rhone –
when it has twined cool limbs with the Sorgue – eagerly
waited its true lord, as did the realm that Bari
and Catona and Gaeta moat, where Verde

and Tronto uncoil their voices in the sea;
the crown of the land through which the Danube's currents flow
was already scintillating upon my brow,
and beautiful Trinacria – whose sulphurous
fumes, on the coastline most pummelled by Eurus,
blacken the skies of Pelorus and Pachino
where ancient authors saw titanic nostrils blow –
would've looked for its kings to the kings born through me
had not crooked leaders, who invariably
crush the hearts of the populace on which they lie,
driven Palermo to chorus *die, die, die, die!*
My brother, foreseeing this, could shun the avarice

of Catalonia; by nature ungenerous,
he requires a militia devoted not just
to cramming a maximum of coin into its chest…
his subjects are bent double and can bear no more."
"Because I believe that the profound joy, signor,
with which your voice has filled me is *seen* by you where
all good ends and begins, it is all the more dear;
you have delighted me so enlighten me now,
for your words have raised the question as to how
bitter fruit can come from sweet seed." "If," he answered,
"I reveal a truth, you will have your face toward
what you ask about – not your back, as at present.

He who turns this mountain realm is both provident
and a sculpting force via these immense bodies,
that perfect Mind foreseeing the excellencies
of all of its beings and their well-being too;
if this was not the case, the nine heavens which you
now traverse would not be masterpiece but ruins,
and that would imply a faulty intelligence
had forged the shining minds that mobilize each star...
do you need the truth of this to be made more clear?"
"Not at all... I see Nature can't give out or tire."
"Then tell me," he went on, "whether or not, down there,
one stripped of his citizenship would be worse off?"

"He would," I replied, "and here I ask for no proof."
"And could you want a city without there being
many different men, each with a different calling?
I think not, if your master's taught you rightly.
Thus various effects have a variety
of roots... one is born Xerxes and another Solon,
and one's Melchizedek or he who lost his son
playing truant in the sky. Nature's wheel, sealing
mortal wax, works its art without distinguishing
a palace from a slum; and so it comes about
that Esau's mind departs from Jacob, that devout
but low-born Romulus was once ascribed to Mars...

all natures would run in their inseminators'
tracks, if divine providence didn't intervene.
Now what was behind you should be distinctly seen,
but so that you may know how much joy you bring me
I'll add the bright mantle of this corollary –
when fate puts someone in a place at variance
with his inner being, he has as little chance
as a seed sown on hard ground of proving his worth;
all that's needed for a vital population
is correct discernment of Nature's foundation,
yet you dress in suits those supposed to dig the earth
or even set a crown on the merely smooth-voiced...

thus, straying from the path, you find that you are lost."

9.

When Charles had enlightened me, beautiful Clemence,

he divulged the grave betrayals his descendents
would sustain; but then he said, "silence… let the years
wheel by," and so all I can say is that your tears
will be there for your pain. The life of that holy
light then turned back to the Light which filled it wholly,
as to a good that is supremely sufficient.
Ah, you who glorify what fallen minds invent,
who twist your hearts away from *this*… loveless creatures,
deluded souls! Now another of those splendours
approaches, suggesting by its incandescence
a desire to please – and Beatrice sweetly assents,
her bright eyes once more fixed on mine. "Tender zealot,"

I said, "give my wish fulfilment, and prove that what
I merely conceive can be mirrored into you."
And now the nearing radiance, still strange and new,
spoke from that same depth – its voice as if rejoicing –
out of which the multitude had seemed to sing.
"In that part of our pestilential country
between the sources of the Brenta and Piave,
there rises a modest eminence from which once
a fire proceeded through the land with great violence…
I and it have one root. Cunizza was my name,
and I shine in this star because its rays overcame
me; I forgive myself that destiny's cause

with no remorse, which may appear odd to the coarse
ears of your common mob. The fame of the diamond
beside me – our sphere's precious jewel – yet remained,
and millennia shall pass before the echo
of his voice dies away; a man should excel, so
that when he is buried his essence will resound.
Of all this, the degenerates currently penned
by the Tagliamento and the Adige
have not the slightest idea, and neither do they
repent in spite of the beatings they endure. But soon
a time will come when Paduan blood must stain
the marshes round Vicenza, her people being

so reluctant to do the right and fitting thing;
as for that lordling, his head held high, who goes
strutting where Sile and Cagnano merge their flows…
the net to snare him has already been knotted.
Soon Feltro will weep for her merciless shepherd,
a worse beast than dungeon ever gave admittance
to; he who'd have to weigh out – ounce by crimson ounce –
the Ferrarese blood that this most gentlemanly
priest is prepared to spill to show his loyalty
would be taxed indeed; such gifts, of course, are in keeping
with that land. Above, an order of reflecting
angels flash His judgement down through the crystal zones

so this talk pleases us… I think you call them Thrones."
Here she fell silent, reentering the ring's
vast dance like one who turns to other, stranger things;
the precious stone she had spoken of now became
dazzling as a ruby in the sun's hand, aflame,
for up there joys make a spirit grow in brightness
just as, within hell's blaze, unholy images
darken guilty hearts. "God sees and knows all things," I said,
"and your vision's so at one with His, O blessèd,
that no wish can elude it… why, then, is your voice –
which gladdens heaven always, with the song of those
veiled by the sixfold iridescence of their wings –

not swifter to attend to my thoughts' meanderings?
I wouldn't wait to be asked, if I could see
as deeply into you as you can fathom me."
"The largest expanse that water fills," it began,
"after the blue garland of the outer ocean,
extends so far eastward between discordant shores
that its meridian's where its horizon was.
I lived on the coast between Magra and Ebro,
the former the river whose truncated furrow
separates the Tuscan and the Genovese;
Bougie has the same dawn and dusk as my city,
the port which once slickened its sea-walls with blood. They

who imagined they knew me knew me as Folquet,
a poet marked with the insignia of this
science that bears mine... for the daughter of Belus,
equally wronging Creusa and Sichaeus,
or brute Alcides when he held Iole close,
never burned as I burned before my hair went white.
I don't *regret* this here but laugh with pure delight,
not at offences that no longer come to mind
but in sheer awe at what foresaw and preordained;
we marvel at the wondrous artifice of love,
the stern benevolence whereby the world above
shapes events on earth as a potter at his wheel.

Yet so you may truly finish with and fulfil
the passions Venus fosters, I must continue...
you'd ask the identity of the brilliance who
gleams beside me like a sunbeam in clear water;
it is Rahab, highest adept of our order,
at peace within that tranquil flame. She arose
into this sphere – the final zone your dark world shadows,
where that black sword narrows to a point – before all
other worthy souls were raised by Christ triumphal;
how apt it was to set her on a star, a palm
of the victory won by His pierced, vanquished palms,
considering her role in Joshua's glory

in the Holy Land (a realm papal memory
would seem not to contain). Your flourishing city –
planted and maintained by him whose cupidity
causes such sorrow – breeds and spreads the invasive
bloom which leads souls astray, that makes them come to grief...
the coin that can put a wolf in a cashmere suit.
Now popes dedicate themselves to greed, dissolute
cardinals neglecting the prophets and the saints
in favour of what their imagination paints;
not one thought flies to Nazareth, where Gabriel
opened his wings' silence, though soon our ignoble
Vatican – the grave of Peter's sacred army –

will finally be freed from this adultery."

10.

Regarding the child with that love which the one

and the other breathe – a ceaseless respiration –
the first and unspeakable virtue created
all things with an order that can't be contemplated
without scenting something of the Beloved's face,
as they turn in the twin eternities of space
and the human mind. Readers, lift your eyes with me
directly to the spot where the immensity
of one rotation strikes another wheel just so,
starting to marvel at the art of the Maestro
who, deep in His enamoured being, does not take
that gaze away a moment. See the oblique
and planet-bearing circle branching off from there,

to please the world that cries for them; for without their
twisted path, the skies' teeming energies would be
in vain, and our earth's rich potentiality
frozen; if, conversely, there was any more or less
deviation from the straight track, the world would miss
much of its wondrous structure, below as above.
Stay where you are, dear shadows, if you wish to have
delight before you sleep, meditating on this
foretaste fate has given you... those hard benches
are good seats to feed yourselves with the feast I've laid,
for the almighty theme by which I have been made
a mutterer and scribbler now calls me again.

The highest-ranking minister of Nature's reign –
who emblazons earth with images of heaven
and divides our lives with fire – was in conjunction
with the gyre I have spoken of, spiralling through
the movements that ensure each drop of April dew
globes his shining likeness a shade sooner each day;
and I was there too, the ascent as swift as a
thought you're not aware of until it's come and gone,
for Beatrice is one whose instantaneous action
conducts from fine to finer without the need
of time. How undimmed in their own selves must have been
those who were within the sun when I entered it,

apparent not by tone but light. I summon wit
and practice, the craft so long to learn, and yet still
can't *say* it in a way that makes it visible;
though it can be believed, and the sight thirsted for,
and if mental pictures fall short it is no wonder…
what eye has ever seen gold more dazzling than the sun,
where the holy Breath of the Father and the Son
gives the Most High's fourth household satisfaction?
"Send praises to the unseen orb," she then began,
"who has raised you to this coarser one with His grace."
Hearing these words I immediately place
the fullness of my love in Him, to the extent –

surrendering this heart with absolute consent –
that brief oblivion eclipses even her.
Beatrice showed no displeasure but laughed, the splendour
of each eye refracting the thinned beam of my mind;
almost as bright to sight as they were sweet in sound,
I now saw a multitude of quick brilliancies
crowning and surrounding us (as, sometimes, one sees
girdle the murderous moon when the midnight air
is damp). There are many jewels in bliss's court, where
I have lately been, of such unearthly beauty
they cannot be transported from that high country –
the incantation of those lights was such a stone,

and you on whose shoulder blades feathers haven't grown
will only hear of it from them who can only
sign. The luminescent bodies then seemed to me,
having circled us three times like stars near the pole,
like dancing girls who pause in sudden quiet until
a fresh tune fills their ears. "Given that grace's ray,"
I heard a voice from within one both sing and say,
"by which true love's lit and which loving tends and feeds,
so sounds or resounds inside your soul that it leads
up that ladder – the golden chain – no survivor
descends without climbing it again, whoever
denied your thirst some wine out of his flask would be

like a stream that withheld its waters from the sea.
You wish to know the plants in this garland, adoring
the beauteous woman who is tempering
your steel for the heights; at my right hand is my own
master and blessèd brother, Albert of Cologne,
and I am Thomas Aquinas; the next flame blooms
from the smile of Gratian, who served both forums
and thus delighted heaven; beside him in our
choir is that Peter who offered up his treasure
to the Holy Church, like the widow and her mite,
and beyond him's the fifth and comeliest light
of all… love wed wisdom in his matchless song and mind.

Beside him see the light of a taper assigned
to this sphere for witnessing the angels' ministry,
and in the next flame laughs one whose advocacy
of the Christian age was crucial to Augustine;
within the eighth light, rejoicing at the pristine
vision of the Good, is the scholar who makes clear
the false world's transience to those with eyes to hear…
he leapt straight to peace from martyrdom and exile.
The next glowing flame is Isidore's smile,
and beyond her is Bede then Richard who was more
than man in contemplation of the stars, in awe;
and this last one, from whom your gaze returns to me,

is he whose grave thoughts reckoned death came tardily…
it's the deathless intelligence of Siger, who
used logic to illumine the eternally true."
And now – like a clock whose pure chime in the darkness
before dawn awakens the bride, who rises
and softly mouths an aubade to the groom, to Him,
the note struck by the hidden mechanism's rhythm
so sweet that a well-ordered spirit swells with love –
I saw the majestic wheel slowly start to move,
deep calling deep, voices answering voices,
an unutterable mood of wild gentleness
which cannot be remembered or known except where

the sapience of joy is multiplied forever.

11.

Ah mortal spirits, both anxious and unfeeling,

justifying flight from God with warped reasoning!
One dissects a pale corpse and one crams legalese,
and one craves priestly garb and another studies
the arcana of rule by propaganda or
force; she dips for wallets and he fashions speeches,
another toils in silken beds, and this one is
a scholar of the art of perfect idleness –
whilst I, set free from all such things, am with Beatrice,
gloriously received in the heart of the sky.
Each radiance stopped like a small flame on a high
chandelier when it came to where it was before,
and then the glow that had already addressed me –

smiling and brightening – spoke once more. "I can see,"
it commenced, "as I mirror the eternal ray
and regard His light, that your doubts would have me say –
in language trued to your ear's labyrinthine shell –
more of the path I walked, *where a soul shall fatten well
if it doesn't stray*, and of the man whose heart shone
in song I said was matchless; discrimination,
here as always, is essential. The providence
that steers the world ordained one and another prince
to guide the church on either side… the first akin
to the seraphim, the second like a cherub in
the resplendence of his understanding.

I'll talk of the first, for their works and days were aiming
at a single end; to praise one is to praise them
both. Between the Topino and the stream
whose source is the hillside now known as Ubaldo,
there slopes the tall mountain from which Perugia's snow
and June heat descend; on this slope a sun once rose,
just as this sun's sometimes born where the Ganges flows…
when we name the place let us not say Assisi
but rather Ascension, to speak accurately.
His gold was still low in the sky when he began
to make the bleak woodland of the world bud and waken,
defying his father for the love of her who –

like death – no one ever willingly opened to;
before the spiritual court and the Father
they were united, and he loved her more and more
with each passing day. She, having borne eleven
hundred years since her first husband rose to heaven –
a millennium of scorn and obscurity –
had not been wooed till then; it hadn't helped when he,
Caesar, who made nations tremble with his voice, found
her and Amyclas sitting fearless on the ground,
or that her ardour was so constant and so fierce
that she bled and wept with our Lord upon the cross
while Mary stood below. But I rhyme too darkly,

and I'll tell you that Francis and blessed Poverty
are the couple of my perhaps longwinded speech;
the harmony between them – the happiness each
so clearly gave the other – and their mutual
delight, the joyed glances, the looks of love, led all
who set eyes on them to think of all that's sacred,
the first to go barefoot being aged Bernard
who, running after such peace, still felt he moved slow
as one dreamt wolves pursue. And now Egidio
kicks off his shoes, and Silvestro too... all after
the groom, so beautiful is the bridal laughter!
O unimagined treasure, who would ever know?

Thus he goes his way, that *padre*, that maestro,
his lady and family belted with the cord,
and when the poor flock behind him swelled to a crowd –
having not allowed any cowardice of heart
to weigh his forehead down, some calling him an upstart,
and having declared his intent with such regal
mien and received a seal from Innocent – the will
of this sublime shepherd was crowned a second time,
the Spirit working through Honorius's palm;
and when he preached, in his desire for martyrdom,
the gospel of Christ and all those who follow Him
in the Sultan's elegant presence, finding they

were unready for conversion, he didn't stay
but returned to the green spires of his native land...
settling on a black crag in the Appenines, and
receiving on his naked flesh the ultimate
mark. When the One who'd preordained him to such great
humility deigned to take him to Himself, he
told his brothers to love his darling faithfully
and commended her life to them, the rightful heirs;
and then, from her white breast, his perfected soul soars
back to its own kingdom on the bier of a stone.
Now you consider what he was, another one
worthy to steer Peter's ship by the truest star –

this was *our* patriarch, and therefore whoever
proceeds as he commanded carries priceless goods...
yet his fleet, grown greedy, disembarks in strange woods,
and the longer they roam the drier they become;
assuredly, there are some who for fear of harm
stay close, but so few you could hide them with a sail.
If you've listened attentively, and if you will
remember my song – and if my language has been
less obscure than clear – you'll certainly have seen
something of the tree from which the twig was broken,
and perhaps will intuit what my unspoken
words meant when I said or I neglected to say

where a soul shall fatten well if it doesn't stray.

12.

When that blessèd fire had mouthed its last, the millstone

of the heavens yet again began to turn;
before it had completed a circuit, a second
wheel enclosed it round, matching sacred sound with sound
and motion with sweet motion... paeans which surpassed
those of our muses and our sirens as the first
splendour surpasses its image or its echo.
As through diaphanous cloud a double rainbow
curves in parallel, circling as it were the square,
the outer the inverted ghost of the inner –
like the voice of that far-wandering nymph whose one
desire consumed her life like vapour in the sun,
and making them who read the changing skies recall

the covenant which promised that such torrential
rain would never fall again – so the twin garland
of ever-blooming roses whirled about us, and
their slow dance was a kind of litany of light.
All that measured movement, this festival of white
song and singing flame, radiance on radiance,
joy and grace together, suddenly ceased at once
as eyes glance in unison on a shining face –
and from the heart of one of the new lights a voice
now made me spin round, atremble, like a needle
to the northern star. "Love, whereby I'm beautiful,"
it said, "compels me to praise the other prince's

greatness, such honour having been paid to Francis...
they fought together, let their glory shine as one.
The army of Christ, whose holy ammunition
was bought at such cost, straggled behind the standard –
slow, riven with mutual suspicion, scattered –
when that Emperor whose rule is everlasting
provided for His helpless militia, acting
not because they deserved it but through grace alone,
and sent His bride the one and other champion
to bring, by means of what was said and what was *done*,
a lost people back to themselves. In that region
where the reviving breath of Zephir rises to

unfurl the fresh leaves with which Europe's dressed anew –
not far from the clashing of the white surf where
the sun, at certain times in its flight, will disappear –
there sits favoured Calareuga, protected
by the lion that subjects and is subjected;
the lover of the Christian faith was born there,
a dancer, God's athlete, he who was full of care
for his own and yet unrelenting to the foe...
his mind, as soon as it was conscious, being so
alive it gave his expectant mother foresight
(she saw a dog, mouth ablaze, set the world alight).
When he was betrothed to Faith at the holy font,

health augmenting health, the lady who gave consent
had dreams of the stellar fruit that would stem from him;
and, so word and act might conform, the seraphim
sent him the possessive of the One whose he was
entirely... he is Dominicus, one He chose
to labour side by side with him in his vineyard;
he truly seemed to be Christ's familiar, the hard
path of true poverty being his first declared
love, that first and most precious counsel of our Lord.
His nurse often found him kneeling as if to kiss
the earth, wakeful, as though to say *I came for this*.
O blessèd father of the child, Felix indeed –

and Johanna his mother, if interpreted
rightly! Not for the world's sake, for which slaves labour,
but rather for love of the authentic manna
he became a great teacher – watering the plants
that quickly wither in the gardener's absence –
and asked the seat which showed no kindness to the poor
because of the sly apostate who squatted there
for permission to fight against mundane error,
to defend such seeds as eventually bear
plants like the twenty four that now surround you; then,
armed only with his iron will and high doctrine,
he swept like a torrent fed by the deepest source

and where lies grew thickly he was the most zealous…
the streams that nourish our universal garden,
so its saplings gleam with life, have their origin
in him. This was one wheel of the chariot which
both defended and waged civil war for the Church,
the other's excellence having been made quite clear;
yet now the track or orbit scored by the outer
rim has been abandoned, so that a grey mould grows
where good wine's crust should be. The one once in front throws
seed under the trampling feet of them who follow,
and soon the very thistles shall protest that no
space is made for them in the royal granary;

such a culture's the harvest of poor husbandry,
as anyone versed in Tradition might tell you.
Despite this, I would say that all who search through
our book can discover pages where *I Am Still
What I Was* is charactered in fire, but it will
be one from neither Acquasparta nor Casale
where the Word is avoided or explained away.
I am the life of Bonaventura, who,
in the midst of fulfilling high offices, knew
how to keep in their place both riches and honour;
Illuminato and Agostino are here,
amongst the first of the barefoot brethren to become –

roped round like beasts – the familiars of God; with them
are Hugh of St Victor and Petrus the Bookworm,
and Peter of Spain – whose superlative wisdom
still shines in twelve volumes on earth – and then Nathan
the prophet and repentant Chrysostom ('golden-
mouthed'). Anselm's next, deep yet precise, then he who deigned
to take grammar – the art of sculpting speech – in hand;
Rhabanus is with us, and beside me there glows
the fine abbot Joachim, who *sees* and who *knows*…
the spirit of prophecy, I mean, is within
him. I was moved to praise so fair a paladin
by Thomas's words, his luminous courtesy,

and this whole company moved and was moved with me."

13.

Imagine, you who would conceive what I now see –

and clasp the bright image as I speak, fixedly,
as though it was the black centre-stone at Delphi –
the fifteen stars that glint with a diamond clarity
undimmed by the dense and intervening air;
then imagine that Wain which the broad breast of our
sky contains both day and night – never too narrow
for the rotating shaft – and imagine the O
of that open-mouthed horn that is blown where there is
the eye of the heavens, the place of the axis;
and now picture all these, from each zone of the sky,
creating two tiaras like the crown made by
Minos's daughter when her death transfigured her –

and let the rays of one encompass the other,
and both wheel so that this will lead and that follow –
and you'll nearly begin to sense a shadow
of the true constellation and the double dance
circling round me, surpassing mere experience
as the uttermost crystal outstrips a muddy stream.
Their theme was not Bacchus, they were bleating no hymn
but articulated praise of the threefold One,
of human and divine coexisting in one
shining man. They sang and span the tender measure
to its end, and then – as if it spelled rare pleasure
to go from care to care – those sky-saturated

presences turned our way. "An ear of wheat," one said,
the total silence broken by the light that had
told the wondrous tale of the vagabond of God,
"has been threshed and its gold grains stored safely; now love
urges me to beat at the second. You believe
that the breast which gave a bone to fashion the fair
face whose questing palate would cost our world so dear –
and the one which, pierced by the miraculous lance,
outweighs all past and future ills in the balance –
was infused with as much of its Maker's vital fire
as man's nature can admit; you marvel, therefore,
at my saying that the fifth light's awakened

mind was matchless. Open your eyes to my reply, and
you will find that your belief and these words meet
just as, at the centre of a circle, complete
truth abides in stillness. Those who must endure death,
and those who don't, are nothing but the showing forth
of that Idea which our most gracious Lord conceives
in joy; for the sentient light – which, when it leaves
its source in His splendour, knows no separation
from it or from the Love that unites three in one –
refracts its conscious ray through nine existences
whilst staying, eternally, what it *always* is,
descending from act to act down to those final

substances that are unsteady, ephemeral…
such generated things as the vast skies produce,
with or without seed, by the movement of the stars.
Neither that dim sublunar wax nor the bodies
which guide them ever tend to rest, so the Idea's
emblem illumines some things more and others less;
and thus it comes about that two adjacent trees
can swell with the sweetest and the bitterest fruit,
that one man's a genius and one but a wit.
If the dark wax was perfectly prepared – and the
force of the transmitting star at its apogee –
the sign's white light would be printed in completeness,

yet Nature is an engraver whose *habitus*
is often undermined by a trembling hand. Hence,
where the lucid love and supreme vigilance
of the first power clears the ground and sets its sigil,
every virtue is acquired; by such means was soil
given the unearthly perfection of the soul,
the Virgin sown with silence, and man never will
approach what he has been in the flesh of those two.
Was I to go no further, I can tell that you
would now ask how it is the fifth light's had no peer –
but consider, so what's implicit may appear,
who Solomon was and the true reason for his

requesting what he did instead of years or riches;
a king demands the wisdom proper to a king,
the intelligence of the heart's understanding,
not for idle knowledge such as how many
angels turn the spheres, or whether any
motion that animates itself can be conceived,
or if conclusions sired by happenstance should be believed;
regal prudence, then, is that quality of sight
which the loosed arrow of these words intends to strike,
and if you clearly regard my 'matchless' you'll see
it refers to kings alone, who come as cheaply
as the genuine are few… take this distinction,

and stand it with your image of the primal man
and our beloved. Proceed as though you'd lead
shoes upon your feet, slow (as though you were half-dead
from weariness) to leap to either *Yes* or *No*
before you view things clearly. A person ranks low –
is set, in fact, with fools – when he praises or negates
in the absence of the eye that discriminates…
spun by second-hand opinion, effectively blind
and emotional reaction hobbling his mind;
to fish for deep truth without art and expertise
is worse than just a waste of time, since the seas
will return a soul to shore peculiarly

changed. Parmenides, Melissus, Bryson and many
more who voyaged compassless furnish proof of this –
as do Sabellius and Arius, the face
of God's word warped in the metal of a sword…
and let the wise's judgement not be too forward,
like a man who chews and spits out the still-green corn,
for I have seen the brittle and ferocious thorn
utter at long last a crimson rose upon its tip
yet I've also known a swift, haughty clipper ship
cut halfway round the globe then wreck itself in port;
no dupe should presume to think he knows His thought,
seeing one man sacrifice and another steal,

concerning who shall rise to life and who will fall."

14.

From the round edge to the sleeping centre, or from

the shattered centre outward to the bounding rim,
water in bronze vessels trembles in accordance
with a dropped stone or tap at the circumference;
this image immediately entered my mind
the second that Thomas's speech came to an end,
picturing as it did the relation between
his words and the answering discourse of my queen.
"He needs," she said, "though neither mouth nor even thought
has made it known, to go down to the potent root
of yet another truth; say if the resplendence
with which your substance blooms will remain with you once
all bodies rise – and, if so, say how it can be

that when you have eyes again it won't hurt to see."
As, both fired and drawn by a growing happiness,
the lithe dancers in a ring lift woven voices
and pace more eagerly, so her devoted prayer
seemed to give the sacred circles new joy in their
wheeling and that wondrous song; ah, you who lament
our worldly deaths have not witnessed what refreshment
descends in those skies with the sempiternal rain!
The One and Two and Three that will endlessly reign
and shall live forever in Three and Two and One –
circumscribing every breathing thing and everyone
but itself unconfined – was now hymned by each

of those spirits three times, the melodies of such
subtlety as the merest glimpse would reward
the most deserving. When this concluded I heard,
from the smaller ring's brightest light, a gentle voice.
"Ardour will coruscate these garments around us,"
it said – in a tone perhaps not unlike the one,
calm yet compelling, of the Annunciation –
"as long as joy's festival lasts… their distinctness
fed by love, and love fed by that clear sight which is
wealth beyond the merit of any single soul;
we'll be the more pleasing for our being whole
when flesh's spiritual body reinvests us,

and so what the Good grants of gratuitous
light will increase… that light, in turn, which shines on Him.
Thus insight deepens, and from vision, in rhythm,
the passion it kindles becomes far greater too –
and then, at last, the love-lit glow. Just as coal's blue
flame is less brilliant than the incandescent heart,
its own golden outline still lucid and apart,
this circumambient radiance will be surpassed
by the dazzling forms that are now arrayed in dust…
and the luminous excess shall not weary us, for
such skin's equal to delight as fierce as terror."
So swift were the two wheels to chorus *Amen!*

that they showed their longing to wear those robes again –
not just for themselves, perhaps, but for their mothers
and their fathers… for the sake of *all* the others
who were dear to them before they turned to fire. Now,
on every side, another gleam began to grow
much as the horizon will brighten near dawn – yet
like twilight too, in the aftermath of sunset,
when stars you think you see scarcely seem to be there –
and it appeared the two circumferences were
enclosed by another lucent ring. O flashing
of the Holy Spirit, so sudden and dazzling
my eyes were overcome! And Beatrice's beauty,

ineffable to the extent that memory
has no record of the sight! Looking up once more –
for her face gave an influx of new strength – I saw
we'd been transposed to a higher state of bliss,
the sphere's fiery smile of an unusual redness,
and declared with my entire heart (and in those words
which are one tongue) my deep gratitude for the Lord's
latest gift or grace. The burnt sacrifice was still
smoking when I knew it had been acceptable,
for there shine out, between two rays, such marvellous
ember-coloured splendours that I shout *Elios,*
you armour them in glory! As the galaxy pales,

perplexing the wise, between the mighty heavens' poles,
freckled with both distinct and indistinct stars,
so those twin beams of light in the chasm of Mars
drew the sign one makes by quartering a circle –
and here my memory quite vanquishes my skill,
for that cross blazed Christ and yet still I can find no
speech equal to it... take up *your* cross and follow
and you will experience what I must leave blank,
seeing the glancing forth of Him on dawn's clear brink.
From the base to the summit, from horn to horn, those
lights are weaving and when they pass each briefly glows –
as, in the civil dark that wit and art contrive,

a single straying ray is seen to be alive
with tiny gilded motes of dust... some quick, some slow,
some crossing the bright path and some seeming to go
right up its length as if making for the sky,
and all like constellations shifting ceaselessly.
As the violin and harp, played in harmony,
tintinnabulate before the ear's inner eye
even in the case of an unfamiliar song,
so now I could perceive – streaming swiftly along
the arms of the cross – an enchanting melody
which was strange and hard to grasp yet captivated me;
I knew, though, that it was a psalm, exalted praise,

since there sprang to mind the words *Conquer* and *Arise*
as to one who receives without understanding,
and soon I had such love for it that surely nothing
has ever entangled me in so sweet a snare.
Maybe my words seem too bold, as though placing her
incomparable eyes below that martial air –
those eyes which to gaze upon stills base desire –
but if you're aware beauty's living seals have more
power the further one ascends, from sphere to sphere,
and that I hadn't turned around to see them there,
you will forgive me as I accuse myself here;
for pleasure is nowise excluded from this fire,

but – as we mount the sky – is increasingly pure.

15.

The benevolence that flows from a love which breathes cleanly –

as surely as imbalance from cupidity –
now imposed quiet on that sweetest lyre, the holy
strings that are tuned by the strong hand of the sky
becoming still as one so as to prompt my request…
all those who, for the love of things that turn to dust,
lose this higher love will justly grieve forever!
As it sometimes happens an unexpected fire
traverses the serene, cloudless face of heaven,
jolting man's obdurate eyesight to attention –
you think it is a migratory star, but then
there is no absence at the place where it began –
so from the constellation shining on the right

horn of the giant cross there darts a living light,
down to the foot along a radiating line;
thus did Anchises' shade reach out, if the divine
scribe deserves our credence, when he turned and saw
Aeneas in Elysium. *Father, how you pour*
forth the plenitude of your illuminating grace!
For whom, O blood of mine, has the gate of the skies
ever swung open not only once but twice?
These were its precise words, and now I shift my gaze
back to my lady… such a smile within her eyes
I thought the very depths of my own paradise,
my soul's innate glories, were present before me;

then, wonderful not just to hear but to see,
it continued with an utterance whose sound
surpassed all understanding – discourse as profound
as *claritas* rather than mere secrecy veils,
the conception that far above the mark of mortals –
so I felt myself hemmed by amazement on each side.
The first words, in fact, I actually descried,
when the parabola of his speech had fallen
somewhat to the height of human intellection,
were *Blessings to the Lord, both unity and three,*
for treating my descendent with such courtesy!
"Your appearance in this light," he went on, "my son,

gives a sweet, protracted hunger satisfaction,
thanks to her who graced you with plumage for your flight…
a hunger drawn from reading in the book whose white-
on-black hieroglyphics know no alteration;
you imagine your thoughts come to me from the One
who is the calm fulcrum of all things, exactly
as five and six ray forth from singularity,
and therefore you don't ask me who I am or why
I seem – more than all other spirits in this sky –
to be so full of joy. What you believe is true,
for the greatest and smallest creatures gaze into
that mirror within which, before a thought's unveiled,

it already stands wholly naked and revealed;
though in order to gladden the love where I wake
with an eternal sight – a love that does not slake
thirst for Him but charges with that thirst's wild sweetness –
let your voice express, child, confident and joyous,
the question my response to which is scored with fire."
I didn't even speak, yet she heard my desire
and smiled a sign that gave it wings. "Intelligence
and affection," I said, "when the primal balance
of our Lord came before you, became of one weight,
the igniting sun bestowing both heat and light
with a parity that is incomparable;

mortal faculties, however, and mortal will
are feathered differently for reasons which are plain…
and I, a dying creature, apparelled in pain,
can find no words equal to the gratitude I feel.
Sentient topaz, adornment of this jewel,
I just ask that you tell me who you are." "Green leaf
of my own root," he began, "who, with patient love,
I've long regarded while I waited for you here!
He you take your surname from – your great-grandfather –
was my dear boy, who for more than a hundred years
has circled the sacred mountain's lowest terrace;
how apt it is your labours should shorten his.

Within her ancient walls, Florence dwelt in quietness
and modesty; she had neither bracelet nor crown,
no belt or elaborately-embroidered gown
such as will outshine the face of those who wear it;
from the moment of their birth, daughters didn't yet
fill their fathers with dread... marriage-age and dowry
not having passed the bounds of all propriety
(the one hastening down, the other to the skies);
vast piles did not stand empty of their families,
and no Sardanapalus had come to reveal
how depraved man can be in a basement, how vile;
I saw Bellincion Berti dressed in furs, saw

his lady step softly away from the mirror
secure in the natural beauty of her face.
Ah, happy women... sure of their burial-place,
safe in the devout embrace of the blessèd bed!
This one keeps watch over a baby's sleeping head,
and if he stirs or wakes she'll console him with those
first lilting sounds from which a world of words follows;
and this one, as she draws the fine threads through the wheel,
recounts to her children a legendary tale...
a story of Troy, or of Fiesole, or Rome.
To such tranquillity, to such a gentle home,
to such a loyal people and such holy days,

Mary gave me – my mother called her with loud cries –
and in your ancient baptistery I became
Christian by faith, Cacciaguida by name.
My brothers were Moronto and Eliseo,
and my wife a gift of the valley of the Po
along with the appellation *Alighieri*.
Later on I followed Conrad, who knighted me
for the favour I had gained whilst in his service,
fighting the iniquity of the law whose vice
has occupied the kingdom that is yours by right;
an infidel severed me from that sunlit night –
the false, deceiving world which warps with its disease –

and I leapt from martyrdom to this peace."

16.

It can never now be cause of wonder to me

that we glory in our meagre nobility
down here where wills are feeble, given the delight
I took in my lineage there where appetite
does not turn aside – in that sphere, I mean to say –
though gentle birth's but a cloak which, unless each day
restores it, is soon ruined by the shears of time.
With the honorific once used in ancient Rome,
and seemingly unknown to her descendants,
I then began to speak, whilst – somewhat at a distance,
and smiling faintly – Beatrice momentarily
brought to mind a cough and Guinevere's first folly.
"You are another father," I said, "and you give

fresh courage with your discourse, raising me above
this poor self, filling my consciousness with gladness,
feeding it from so many streams it rejoices
to sustain the lucid current without being
blown; tell me of your ancestors, my own dear spring,
and of the years that your childhood records… tell me
of the sheepfold of Saint John, and who were worthy
to sit in its highest chairs in days of virtue."
As, in the silent wind, an ember glows anew,
I saw that light reillumined by my supple
speech; and, having slowly become more beautiful,
it replied in a voice of a delicacy

unlike our lapsed tongues. "Five hundred and fifty-three
times," it began, "this blaze had been reignited
by the Lion's paw, from the day *Ave* was said
till the cry with which my mother – who is now blessed –
delivered that weight which is of all things lightest.
My ancestors and I first drew breath at the place
where the last ward is reached in your annual race…
though as to where they were from originally,
and their identity, it is better that we
keep silent. The number of souls who could bear arms
was a fifth of those living their deaths in these times
between the old statue of Mars and the Baptist,

yet our blood was pure down to the humblest artist
in metal or stone, an integral populace
not mixed with an alien and resentful race
from Figline, from Certaldo, and from Campi –
how much better it is for your neighbours to be
your own kith and kin, to stroll at dusk upon a wall,
than be compelled to endure the stink of all
out for what they can get by either force or fraud;
just as a body's made unwell by tainted food
or eating in excess, it's inevitable
that cultures are killed by a polyglot babble…
a city or country without a boundary

is no different from someone with no immunity.
See how Urbisaglia's crowds are now ashes,
and know the same fate awaits London and Paris –
that cities, in other words, have a life *and* death –
and it won't seem so strange to you that the breath
of a true aristocracy can cease as well;
every single thing in your fading world's mortal,
though an empire or age can keep that fact hidden
by its sheer wealth of days in comparison to men…
just as the rotation of the pale lunar sphere
unendingly veils and reveals the ruined shore,
thus fickle Fortune deals with our Firenze.

Bear this in mind, so that what I proceed to say
of those whose fame is lost in time will be far less
hard to believe. I have witnessed illustrious
houses in slow decline, and also families
whose actions were in tune with ancient pedigrees;
the Ravignani dwelt over the gate that lately
is weighed with such crimes we are likely to see
a sunken city; de la Pressa knew how to rule,
and Galigaio's gilded hilt and pommel
shone on his white walls; the axial column of grey
fur was already standing tall, and also they
who must redden to remember the doctored

measure; the Calfucci's stock flourished forth hard wood,
and both the Sizii and the Arrigucci
had been called to the seats of the magistracy.
How truly great were those now brought low by their pride,
when the flower that Florence once was opened wide
in the warm glow of the Lamberti's golden spheres;
such, child, was the calibre of the forefathers
of those souls who, whenever the church stands empty,
gorge themselves like suited pigs in consistory.
That vulgar crew which plays the dragon to the weak,
yet is instantly cringing to any that speak
with a flash of sharp teeth – or who flash their money –

was coming up from the gutter, and already
Caponsacco had slunk down from Fiesole's stones;
Infangato and Giuda were good citizens,
and one entered into – incredible but true –
the sacred precinct of our encircling walls through
a gate christened after the Pera family;
all those knighted by the Marquis of Tuscany –
whose name and whose praises are made new again
when the light's at its least – bore his lovely token,
the very one that now like a gilded lily
is worn by no pious force but popularly;
the Gaulterotti and Importuni were there,

already living on the tranquil Borgo where
arrivals now squabble like importunate apes,
and the house because of which the whole city weeps –
due to the righteous anger that has turned us all
into walking corpses, destroying what's joyful –
was honoured with its friends and associates too…
O Buondelmonte, how unfortunate that you
fled from union with it at another's prompting,
yet the grand scheme called for a savage offering
at the foot of the bridge's disfigured stone. With these
and other nobles our Firenze knew peace,
days so glorious and just that the Ghibelline

blossom gleamed ghostlike, not some dark and blood-soaked sign."

17.

The one who made fathers eternally wary –

wary, that is, of a wayward son – hastened to see
and to receive confirmation from Clymene
when low talk had him doubt his high paternity;
so I was now and so was I perceived to be,
not only by Beatrice but by the holy
radiance which had changed its place for me before.
"Speak," my darling said, "your desire's total ardour,
printed with the emblem of your hidden spirit…
not in order for *us* to be informed by it,
but to make your thirst for Him more articulate
so that one who hears you may pour the nectar out."
"Gnarled root of my body's great tree," I began, "who

are so remotely placed that – as we can see two
obtuse angles will not fit in a triangle –
you view the infinitesimal point where all
time and place is simultaneously present…
when I was with Virgil, hazarding the descent
far down into that executed world and then
ascending the hard and soul-restoring mountain,
grave words were said about the life ahead of me;
though I feel solid and foursquare, immutably
centred in myself, safe from chance's every blow,
I would nonetheless be reassured to know
what nears… does a watched arrow not fly in slow motion?"

This is how I addressed the light that had spoken,
confessing – as Beatrice wished – my entire desire;
and now that paternal love replied, the fire
of his smile's epiphany veiling him from sight,
and his language precise and the words clear and bright
and wholly unlike those labyrinthine sayings
where oracles once housed inexpressible things…
what madness reigned before the Lamb of God's healing wound!
"Happenstance," he said, "which does not extend beyond
your little world's bound and illuminated book,
is portrayed in detail in the unending look
that is our Father's mind – this doesn't, however,

mean these events *have* to be, no more than a river
and all its sails is swayed by the glint of your eye –
from which my sight derives, as the vast harmony
of an organ takes the ear, the times that'll soon
unfurl. Just as Hippolytus was once driven
from Athens by his cruel stepmother's treachery,
so you'll be exiled. This is willed, has already
hatched in the brain of one who dedicates his days
to selling out Christ; the shout of blame, as always,
will attach itself to the offended party,
but vengeance shall in the end be testimony
to the truth that dispenses it. You must leave

behind you everything which you most dearly love –
exile shoots this arrow first – and you'll taste the bread
of a strange land, discovering how it's salted
by your own tears; your feet shall labour down and climb
an alien stair, shoulders and each leaden limb
weighed most of all by the malign stupidity
of those with whom you will fall into that valley…
they who'll then turn on you, unhinged and ungrateful;
the shame, though, will soon be theirs, the eventual
outcome giving proof of their degeneracy
and that you were wise to be a one-man party.
The hospitality of the great Lombard shall

shelter you a while, he who bears the sacred eagle
at the ladder's top; you will encounter, with him,
one so profoundly marked by our warlike rhythm
that eternity will record what he'll devise –
as of yet no one knows his name, for these skies
have only wheeled around him nine times, though flashes
of unearthly strength and virtue are seen in his
indifference to hard work and heaped treasuries…
his worth shall be acknowledged by his enemies.
Look to the beauty of his beneficent face,
the radiance whereby rich and poor will change place,
and inscribe upon your mind" – but here he spoke of

things which, though witnessed, will occasion disbelief.
"Child," he added, "these are the marginalia
on what's been said to you before; behold the danger
the merest flick of heaven's volume now conceals,
yet don't succumb to envy for your fellow-souls…
after their punishments and their very crimes
have long been forgotten, your star's ever-virile beams
will still be travelling light." Here the song ended,
that reverent soul showing it had drawn the thread
right the way through the warp I'd held out to it;
and now I began, like one whose doubtful spirit
needs counsel from one who loves and sees and *desires*

what is true. "I discern, father, how swift time spurs
towards me, preparing to deal those blows that fall
hardest on the unready; it is just as well,
it seems, for me to arm myself with foresight, so
as not to be cast – for the sake of a canto –
from all other places and not only our dear
city. Down into that world venomed with self-fear,
then around the terraced mountain from whose lovely
summit I was raised by the eyes of my lady,
and lastly throughout these skies, light succeeding light,
I have seen and learned things which merely to relate
will displease many; yet if I'm truth's timid friend,

my name in times to come shall not be reckoned
with those who never die." "A dark conscience," he replied,
flashing gold like a mirror in the sun, "may indeed
flinch at your every word… and yet, in spite of this,
put falsehood aside and manifest in fullness –
the unclean, of course, will scratch – the vision you've seen.
Your voice might at first stir up both outrage and pain,
but, digested, shall be nutrition for the soul;
a hurricane, the vortex of your lucent howl
will purify the fouled peaks – and *that* is no small
ground for honour. For this simple reason, all
you've encountered are known to fame or infamy…

whose faith would be fixed by proofs that grew obscurely?"

18.

That sacred mirror was already rejoicing

in its inwardness – the lost word, the single thing
which can never be uttered yet impels all speech –
and meanwhile I was caught up in my own mind, each
bitter reflection offset by one that tasted
sweet. "You should change these idle thoughts," a voice then said,
the bracing voice of her who was conducting me
to God, "and consider I'm perpetually
near the One who makes our every burden light."
I turn sideways at this tender sound, and the sight
of those loveliest eyes is such that I must here
discard any hope of expressing what they were…
not for lack of the right phrase, but because the mind –

without a higher guidance – cannot rewind
or rather reascend to altitudes so far
above its meagre self; yet, contemplating her,
my mad heart was liberated from low desire,
content with the semblance of the eternal fire
of His delight imaged in the features of her face.
"Turn round and listen well," she said, "for paradise
resides in places other than beloved eyes."
As sometimes, down here, we see passion in a gaze,
if strong enough to take possession of the soul,
so by that flame's intensity I could now tell
it wished to talk with me some more. "In this fifth thresh-

hold," it began, "of the perennially fresh
and fruit-bearing tree – drawing life from its summit's
lucid gold – there move and breathe such blessèd spirits
as whose least gesture was the stuff of poetry.
Watch… the one I call upon will dart as swiftly
as fire within a cloud to the horns of the Cross."
The instant Joshua was named there sped across
those arms a vital glint, and immediately
there sounded the name of the great Maccabee
another brilliance span like a top whipped by joy; as
one's eyes pursue a hawk in flight, my rapturous
glance followed Charlemagne – Roland – Robert Guiscard –

Duke Godfrey – Count William – the mighty Rainouart –
and then, rejoining all that living radiance,
the spirit I had talked with showed me how to dance…
a true artist amongst the singers of the skies.
And now I turned to my right, to see if Beatrice
would indicate what I should do by word or sign,
and saw her smiling eyes so dazzling that their shine
wholly surpassed all they had ever been before.
As men grow, day by day, in virtue and vigour
through the pleasure consequent on labouring well,
so I then perceived – observing this miracle
get still more beautiful – that the vast arc of my

rotation had increased with the rotating sky;
and, like a pretty face's instantaneous
transformation when hot shame departs, the redness
of that warrior star was exchanged for the clear
and brilliant pallor of the temperate sixth sphere
whose light now received us. A scintillating love
was making, within that majestic torch of Jove,
the overt speech which is distinguished by the eyes;
and, just as a multitude of birds, when they rise
in wordless exultation from lake or river,
will move first in one dark shape and then another,
so as those holy creatures fly and sing and flow –

each one contained yet not restricted by its glow –
they form the letter *D* and then *I* and then *L*,
every soul leaving off its individual
note for as long as they pause in quiet formation.
O you who grant genius, divine Pegasean,
immortality and glory as its words give
to cities and empires the light by which they live –
illumine me so that I may articulate
those forms as I conceived them, allowing your great
intelligence to shine through these self-renewing
lines! This, then, is what they displayed, multiplying
five by seven with vowels and consonants,

my role being simply to jot with diligence
each given part: *DILIGITE IUSTITIAM*
are the first words, and *QUI IUDICATIS TERRAM*
were the last, and then they held that final letter...
a golden mark on the silver page of Jupiter.
Now other lights swoop to the apex of the *M*
and gather there singing, and I believe their theme
was the Good that impelled them; next, as when sparks fly
from a kicked ember into an autumnal sky,
fleeting script within which idlers might read meaning,
I seem to see more than a thousand gleaming
points of light ascend – some rising far, some less so,

demonstrating by their settling high or low
the degree to which they were kindled by God's sun –
and suddenly I saw the representation
of an eagle's neck and head, distinct in trembling fire...
there is nobody to guide the One who draws there,
but his guidance is His inmost self, much as He
guides the remembrance whereby birds infallibly
construct their circling songs. *O sweet star, what priceless*
and plenteous gems declared how earthly justice
is effected via the heaven you adorn;
hence I beg that Mind, the light your force and motion
are initiated by, to regard and raze

the infernal towers whose smoke obscures your rays
and once again strike out with a righteous fury
at all who've turned the Lord's sacred sanctuary –
where every stone's a miracle or martyrdom –
into a tinkling mall. Militia of the dome
whose stars I meditate, voice prayers for those who stray
behind the simulating toys which lead the way
not to life but death; in the past men brandished swords,
yet now we wage a subtler war with such sly words
as blind us to the living Word, our Father's bread.
Ah, Petrus Romanus, just recollect the 'dead'
Peter and Paul are blossoming around you... they

battled for the vineyard that you would give away.

19.

The beautiful image those souls had created

was glittering before me with its wings outspread,
joyous in execution and the fruit of joy,
each spirit like a little ruby which a ray
of sunlight flames so bright your eyes are set on fire.
That which I will now proceed to state has never
been framed by human voice or falsified in ink,
is stranger than any thought a mortal brain can think
or our dark imagination could conceive...
for I didn't merely witness the great beak move,
but heard it say not *we* and *ours* but *I* and *mine*.
"For being just and most merciful," it began,
"I have been elevated to this glorious

place that nothing human longing paints can surpass;
the wicked down on earth pay lip service to me,
mimicking my form and my appearance only."
As one feels a mingled glow from a multitude
of coals, so from the shimmering symbol issued
that single sound of many loves. "Perpetual
flowers," I then replied, "of our Lord's eternal
bliss – breathe forth the chord of your scent and deliver
my soul from the immense hunger that won't ever
find sustenance on earth; perhaps some other sphere
reflects almighty justice, yet I sense that here
it is not apprehended through a verbal veil...

you know I'm ready and able to listen well,
and what uncertainty and thirst I carry."
As a falcon, released from its hood, rapidly
twitches its head, applauding itself with its wings
as if aware of being one of God's finest things,
so shivered that sign woven of His grace's praise
and the songs solely known to those who can rejoice.
"He who traced," it began, "the spherical limit
of the limitless world, devising within it
such wondrous beauty both hidden and plain to see,
did not for all that impress the entirety
of what He is on the created universe;

the Word escapes it utterly, the proof of this
being that the acme of creatures – and the first
to swell with pride – fell unripe, eternally cursed
for lacking the patience to attend the light…
from which fact we can conclude that the infinite
virtue of the One, who measures only His own self,
transcends the capacities of the vastest gulf
as the Pacific does the thimble of your mind.
Our vision, therefore, a single beam of the Mind
with which each thing is replete, cannot but discern –
be it howsoever strong – that its origin
and principle are far beyond the apparent

world, fathoming supreme justice to the extent
your frail human eyesight can penetrate the sea;
for though, from the shore, it sees the bottom clearly,
the open ocean's inconceivable deepness
conceals the abysms which are *there* nonetheless.
Any light but that of the imperturbable
radiance of His sky is a lustre able
to trap your bodies in the shadows that they cast;
and now the lair of justice lies open at last,
the lair you've interrogated so many times.
'A man,' you have said, 'is born and raised by the streams
which flow into the Indus, where no one speaks for

or writes of Christ. His actions and desires are pure
as far as human reason sees, his lips shape truth,
but he dies unbaptised and a stranger to faith…
by what right would loving justice then condemn him?'
And yet who are *you* to sit in judgement, your dim
surveillance stretching far as the width of a hand,
the defendant in a thousand-mile-distant land?
Was scripture not luminous above you there'd be
ample room for clever doubts, unquestionably;
animal men, with your mechanistic thinking!
The primal will, inherently good, unchanging,
creates all value by its own radiation –

justice is a measure of harmonization
with this pole that never moves but which moves all things."
As when a mother stork soars in gracious circlings
above her just-fed young, and they gaze up at her,
so I lifted my brow and I looked in wonder
as the image beat wings which uncounted counsels
wove. *Eternal judgement*, it sang, *is to mortals
what the hieroglyphics of my notes are to you.*
Then the Holy Ghost's incandescent splendours grew
still once more, once more displaying the sacred sign
that made Rome revered and will make Rome rise again.
"No one," it went on, "who did not believe in Christ

was ever translated to this realm of the blessed –
whether after or before He was nailed to the tree –
yet at that final moment, there are many
now mouthing *Christ, Christ!* who'll be further from Him than
some who never heard it… the Ethiopian
shall condemn such hypocrites as each company
goes its fated way, one of them unendingly
rich and the other one penniless forever.
What will Persia say to your kings then, the cover
of the book of life being opened to her shame?
In it shall be viewed, with Albert's works, the great name
of Prague made desolate, and out of it will shine

the suffering caused along the banks of the Seine
by monetary fraud; there shall be seen the pride
which will drive the Scot and the Englishman so mad
that neither can respect his rightful boundary,
and there we will witness the soft debauchery
of those rulers of Bohemia and of Spain
who knew no heaven higher than freedom from pain;
we shall behold the cripple of Jerusalem,
branded like a heifer with an *I* and an *M*
for his singular goodness and manifold vice;
there will glow the cowardice and the avarice
of the king who has the island of spewing fire –

where Anchises' long life ends – and to make quite clear
how marvellously insignificant he is,
the type will be too small to read without glasses;
and then all shall witness the sordid works and days
of his uncle and his brother, the true dispraise
of those who would bastardize so fine a nation;
they of Portugal and Norway shall be seen and known,
and that king of Rascia who will ape the coin –
harming only himself – of the Venetian.
Heroic Hungary, if able to resist
the profane crusade that'll pour into the West,
and blessèd every country which has natural

barriers to protect its culture, its people!"

20.

When the great lord the world's illuminated by

redescends below our hemisphere, the sky –
day on every side being swallowed up in darkness –
shines not with a solitary brilliance but is
gradually resplendent with myriad fires
that are, you might say, the one light's dazzling mirrors;
this superhuman drama came to mind, as
the sign of the world and of its rightful rulers
shut its blessèd beak, for the radiances then
blazed their vital splendours more brightly and began
to sing in ways that slip and fall from the memory.
Sweetest love, your veil a smile, how passionately
you played within those flutes animated just

by the breath of thoughts of all that's holiest;
then the jewels studding the sixth sphere were silent,
and it seemed I could hear the crystalline descent
of a mountain stream as it gabbles down through stones
and pronounces the power at the heights. As tunes
take their character from the neck of a guitar –
or as a pipe's finger-holes give form to formless air –
so that inarticulate murmuration rose
as though the bird was hollow and became a voice,
the huge beak once more uttering, with supreme art,
such words as are fit to be engraved on the heart.
"That part of me," it said, "with which earth's eagles see

deep into the sun must now be watched intently,
for the lights that comprise this living mosaic
are there the most exalted. He who bears the Ark
from age to dark age is the lambent gleam you spy
dancing at the centre, in the pupil of my eye,
the worth of his spiritual song – insofar
as he put his lost soul into it – being made clear
by recompense proportioned to its holy fire;
of the five who ring that blackness, the sparkle near
my beak is he who consoled the poor widow…
he understands what it costs not to follow
Christ, through first-hand knowledge of joy and joy's absence;

next on the upper arc of the circumference
is someone who, repenting, had his own death wait –
now he knows that prayer can make time procrastinate,
without thereby changing an eternal decree;
then is the one whose pure intentions bent your tree
with bad fruit, turning the law and my own self Greek
so as to give precedence to the sacred crook,
knowing now how a well-meant act can waste the whole
world and yet not singe a single hair of the soul;
passing on to the lower arc, the glow you see
is he on whose account the perennially-
darkened land mourns... at this altitude he knows why

our skies adore a just and wise king, showing by
the brightness of his face what intellection does.
Who'd have imagined that the Trojan Rhipeus
would be the fifth beatific light in this ring?
Now he witnesses God's grace in ways your straying
earth cannot comprehend, although even he
can only see so far into that infinity."
Like a lark that climbs a pale blue heaven, at first
singing then silent as if brimful with the last
wild phrase – too mysterious even for itself –
so seemed to me that mark or imprint of the Self,
the eternal joy through whose fathomless desire

we come in good time to be what we really are;
despite the fact that my deep perplexity was
clearly apparent as a painting under glass,
I couldn't wait quietly but cried "how can this *be*?"
Rejoicings glance forth in response, and, the beauty
of its eye rekindled, the wondrous sign replied
as if loath to keep me looking that stupefied.
"You accept all these things because of what I say,
yet – not *seeing* them with your immortal flesh – they
aren't the objects of knowledge so much as of faith;
you're like those who know things by name but not in truth,
who need others to portray their inner suchness...

this being, crudely put, all that human art is.
A burning love and vivacious trust overcome
the divine will, storming bliss's pristine kingdom
not as a man might fight and conquer other men
but because it lets this thing be done; then, broken
into, *it* conquers with its vast benevolence.
You marvel that my eye's first and fifth radiance
are shown in our angelic realm, yet they stepped forth
from their skin not as infidels but in firm faith…
one of them returning to his bones from that place
where every will is bent – I mean, of course, hell's blaze –
and this was the consequence of unceasing hope,

hope which gave such strength to his pleas to raise him up
that His hand was forced; briefly reinhabiting
its flesh, the noble spirit of which we're speaking
believed in transcendent aid – and, in this belief,
was set alight with such flames of authentic love
that, from a second death, it came to heaven's joy;
the other, due to that grace no created eye
ever glimpsed the source of – so deep's the primal spring –
devoted his heart and soul to righteous living,
and thus, from grace to grace, God granted him vision
sufficient to behold our future redemption,
until he could endure that pagan stench no more

but rebuked the crowds' perverseness. Those three you saw –
the beauties by the right wheel – were sponsors for him,
over a millennium before baptism
began. O strange predestination, how remote
from them who do not view the First Cause is your root!
Restrain your judgement, mortals, for we who direct
our sight on the Lord *still* don't know all the elect…
such lack being sweet to us, because, in this good,
our virtue is refined: we wish what's wished by God."
Thus that divine image gives subtle medicine,
whilst – like a lute-string's intent reverberation –
the two holy radiances flicker in time

and, as the words are formed, so moves each living flame.

21.

Here my eyes are once again transfixed by her face,

my spirit quite unaware of both time and place.
"Was I to smile," she then declared, "you'd instantly
be turned, like Semele, to ash; for my beauty –
which, as you have seen, blazes ever more fiercely
as we approach the palace of eternity
up this stair – contains such power that your mortal
faculties, subjected to its lightning, would all
shrivel like a tree at the storm-god's kiss. We're now
in the seventh splendour, which, at this time, below
the breast of the burning Lion, radiates down
mingled with its force. Set your mind behind your own
eyes, making each of them a living reflector

for the image which shall manifest in this mirror."
Whoever knew what sweet sustenance her aspect
gives my sight, would also know (as I redirect
my mind) the joy of obeying that stellar guide,
balancing the one against the other side.
Within the crystal that bears the name, as it rings
our world, of him who vanquishes all leaden things,
I saw a ladder the colour of sunstruck gold
stretch upwards further than my weak light could behold;
and I saw, descending by degrees, so many
resplendences it seemed that the heavens' every
star was streaming out. As, in their unerring way,

magpies arise together at first break of day
to warm their chilled feathers – some then disappearing,
some landing back where they began, others soaring
raucously about – the scintillating throng
went in wild unison from rung to burnished rung;
the one closest to us was so incandescently
brilliant that I thought, "the love you signal to me
is clear, yet she who disposes sound and silence
is now silent herself; despite the vehemence
of my longing, I dare not speak." And she, seeing
that silence in the sight of Him from whom nothing
is concealed, said to fulfil my fervent hunger.

"Not for my own merit," I began, "but for her
sake, tell me – blessèd sentience cocooned in joy –
why you have approached this near to us, and why
the symphony of paradise is silent here
yet loud with adoration in every other sphere."
"Your hearing's as fragile as your sight," it replied,
"and we refrain from song for the reason your guide
must curb her smile; I've come down our sacred stairway's
twelve degrees to welcome you with speech, with the rays
of light I'm mantled by... not moved by greater love,
for hearts burn with equal intensity above –
as those flamings demonstrate – but the charity

that makes us serve the Helmsman with alacrity
decrees lots (as you can see)." "I understand," I said,
"how in this court a fully free yet devoted
love is enough to make you follow Providence...
but why, amongst those united in this silence,
were *you* predestined to this role?" The final word
hadn't passed my lips before the pure nimbus whirred
like a millwheel, centred on its hidden axis,
then replied in the tones of the love which it is.
"A beam of divine light focuses upon me,
penetrating this bright womb, and that potency –
allied with my vision – raises me so far

above myself I can *read* the essential fire
out of which it flows; here is the source of my joyous
flames, their blaze commensurate to the clearness
of my sight. Yet the night's sublimest seraphim,
or she whose gaze is absolutely fixed on Him,
couldn't answer this; what you desire to know lies
deep in the beyond of His eternal abyss,
apart from all created eyes. When you turn back
to the dying world, bear this doctrine on your back;
apes' feet should not presume to near such mystery,
for the mind which gleams here is there dim and smoky...
how could it comprehend things that it can't even

attain to when it assumes the cloak of heaven?"
Circumscribed by these words, I check myself and merely
ask who he was. "Between the coasts of Italy,
not too distant from your fatherland, bare crags rise
so high that when thunder re-echoes through the skies
the rumbling's far below you. Beside a ridge
called Catria, there is an ancient hermitage
once wholly given over to prayer and praises;
here I became so established in His service
that olive-juice sustained me through the frost and heat,
content in the glory of contemplative thought.
The cloister used to yield fine harvests for this sky,

though now it is barren... Peter Damiani
was my name. When Simon came, and the great vessel
of the Holy Ghost, the most decrepit hostel
was sufficient for their lean and shoeless spirits;
a modern pastor's more well fed, and when he sits
on horseback he requires a boy at either flank
to buttress his quivering flesh, to steer the tank;
a silken mantle covers both man and horse, so,
snug beneath a single skin, *two* animals go.
O patience, what you bear!" At this last phrase, I saw
innumerable flames spin down from stair to stair –
with each turn more lovely – then utter such a cry

as surpassed all thought and conquered me entirely.

22.

Oppressed with consternation, I turn to my guide

as a frightened child will always run to the side
of the one who can make him feel secure; and she,
like a mother whose calm voice immediately
soothes her pale and breathless boy, said: "Don't you realise
that we are in His heaven, that throughout these skies
everything is holy, and everything is done
with fine zeal and pure intent? The transformation
had they sung, or attendant on my slightest smile,
you can conceive by how that shout has made you reel;
a cry in which, if you understood its plea,
you'd already have discerned the vengeance you'll see
before your death. God's sword's never swung in haste or late,

unless from the perspective of people who wait
with impatience or fear… now redirect your sight's
beam, and you'll witness many illustrious sprites."
I turned around as she had commanded, and saw
a hundred little spheres making each other more
resplendent with the light of their mutual glow;
I stood like one who fights with longing's punctum, so
much does he dread to overstep propriety,
until the pearl that shone the most luminously
came forward itself as if granting my desire.
"If you knew," I heard said deep within it, "the fire
of sheer love that burns among us, you'd have expressed

those thoughts; to save you from delay in your noblest
aim, I will now answer the question that you hide.
The mountain bearing Cassino on its side
was once frequented, at the summit, by an ill-
disposed and resolutely ignorant people;
I was the saint who planted there the name which He
brought to men that they might be exalted, be set free,
such grace then flashing down upon me that I drew
the surrounding cities from worship of one who
had seduced the world to arbitrary praise, false rites.
They were all contemplative souls, these other lights,
possessed by that flaming passion that gives birth

to flowers and fruit that are the glory of earth.
Here is Romauld, and here is Macarius,
and my brothers who paced the stone cloisters with us
and whose hearts stood firm." "The love you demonstrate
in addressing me," I said, "and what I see and note
of your fire's benevolence makes my own fire bloom,
as sunrays unfurl a rose's voice on its stem;
and hence I ask you, padre, to tell me whether
I shall one day gaze directly at your face." "Brother,
this great desire will be fulfilled in the final
sphere, where prodigious thirsts are sated – mine as well –
all that the heart has ever dreamt being wholly

perfected, entirely ripe. There alone, every
aspect's where it has always been and always *is*,
for joy is not in space and spins on no axis…
our stairs are the bridge from *I* to *Thou*, which is why
they appear to your sight to vanish in the sky;
the patriarch Jacob once saw them bend into
such heights when angels were descending through the blue,
but who now dares or cares to step off earth and climb?
The illuminated script of my Rule's become
barren text, the abbeys black and unwholesome caves,
a monk's habit a sack in which a fat wraith craves.
Usury was never as contrary to God

as that fruit which makes monastic hearts go mad,
for what the Church has in its keeping is for those
who implore in the name of the Lord and not His foes;
mortal flesh is so weak that, faster than it takes
an acorn to grow and to scatter little oaks,
the best of beginnings has become a sorry
end. Peter commenced in his native poverty,
and Francis in humility and I with prayer,
yet – just look at each order's source, and then think where
it is now – you must see how white has run to black.
Truly, the vision of the Jordan flowing back
would be stranger than an intervention here." Thus

he spoke then rejoined his peers, the harmonious
hurricane ascending; and now my sweet lady
thrusts me starward with a subtle sign, completely
mastered by her virtue's light, supernatural
flight which earth's deftest hummingbird could not equal.
In the name, brave reader, of my thirst to return
to that sacred triumph on whose account I burn
with shame for my sins, I swear I was instantly –
in less time than is needed for the brain to be
told by a fingertip how ardent embers are –
inside the house that follows Taurus. *Natal star
or stars, pregnant with the force from which everything*

*that comprises my ambiguous cunning
is ultimately derived – this much I recognise –
you who were tempering sunset and sunrise
when I first sensed the open air, and whose region
received me when I entered the vast rotation
by which your shine is spun, my spirit devoutly
asks for power equal to the difficulty
of the final pass.* "You are so close," said Beatrice,
"to bliss's wide haven that you must keep your gaze
keen and clear; before we go any further, see
what realms I have placed beneath our feet already."
I regress then in vision through all the seven spheres,

smiling at how paltry this semblant world appears;
he who values it least is he who counsels best,
his soul erect and his mind set on the highest.
I view the splendour of the light side of the moon
then endure, Hyperion, your incandescent son
with Maia and Dione circling him closely;
I see Jupiter between ice and fire, and see
the shape of their ever-moving, never-changing dance,
each science demonstrating just how immense
its body and speed and distance from us is.
I scan the little threshing-floor that makes men fierce,
from the river mouths to the peaks which pierce the skies,

and then I turn back to those loveliest of eyes.

23.

A bird in a great tree's tremulous charity,

throned upon its nest and its brood through the lonely
night which hides all things, yearns to see their small faces
and to root for nourishing food in dark places,
such hard labour being sweet, anticipating
the unutterable sun with silent longing,
waiting, on a bough's bared arm, for first light to start:
just so my lady was alert, turned to that part
of the sky where the midday sun crawls slow, whilst I,
observing her in her eagerness and suspense,
became as one inside whose bleak soul an intense
hunger for the unknown is calmed by hope. The sky
grew ever more brilliant, time flowing seamlessly

between the Nows of vision and expectancy,
and then at long last Beatrice spoke. "Behold," she said,
"the hosts of Christ triumphant, the fruit harvested
from the rotation of these spheres!" It seemed her face
was ablaze, such joy irradiating her gaze
that I must move on in silence. As in a night
when the skies are serene and the rounded moon bright –
Trivia's white laughter dimming the eternal
nymphs who paint the ceiling of the dark's banquet-hall –
I see above thousands of lesser lights a sun
which enkindles all of them, just as the one
lantern of the lower world ignites the vassal stars,

and through its sentient splendour the substance glares
too dazzlingly for my weak eyes to endure it.
O Beatrice, loving guidance, gentlest spirit!
"This overwhelming sight," she said then, "is a virtue
and strength you cannot keep from breaking in on you...
there's the Wisdom and Power which opened a path –
the path so long desired – between heaven and earth."
As thunderclouds expel the bolt that has outgrown
its cell, fire darting instantaneously down
against the current of its nature, so my mind –
in the presence of that strange feast – seemed to expand
and become, in ecstasy, something I can't name

or even remember. "Regard me as I am
with unveiled sight… what you've seen will have given you
the strength to sustain my smile." I was like one who,
emerging from a rapidly-fading vision,
struggles to recollect it but struggles in vain
when I heard this offer that nothing shall erase
from the book of past time. Was I to sound its praise
with every single one of the hundred thousand
tongues which Polyhymnia's sisters have quickened
with their richest milk, still my song would not come near
to that smile's truth and how it made her face appear,
to a fraction of the shine of her holy eyes;

and thus this sacred poem, limning paradise,
must proceed with light feet as though vaulting a tomb.
Yet those who consider the graveness of my theme,
and the mortal shoulder that has taken it on,
will not blame me if I shake beneath the burden –
it is no voyage for a coracle, this one
my audacious prow is cutting, or a helmsman
who goes easy on himself. "Why is it my face
so enchants you that you don't turn to where Christ's rays
are making the inviolable garden bloom?
There's the rose who dressed the Word in flesh, the perfume
of the lilies which draw us to the royal way."

Ever swift to react to all that she might say,
I set myself to raise my feeble lids once more.
As I have watched, lancing through tattered cloud, a pure
sunbeam illuminate a meadow of flowers –
my gaze mired in shade – I now saw countless splendours
struck as by lightning from above, but couldn't see
where the ardent flashes had their source… benignly
brutal force that seals them, you'd retreated on high
to grant a breathing-space or respite to an eye
not yet strong enough to bear your love! The sublime
name of Her I call both morning- and evening-time
then focussed my soul upon the consummate fire,

my two living eyes portraying that living star –
its nature and its magnitude – which possesses
victory in bliss as it did in this darkness,
as meanwhile, from the heights, there comes spiralling down
a bright orbit of sparks in the form of a crown,
circumscribing her and spinning round her slowly;
our most dulcet-toned, spirit-stirring melody
would surely, if set beside the sound of the lyre
that anointed the heavens' world-spangled sapphire,
seem harsh as the boom of colliding clouds. *I am
angelic love, environing the joyous womb
which housed our desire, and hence – Mother of the Sun –*

*I will wheel about you till you follow your Son
and exalt, by your mere entrance, the supreme sphere.*
Thus that melody came to a close, the other
lights answering with an immense cry of *Mary!*
The sovereign binding of the planetary
book, spun and vivified by one breath and being,
was still such a distant beach that the ascending
crown of fire – following its seed into His skies –
outpaced my comparatively powerless eyes;
as a baby that, having fed, stretches pale arms
up towards its *mama* like little fleshly flames,
each of those brilliances now swayed its tip above

in unambiguous display of their deep love,
and then sang *Rejoice, Queen of Heaven* too sweetly
for the ineffable taste of it not to be
forever with me. How great is the abundance
contained in these precious arks, all those who were once
diligent ploughmen for the sowing of the Word!
There they live and exult in that treasure acquired
at the small cost of endless tears in Babylon;
there now rejoices, under the majestic Son
of Mary and of God, with the old assembly
and the new – eternally victorious – he
who holds in his hand the golden and silver keys

needed to enter such celestial glories.

24.

"Elect company of the Lamb's marriage-feast,

wisest revel where every craving ends in Christ,
if by divine grace this man has had a foretaste –
in advance of death – or mere crumb from your repast,
consider his colossal hunger and bedew
his face with a drop or two; think, starry souls, you
drink always from the source at which his whole mind aims."
So Beatrice says, and then each blessèd spirit flames
and spins in the form of a globe on its axis;
and – as a clock's wheels appear to him who watches
to be either motionless or too quick to see –
these animate carols, dancing variously,
enabled me to gauge their inward wealth. Above

and all around the one that seemed most lit with love,
a joyous glow of an unparalleled lightness
was flickering forth; three times it circled Beatrice,
with song so sublime that my ingenuity
can't give the barest outline of it back to me…
here, then, my pen will do a leap where it won't write,
our phrases and our fantasising far too bright
for such fine convolutions, those subtly-shaded
folds. "Holy sister," the fire articulated
when it had slowed and stilled, "your steadfast, ardent prayer
and fierce affection have detached me from that sphere."
"Deathless light of the heroic soul," she replied,

"bequeathed the keys to exultation by our Lord,
try this pilgrim with basic or more arcane points –
as it pleases you – concerning that by which once
you paced briefly on the sea. The drift of his loves,
and the quality of his hope and his beliefs,
are not concealed from you but viewed where all is shown;
yet since in this realm one becomes a citizen
through the only faith, why not increase its glory
by giving him a chance to expound it clearly?"
As bachelors arm their minds though keep their mouths closed,
observing the master till a question is posed –
and even then talking for analysis' sake –

so I equip myself, as I listen to her speak,
with an array of freshly-sharpened arguments.
"Say, good Christian... what *is* faith?" At this, I glance
at the light that breathed these words and then at Beatrice;
and she, sweet encouragement shining from her face,
emboldens me to pour forth my soul's secretness.
"May the Grace," I began, "by which I confess
to the supreme standard-bearer, let me now give
adequate expression to all I can conceive;
as your fellow apostle, father, has written –
setting Rome on the path with his veracious pen –
authentic faith is the substance of our longings,

the argument and evidence of unseen things...
this, it seems to me, is its quiddity." "Correct,"
came the response. "The marvels I see with direct
and, as it were, deep apprehension in these spheres
are veiled from man's eyes upon earth; their truth appears
solely in that belief on which our hope is built,
and thus faith's a substance. From faith, the difficult
work of higher logic proceeds as someone who
travels by moonlight... hence faith is rational too."
("If," I heard, "everyone had this grasp of doctrine,
no suave atheist could inure the world to sin.")
"We have," that burning love exhaled, "now inspected

"this coin's alloy and weight, yet you never said
if it sits within your purse." "It does," I reply,
"and its golden glare and round shape both testify
to genuineness, the royal mint where it was struck."
"And this most precious jewel, every virtue's rock...
it came from in the ground?" "From the Holy Ghost's rains
torrentially drumming on the old and new skins,
such syllogisms as outshine all other talk."
"The texts or propositions, modern and antique,
upon which your conclusion is based... why is it
you regard them as the speech of a divine spirit?"
"The proof," I replied, "is in the miracles

Nature cannot ever make upon her anvils."
"And tell me – who assures you that these works occurred?"
"The whole world," I replied, "converted to Christ's word
without signs and wonders having to intervene,
a fact eclipsing anything that could be heard or seen;
for you came into the field both poor and hungry
and sowed the good plant, the vine originally
laden with grapes yet now bristling with thorns."
When I'd said this the spheres resounded with the tones
of *Praises to Thee, O Lord,* that transcendent court
shaping those melodies which stagger human thought;
and here the baron, who, in examining me,

had led, from branch to branch, to the last leaves of the tree,
spoke again. "The grace that allures your mind," he said,
"has opened up the mouth in an obdurate head
and I approve of what's come out... now, though, declare
what it *is* that you believe in, then tell me where
such faith was found." "O devout father, you who see
with crystalline sight what you believed so wholly
that you stepped past younger feet into the tomb... I
trust in the one eternal God who turns the sky
with love and vast desire yet is Himself unmoved,
this being a credence marvellously proved
by physics and metaphysics and the holy

voices of the psalms, the four Gospels, prophecy –
all who wrote and shall write when filled with the Spirit –
and I believe in three Persons infinite,
an essence at the same time both One and Trinity.
Concerning the nature of the divinity,
my mind has been as warm wax to scripture's sigil;
and this is just the beginning, the spark that will
gradually grow into a vivacious fire
and gleam in our inner sky like the dusk's sole star."
Like a lord who listens then embraces one sent
with long-awaited news, when I fell silent
I was circled three times by that apostolic glow...

the form and substance of my speech having pleased him so.

25.

If it ever comes to pass that this sacred

song that has made me lean and kept me from my bed –
this chant on which heaven and hell laboured long and hard –
undoes the evil through whose scheming I was barred
from the sheepfold where I slept as a lamb, a sworn
enemy of the wolf by whom our days are torn,
I'll return with altered voice and different fleece
and, at the same font where my baptism took place
and I entered the faith that presents souls to God,
will receive the golden wreath upon my head.
Now another flame moved towards us from that sphere
out of which there had approached Christ's firstborn vicar,
and, her words full of tender joy, my lady spoke:

"See the lord for whom they stream to Galicia… look!"
Much as when a white dove alights beside its mate,
and – with bobbings and low murmurs – they demonstrate
the love they share, so those two mighty princes neared
and warbled strange paeans to celestial food;
greetings over, they turn on me a silent gaze
and such is the soft intensity of that blaze
my sight cannot endure it. "Illustrious
soul," Beatrice said then, smiling, "by whom the largesse
of the square basilica was transcribed to man,
make hope resound in these heights. If anyone can
it's you, who embodied it three separate times. "Raise

your head and rest assured," came a voice, "for our rays
ripen all that rises here from the world below."
It was the second flame who had spoken, and now
I lifted my eyes to the mountains that before
had bowed them with tremendous weight. "The Emperor
wishes that, ahead of your demise, you come
face to face with His noblest in the inmost sanctum,
so that then – having witnessed the truth of that court –
lively hope will flourish in your soul as it ought
and make love grow and spread among men; tell us, though,
what hope *is*… how it blooms throughout the mind, and how
its luminous pollen's blown." So the second light

continued, and now she who has feathered my flight
to such an altitude intuits my response.
"Out of all of the Church's sacred militants,
none has more hope than this man – it is written thus
in the Sun that illuminates each one of us –
and so he came to see Jerusalem before
his departure from Egypt, the end of his war;
the other two points, about which you asked because
it'll make him say how dear to you true hope was,
he can address himself… they will be easier
and give no cause for boasts." Like a prompt and eager
student, confidently seconding the maestro's

exegesis so as to bring forth what he knows,
I then began. "Hope is the firm expectancy,
sprung from merit and His grace, of future glory…
we inherit this light from the manifold stars,
but it was the supreme Lord's greatest of singers
who first distilled its essence in my heart. *Let them
place their trust in Thee*, he says, *that behold Thy name* –
and who doesn't see it who possesses faith like mine?
Besides his, I saw your precipitation shine
so I can rain in turn – out of my fullness –
what you have poured on me." As I spoke, swift flashes
like distant lightning were atremble in the flame

and then it breathed these words. "The love whereby I am
still burning for that hope which accompanied me
to my battle's end, to the palm of victory,
compels my voice again… what does it *promise* you?"
"Both," I replied, "the old scriptures and the new
delineate – for those who have been drawn to God –
the mark the spirit's arrow should hit with a thud;
once, Isaiah tells us, we're in our native land
we shall be invested with a double garment, and
the land is this sweet life; yet more explicitly,
your brother – speaking of two white stoles – makes us *see*
something of that revelation." As I ended,

the phrase *The righteous trust in thee* was sung or said
far, far above and each carol sang in answer;
one of them shone so resplendently that Cancer,
adorned with such a gem, would make a single day
of winter. As a pure and joyous girl might pay
honour to the couple by entering the dance,
now I beheld that newly-brightened luminance
approach the two revolving to Love's melody.
"This is he who lay," said my lady, fixedly
observing them – a silent and motionless bride –
"on our pelican's breast, and who was dignified
by being chosen, from the Cross, for that great task."

Like one who stares, in an eclipse's eerie dusk,
at the half-veiled disc of the sun and is made blind,
I squint at that fire as her words rise in my mind.
"Why dazzle yourself," it asked, "to see what's not there?
My mortal parts are sprawled in dust's apparel, where
they'll remain until our number is correct; just
two lights wear white stoles in the cloister of the blessed…
a fact you will report when you fall back to earth."
Then both the fiery circling and its triple breath
cease at once, as oars hold still at a whistle's blow,
and I turn and I realise that I don't know –
in that sudden loss of sight – where my Beatrice is

though I sense her presence like a glow of happiness.

26.

In the midst of dread that I'd gone blind, there came

an articulate respiration from the flame
which had dazzled me. "Until," it said, "you get back
the light that's been consumed by mine, make good the lack
with speech; say where your spirit's rays converge, and be
reassured the loss of sight is temporary…
the one guiding you through His day, this clear brilliance,
has the same healing virtue in her merest glance
as humble Ananias's hands." "In that case,"
I replied, "let the remedy for my stunned eyes –
the gates where she first entered with a deathless blaze –
come as and when she pleases. That which satisfies
this court is the Alpha and Omega of all

the words Love reads to me in tones loud or gentle."
"You should sift," said the voice that'd managed to give
some relief from my fear, "with a far finer sieve…
tell me who it was who aimed your bow at that eye."
"A higher logic and divine authority
have both, as it were, published love within me;
for the good's inherent goodness immediately
kindles passionate flamings when it's seen and known –
love being in direct proportion to one's own
power of comprehension. It follows, therefore,
that – more than to created things – the mind must soar
lovingly toward the Essence which surpasses

everything to the extent that all we treasure is
a fading beam or trace of its vast radiance…
at least, that is, in anyone who understands
the truth on which this proof rests, demonstrated by
he who sets forth the primal love that draws the sky
(the intelligences centred on the changeless).
The scriptures' real author unfolds it to Moses
when he declares, speaking of Himself, *I will
make all my goodness pass*. You bring it forth as well,
commencing your exalted poem which cries out –
to open eyes on earth – the majestic secret
more starkly than the other heralds of the Word."

"As proclaimed by human intellect," I then heard,
"and the authorities with which it's in accord,
man's inmost passion – your one true love – looks toward
God unceasingly… but say whether you're aware
of the diversity of ropes that pull us there,
the rows of sharp teeth with which this thirst bites the soul."
I could discern the intention of Christ's eagle
and where he wished to lead me, hence I spoke again.
"Everything that tears hearts and makes them turn, in pain,
to Our Lord has colluded in my love; the mere
existence of the bright world, my being present here,
the death He underwent so that I might live –

and the hope which shines in those who, like me, believe –
have all drawn me, together with the aforesaid
vital knowledge, from that stormy sea of twisted
yearning to a shore where love's palm grows straight and tall;
in the measure of the good with which the eternal
gardener illumines each individual leaf,
the walled garden of creation receives my love."
As I fell silent, the entire heaven was filled
by singing of a sweetness unknown to the world
and my darling's lips were moving too. *Holy,*
Holy, Holy! As a man wakens suddenly
when a candle is lit, because the visual

spirit rushes eagerly through each carnal veil –
his features scrunched up like a little child's until
the mind comes to succour him – so every single
ash-speck and inhuman scale now fell from my eyes,
put to flight by the wild effulgence of Beatrice
which had been multiplied a hundred thousand times.
Like one uncertain if he wakes or if he dreams,
so greatly enhanced was my clarity of sight,
I asked her the identity of a fourth light.
"Inside those beams," my lady replied, "is the first
soul the primeval Virtue spoke into the dust."
A cypress in the path of the bodiless winds

bows down its slender tip, a dark green spire that bends
back with the vigour of its own sun-seeking force,
and thus I swayed at her words; sheer passion restores,
in those its sap quickens, the faculty of speech.
"Fruit who alone was born ripe, you to whom each –
ancient father! – bride is daughter *and* daughter-in-law,
you see and so I do not say what I wish for
but ask, with deep devotion, that you talk with me."
Beasts transmit their joy through every hair; similarly,
that primordial soul conveyed with its fleece
of incandescent rays how it desired to please.
"Without you even speaking," it then exhaled, "your

wish is seen more clearly than whatever's most sure
within a man's self-regard, for I witness it
in the unclouded mirror that some call Spirit
and which shows all things yet which nothing can reflect.
You want to know about the living dialect
I wielded and forged, the true cause of His fury,
and how long my clean glance strayed delightedly
in the high garden where she prepared you for the climb;
it's not the tasted fruit that instituted time
and exile, but the fact of transgression itself;
I pined for this assembly – in the same dim gulf
from which your mentor was summoned – for four thousand

three hundred and two solar revolutions, and
nine hundred and thirty times as I paced the earth;
my argot died before Nimrod tried to bring to birth
the impossible oeuvre, fallen language being
no longer a divine but a capricious thing;
the supreme Good – which emanates this coat of joy –
was known in former times amongst men as *J*,
and after I'd descended to the infernal
banlieux of the abyss it was renamed *El*...
mortal tongues are leaves that wag only one season.
I lived my morning of purest dissipation
on the summit of that peak, love's winding tower,

from the first to the seventh catastrophic hour."

27.

Glory to the Father and to the Son, the whole

of paradise began to exclaim with a soul-
enrapturing grace, *and to the Holy Spirit!*
Somehow I seemed to see as well as hear it,
as though the living universe both sang and smiled.
O joy! Unutterable gladness, calm but wild,
existence made one with love and peace! True riches,
endless treasure, yet no trace of covetousness…
infinitely tender, invulnerable delight!
The first-seen of those four flames now became more bright,
Jove's plumage having been exchanged for that of Mars;
providence imposed silence on the sacred choirs
in every quarter of the skies, and then I heard

these words. "If my aspect alters, don't be afraid…
all of us will transmute our shades as I speak. He
who's usurped my rightful place on earth – now empty
in the sight and the presence of the Son of God –
has converted my tomb to a gutter of blood
and that sewage so pleasant to the perverse one
who fell from this height." The glow the opposing sun
paints on the grey cheeks of a dawn or evening sky
then suffuses heaven's countenance entirely,
and, like a modest girl whose innate purity
is such that she blushes for another's sake, my
darling's face changed too; such an eclipse, I believe,

once accompanied the execution of Love.
"The spotless bride of Christ," he resumed, with a voice
as different from his former tone as fire from ice,
"was not fed from my own veins – the blood of Linus,
the blood of Cletus – for the sake of the zealous
piling up of coin, but for the acquisition
of this blissful life. It wasn't the intention
of Pius and Sixtus, Calixtus and Urban –
when they shed their noble blood in sorrow and pain –
that their successors sit with the rich on the right
and the poor on the left, the very keys to light
appearing on a battle-standard in the war

waged by the world on the spiritually pure,
nor that my image should be turned into a mere
token for sold favours (because of which, up here,
reddenings and coruscations are sometimes seen).
Rapacious wolves, in every meadow's shrinking green,
stride in the semblances of shepherds! Mighty Lord
of our defence, why don't you waken when our blood
is thirsted for in Cahors and in Gascony?
To what vile end must such a good beginning come?
That high providence which with Scipio, in Rome,
arose to the aid of the dormant world's glory
will soon be our salvation, if I estimate

correctly, whilst you – set back on earth by the weight
of your bones – shall speak openly as I do now."
As December air fills with soft-descending snow
when the horn of the stellar goat nudges the sun,
so I beheld those triumphant vapours adorn
the ether, falling upwards like manna reversed…
my eyes following until the point that the vast
intervening radiance concealed them from view.
"Gaze beneath you now and see," said my lady, who
knew my lofty stare was temporarily blocked,
"just how far you've turned." Since the time I'd first looked,
we had, I perceived in a single sweeping glance,

moved to the first clime's end; I glimpsed, in the distance,
the mad voyage of Ulysses beyond Cadiz
and, closer to me, the shoreline where Europa's
deft limbs weighed so sweetly; still more of man's little
light-sifted threshing-floor would have been visible,
were it not that the sun was a full sign beyond us.
Meanwhile my famished mind, always amorous,
burned more than ever to see her once again;
all that art and Nature have done to try to gain
control over human thought, snaring it with such
miracles of fine-wrought flesh or of the painter's touch,
would seem like a cold convocation of shadows

next to the divine joy that shines on me from those
smiling eyes when I now turn to see them. Virtue
and power flooding me, I am lifted into
the swiftest heaven out of Leda's dazzling nest;
I cannot say which part Beatrice chose – its closest
and its utmost regions being so similar –
but then she began to speak, reading my desire
and as if the Witness was delighting through her
face. "The nature of the world," she said, "whose centre
is the still, dark axis of every spinning sphere,
begins and also has its ultimate end here…
this heaven possessing no location other

than the mind of God, within which the heartfelt fire –
the love that revolves it, the power that is rained
via each star – originates. This sky's contained
solely by the one circle of His love and light
as it contains the others, hemmed yet infinite
(something which only He who holds it understands,
mysterious as a new father's cradling hands
to the child that looks back with such a sober gaze).
Its motion is not determined by another's
but every other's measured out by this, just as
ten is divided or unfolded by its factors;
it has surely been made quite clear to you now

that time's roots are buried in this soil, and how
its subtle leafage spreads throughout the wheeling nights.
Black ocean of cupidity, no mortal sight's
strong enough to raise a head above your currents!
The white blossom of the will uncurls, but immense
torrents of rain rot the plum on the bough; children
keep innocence and simple faith alive, and then
both flee before the days of hairless cheeks are past;
this one, whilst still a babbler, observes every fast,
then eats what he pleases once his clever tongue's set free;
these two – inarticulate now – devotedly
obey their mother's word, and yet the instant they've

learned how to speak will start to hound her to her grave.
Thus our skin blackens in the face of the lovely
daughter of the clear-eyed sun, that king whose deftly-
placed feet turn dusk and dawn to gold; recall how they
who claim to lead humanity lead you astray,
that before January's altogether lost
its accustomed garment of spectral trees and frost –
inching out of darkness with the tremulous years –
there'll be such a wondrous pulsation from these spheres
that south will become true north, that the vessel's prow
will shoot across blue waves where the stern slumbers now...
again the sea shall wear an imperial fleet,

and your flower cede to its long-awaited fruit."

28.

After she who can and does imparadise this brain

had shown me the truth of our present life, the pain
of haggard existence, my memory records –
as when one sees a dancing flame, looking towards
a dark glass so that you are momentarily
unsure what is semblance and what reality,
glancing round to check if a live fire will agree
with the image, as song with written melody –
that I then gazed into those unparalleled eyes
where love's silken noose is tied; and, as I turn back
to see with my own sight what appears in that black
precipitate orb when one examines it close,
I glimpse a mere speck burning with such an intense

light that anybody would squint at its brilliance...
the tiniest star that we see from earth must seem,
in comparison, like pale Phoebe on full beam,
and another fire spins round it at the distance
of a halo on nights when the dewy air's dense.
This igneous circle was rotating fast, fast
enough for the king of the spheres to be surpassed
by its speed; beyond it, a second circle flew
and after that a third one and so on onto
a seventh spread so wide that the explicit glow
of a rainbow would loom less large. Each whirls more slow
as it is remoter from the first, eight and nine –

farthest from the clear, uncontaminated shine
of the central point – possessing the dullest flame
because, I imagine, least lit by that *I AM*
that is He and His name. "On this," said my darling,
observing my rapt attention, "hangs everything
in Nature, depends every single sphere; just see
the nearest circling, whose immense velocity
is a consequence of the love by which it is
pierced." "If the order," I replied, "that I witness
in these wheels was the same as in the universe,
I'd be quite happy with the doctrine you rehearse...
but in our visible world, the heavens' tents are

more divine as one moves *outward* from the centre;
if, accordingly, my desire's to reach its goal
inside this stupendous and angelic temple
which only light and love confine, I need to hear
why pattern and copy have a different measure…
I struggle to comprehend, yet find I cannot."
"If your fingers," she smiled, "are fumbling with this knot
it's hardly surprising, it having become tied
progressively tighter by never being tried.
You have a thirst for understanding… to sate it,
pace around what I'll now say with your slyest wit;
the smallness or amplitude of the incarnate

skies express what powers and virtues permeate
their every part, the greatest structure being
at once the most blessed and the happiest thing
if its perfections extend equally throughout;
the one, therefore, that turns the universe about
answers to the circle which most loves and knows,
there being an inverse correspondence between those
intelligences' insight and the breadth of their spheres."
Just as the entire hemisphere of heaven clears
when Boreas blows from his milder cheek, the pure
splendour of light laughing delightedly once more
in every stellar province, every cloudy stain

purged and that immortal peace dazzling us again,
so I now became when my paramour's reply
made truth gleam distinct as the last star in the sky.
As her words temporarily ceased, each circle
showered luminous sparks like the white-hot crackle
off molten iron in the forge; each fire-seed coursed
down its incandescent track, their number so vast
they would far exceed the delirious doubling
of grain on the sixty-four squares, and then they sing –
choir calling choir – a mighty, joyous paean to
the still point that holds them all, and always will do,
in the orbits where they fly and have ever flown.

"The first rings," she said, perceiving my doubts, "have shown
seraphim and cherubim, whose velocity
within their bound freedom enables them to be
both as close and akin to the infinitely-
small polestar as they can; the other *amori*
are thrones of the countenance of God… all delight
to the precise extent they fathom with their sight
the truth wherein true intellection finds its peace –
the foundation of bliss being what a soul *sees*,
rather than the love that is vision's consequence
(whose measure comes from merit, which benevolence
and grace conceive in turn; such is the whole process,

from step to step). The next triad in this endless
springtime never ravaged by night-lurking Aries
sings a vernal song of three twining melodies –
dominations, virtues and powers are their names –
and then in the final three circular beams
there revolve the archangels, principalities
and gravely-playing angels. These divinities,
these lucent orders kept to this concentric blaze,
perpetually look above with a ninefold gaze
whilst commanding everything beneath them with such
subtle authority, such a lightness of touch,
that all life is drawn ineluctably toward

the unutterable Father, the sole Lord."

29.

Latona's shining children, at that certain time

the zenith hangs them beneath the scales and the ram,
one on each side of the girdling horizon, seem
to tremble in a perfect equilibrium
till the moment passes and they change hemispheres;
for just so long, alight with a smile, Beatrice stares
at the white point which had entirely mastered me.
"I answer without asking," she then said, "since I see
what you wish to hear in the star where every
place and age is anchored; in that eternity,
outside the strange mercy that is time, beyond all
comprehension and containment, the eternal
Love unfurls itself in a hundred billion loves…

not moved, of course, by any want, but so those lives
might flash His splendour back to Him when they say *I*.
Before light feet danced on this sea, He didn't lie
inert but exulted in timeless silentness;
form and matter – mixed and pure – shot into flawless
existence like three arrows off a three-stringed bow,
and, as crystal or amber or glass takes the glow
of a golden sunray instantaneously,
the threefold opus of the one Lord came to be
with no delay between vision and resplendence.
Order was created for each intelligence,
the spirits that are the universe's summits

and from which pure act is led. Mere potential sits
in the lowest position, and between them whirr
the celestial alloys held together
with such a weave as can never be unwoven;
Jerome said that between the angels' foundation
and the birth of the skies great tracts of ages lay,
yet this truth I here expound concurs with what they
wrote at the dictation of the Holy Spirit –
something you can verify, if you search for it –
and is even discerned by reason, to an extent,
for it's clearly absurd that the preeminent
dukes should lack the realm in which their completion lies.

That which I have elaborated satisfies
three flames of your desire… the where and the when
and also *how* these loving powers were made. Then,
in less time than you could count to twenty, a part
of the angels convulsed the lowest element;
the rest of them remained here, commencing this art –
this song you see before you now – with such intent
delight their revolution never ends. That head-
long plunge was caused by the pride of him you saw, dead
fathoms of earth's leaden darkness holding him still;
as much as he was arrogant, these were humble
enough to recognise their sheer existence in

the Good whereby all sight has its origin…
and so their vision was exalted through the fire
of illuminating grace, their will as entire
and immutable as that on which they're centred
(and I'd not have you doubt, but rather be assured
that the reception of God's grace is a 'reward'
dependent on how deeply the heart can be entered).
Revolve what I've said within you, and you shall find
enough to make a sanctuary of the mind;
yet since it's alleged in your universities
that the nature of the angels is such that these
spirits not only know but desire and recall,

I will speak further so that you may see how all
equivocating readings tend to take truth's place.
These substances, from the very moment His face
first filled them with joy – that visage from which nothing
is concealed – have never left off contemplating
the mystery it is, are always wholly here,
and hence they've no need for some abstract idea
to hide or make amends for a lack of presence.
Down on earth, though, whilst seemingly awake, intense
dreams beguile the lives of mortal men; to those who
propagate doctrine which they know to be untrue
attaches greater shame, love of the apparent

making so-called philosophy's paths divergent…
yet even this is a less reprehensible thing
than those who ignore or distort scripture's meaning.
They don't think how much blood it costs to sow the Word
within the world, nor that the soul of it is heard
by a modest innocence; for the sake of show,
they invent ingenious theories which go
the rounds of the preachers while the Gospel's silent –
one claiming, when the sixth hour came, the moon went
back on its track and engendered an eclipse,
disseminating error with his restless lips…
the fact being that light hid itself, which is why

that blackest of portents flooded half the world's sky –
and thus the sheep return from pasture unaware
the grass they digest is a confection of air.
Christ never said to his first followers to sow
trivia throughout the earth, but rather stood them so
securely on the bedrock of a higher truth
that – as they fought to set ablaze the fire of faith –
the news became both shield and lance. These latter days
a priest prefers to get a laugh than call to praise,
though if people could just glimpse the metal bird
nested in his skull's white hood, whispering each word,
they'd grasp the betrayal of their trust. Anthony's

swine grow fat on this, and all who tender monies
with blank faces where Christ's countenance should glow.
Yet we digress… return your gaze to the narrow
path, the sacred road, that our way may be shortened;
the true quantity of angels is far, far beyond
human talk or thought, although a specific
number's veiled by Daniel's multitude. The magic
of primordial light, informing with its rays,
is received and breathed back in as many different ways
as those brilliances are various; love follows
the depth and the degree of what a creature knows,
so every flame's unique… a facet or version

of the immaculate and undivided One."

30.

Six thousand miles away, perhaps, the sixth hour's

grandiloquence is burning, as this world lowers
its vast shadow down to the level of man's gaze...
meanwhile, in the profound abyss above, the sky's
beginning to lighten so this and then that star
no longer reaches its radiance as far
as our bleak floor, the lucent handmaid of the sun
extinguishing night's lanterns one by one by one
until ending with the loveliest of all; likewise,
by degrees, the festival that ceaselessly plays
round the iota which possesses victory –
appearing to enclose the mote it's enclosed by –
faded from my sight, and now my seeing nothing

returns me to love and my eyes to my darling.
If the essence of everything I've ever said
of her surpassing beauty was concentrated
within a single note of praise, still it would be
unequal to the wonder I now had before me...
beauty that transcends human measure, beauty so
beyond our neat categories that surely no
creature – just the Maker – has the full joy of it.
More than any comic or tragic poet
who found a pass in his gruelling climb to beat him,
I'll own myself vanquished at this point of my theme;
for, as the sun's force makes mortal vision tremble,

the simple recollection of that sweet smile
almost seems to sunder my spirit and my mind.
From the very first day that her eyes awakened
a slumbering heart, right the way to this vision,
my verse has sustained its quest and its precision;
but here these words' pursuit of her graces shall desist,
bowing to the unspeakable as an artist
must ultimately do, trusting a mightier
instrument than they will finally express her
and turning to the brutal stone from which I carve
our song. "We've come forth," she said, speaking with the verve
and demeanour of an empress, "from the largest

body to the heaven where the rays are purest…
that intellectual light which love illumines,
the love of the Good in which holy joy then shines,
a joy wholly unlike any other sweetness;
here you shall behold the twin militia of bliss,
one of them with the appearance of what will be
when His justice reigns." With the immediacy
of a lightning-strike, scattering the imps of sight,
a vital radiance flashed around us, a bright
veil whose lucid swathes made me absolutely blind.
The love that quiets this sphere, I heard inside my mind,
always welcomes in this manner those who visit,

preparing the withered wick of man to be lit.
After these brief words I became aware I was
lifted, as it were, above my meagre powers,
kindled with such novel vision that no brilliance
could blind me again; alchemical refulgence,
light in the form of a mighty river running
between banks adorned with the miracle of spring,
now met my eyes, and now out of those eddies came
a multitude of living sparks, each distinct flame
entering a bloom like rubies circumscribed by gold;
then, as if potent fragrances sent them wild,
they reimmersed themselves in the wondrous torrents

(as each one dived, a fresh glimmer emerged at once).
"The sublime desire which swells your soul, urging you
to jot and to understand everything you view,
delights me with its heat and its intensity…
that thirst, however, cannot be quenched completely
until you drink this water." Thus my sun. "The stream,"
she then added, "and all the topazes that seem
to appear and disappear, the flowers' laughter,
are only foreshadowings of the hereafter…
not that they lack ripeness, though, the defect being
a reflection of the fact your still-raw seeing
falls somewhat short of the nameless truth they preface."

No just-awakened infant ever flung his face,
famished from long sleeping, towards the milk than I
bent down to the deep wave so as to make each eye
a better mirror for its soul-perfecting flow;
as soon as they'd been rained on, the stream seemed to go
not *along* the ground but *round* like a watery
wheel; then, like people who are immediately
familiar when they lose the masks which made them strange,
the blooms and sparks rejoice yet more – and, with that change,
both the courts of heaven are manifestly clear.
O splendour of Jehovah, in whose song I saw
the exultant kingdom, grant or rather lend me

vigour to describe it with strong simplicity!
There's a luminescence there whereby the Creator
is apprehensible to every single creature
whose peace consists purely in the vision of Him,
spreading out in a sheer and spherical beam
greater in circumference than the peerless sun...
its entire snow-white semblance balances on one
solitary ray reflected off the summit
of the primum mobile, out of which it
drinks this power and this serene vivacity;
as a hillside doubles itself as if to see,
in the still lake at its base, the tremulous green

of its flower-starred slopes, so I was now shown –
rising in the ambient radiance – more than
a thousand tiers of those who've returned to origin.
If the lower levels gather such light, God knows
the expanse of the farthest petals of this rose
(though my sight wasn't lost but could somehow witness
that breadth and immense altitude of happiness,
there being no diminution with distance nor
increased clarity with nearness where natural law
can't dull or sway and our Father rules directly).
Like one whose silence is eloquent, she takes me
into the pale yellows of the eternally-

dilating rose which ascends degree by degree,
rendering praise's scent to the sun of endless
May. "See the convent of the white robe's nobleness!
See our city and how much it encompasses,
the occupied thrones, the last few empty places;
that seat whose prominence and whose diadem draw
your gaze is waiting for the true emperor,
who'll sit there before this wedding-feast receives you...
the one who shall be righteous upon earth, and who
will try to set an unsteady people on their feet.
Blind greed's bewitched them like a baby that must eat
yet whose very fever, the dark antagonist,

turns its face away from its weeping mother's breast."

31.

So the soldiery that Christ wedded with His

blood was displayed in the guise of a flawless rose;
the other militants, who, flying, sing and see
the glory and goodness of the unendingly-
enamouring One which articulates this host,
are all the while descending deep into the vast
and billion-petalled flower – as worker bees taste
many stamens' dust and then hasten to the nest
where the alchemy is done – and rising again
to where love's day breaks forever... their faces shine
like living flame, their wings are golden, and the rest
is of such a wondrous pallor that the freshest
fall of snow would look unclean if set beside them.

From bright tier to tier, when they reenter that bloom,
they impart with subtle buzzings the quiet and love
they've gathered; nor does that winged multitude above
the lucent rose shadow the splendour of the sight,
for divinity is a penetrative light
that sees through and saturates all that's undefiled.
This joyous but invulnerable kingdom, filled
with children old and young, focuses its vision
and its transfigured thirst or passion onto one
sole mark. *O triple light, who in that single star
can feed them with your sparkling, gaze down here at our
cyclone raging in the night!* If barbarians

marauding south to Rome from the Great Bear's regions
were stunned by the sight of what seemed superhuman,
imagine the awe of one come to the divine
from the mortal, to deep eternity from time,
from degeneracy to a people sublime
in true sanity and an inherent justice...
sheer joy making silence and my own silentness
more than enough. As a pilgrim who, whilst gazing
in his votive temple, aspires to say or sing
the wonder he feels, so my spellbound eyesight strolled
up and down and circled round those ranks of white gold;
each face is suffused by persuasive charity,

every soul's least gesture bespeaking honesty
and lit with its own love and a mutual glow.
Having taken in the shape of bliss already, though
not having paused to examine any part,
I then turn around with a newly-blazing heart
to pose more questions to my lady, my darling –
but where I expect her I encounter something
entirely other, an old man wearing the same
luminous garments as the people of the flame...
his eyes and his presence are joyful yet kindly,
and both the concern and the gladness remind me
of my dear father. "Where," I blurted, "has she gone?"

"To bring your desire to complete realisation,"
he replied, "Beatrice has asked me to leave my place...
look and see the wordless eloquence of that face
in the third circle where her sweet self has set her."
So I lifted my gaze and I saw Beatrice there,
her lovely head bright with an incandescent crown
of the rays we see reflected as they pour down
off the eternal; never was a carnal eye
as far from the thunder-bearing zone of the sky –
not even one lost within the depths of the sea –
as I was from her now, and yet the clarity
of that sight was entirely undimmed by distance

(there being no atmosphere to veil her countenance).
O lady in whom my hope has vigour and life,
and who suffered for my salvation's sake to leave
footprints on the blaze which gives no light, I recognise
that all that I have seen with wide-open eyes –
its operative virtue, its matchless grace – is
purely derived from your strength and tenderness.
I was in servitude... you liberated me
by every mode, by any means necessary;
sustain the masterpiece you've accomplished inside
my soul, so that when my final sinew's untied
and I step from the flesh I am still sane, still whole.

Thus my heartfelt prayer, and I seem to see her smile
and glance at me across that clear immensity
before turning back to where love's infinity
wells forth in silence. "To complete your soul's ascent,"
that blessèd elder then said, "for which I've been sent
by prayer and love, first fly through this garden with your eyes;
beholding it will further fortify your gaze
to endure the raging force of His fire. Heaven's
queen, on whose blue iris my entire spirit turns,
shall be gracious to us... I'm her faithful Bernard."
Like him who journeys from distant lands to regard
the true counterfeit of Christ's lineaments,

discovering an echo can't sate his intense
and immemorial hunger, so I now
look upon the features of one who came to know –
in the world but not of it – the vast, surpassing peace.
"Son of grace," he added, "you can never taste these
joys, this life, if you will not raise your eyes to where
the remotest circles turn, until you see Her
whose perfect light our kingdom is devoted to."
I lift my face, and, as amidst the lucid dew
of sunrise the eastern hemisphere outshines
the shadowed wood where day eventually declines,
I see a place of conquering radiance in

the heights – having toiled, you could say, up a mountain
with my mind – and at its very centre, aflame,
the savage serenity of an oriflamme
dispensing soundless beams in every direction;
surrounding that centre are more than a trillion
angels rejoicing, diaphanous wings outspread
and each one differently illuminated
and unique in the tenor of its sacred song.
Beauty smiles down on this exultant play, the throng
of all the saints portraying it within their eyes,
and even were I able to write as fantasize
I'd still not attempt to describe the least part

of that bliss which lights the smallest chamber of the heart.

32.

Observing me thus transfixed, Bernard returns

his gaze to her for whom his virgin spirit burns;
and now the contemplative, assuming the role
of teacher and doctor, says these words to my soul.
"Mary closed and anointed," he began, "that wound
inflicted by the beauty sitting on the ground
at her fair feet; beneath Eve, in the third rank, see
noble Rachel enthroned beside your Beatrice. She
who was great-grandmother to the singer who cried
God, have mercy on me! – grief-stricken, mortified –
is next; then see Judith, Rebecca, Sarah, moving
from petal to incandescent petal, naming
each matriarch in turn. From the seventh tier

downward, as above that level also, the clear
parting in the hair is made by Hebrew women,
delineating the sacred stair's division
into them whose belief was in Christ yet to come
and them (look, there are vacant places in the bloom)
whose brows were all turned towards the Lord incarnate;
as, on this side, the seats of the immaculate
Lady of Heaven and her kindred draw a line,
so on the other side the throne of noble John –
who, ever pure, suffered desert heat then went on
to endure two years in the black conflagration –
and those of Francis, Benedict and Augustine

mark the separation… consider His divine
foresight, for *both* visages of the faith shall be
balanced in this white garden. Below the degree
that splits the vertical divisions into two,
see the souls of those released before they had true
powers of discernment; neither faith nor merit
placed them here, for each is a little child's spirit –
as their faces and ringing laughter can tell you –
set free by the intercession of people who
loved them more than words could say. But you're gripped by doubt,
caught within a dark network of elusive thought,
and I will now untie these knots by which you're held.

Eternal law establishes all you behold,
the ring slipping perfectly onto the finger,
and therefore no misery or thirst or hunger
or arbitrary cause has a place in this empire;
it follows, then, that those who've hastened to the fire
of the true life aren't illumined without reason...
the king through whom they repose in love's completion,
creating consciousness for each to have the sight
of Him, to attain to ineffable delight,
gives each mind a unique endowment of grace.
Let the fact, beyond vain explanation, suffice.
This is expressly illustrated for you in

revealed scripture, by that story where one twin
wrestles with the other whilst the womb still holds them close;
in the end each receives a wreath of highest bliss
in occult harmony with their very hair's
shade, the two of them located in different tiers
according not to what they *did* but what they *saw*...
the primal acumen that's fully there before
a child is even born. Parental faith was once
enough for salvation, a baby's innocence
being complete; yet when the golden days were done,
a male soul needed the rite of circumcision
to give virtue to its plumes; now, in this current

blessèd age, children – no matter how innocent –
are detained below without baptism in Christ.
But look upon the lovely face whose brightness most
resembles Love, since that radiance alone
can prepare you for the light and presence of the Son."
I saw such joy cascading down upon her then,
borne within the minds made to range throughout heaven,
that everything I'd seen before had not shown me
any sight approximating God as closely
or so suspended me in fine astonishment;
the angel who sang, at the spring of his descent,
Hail Mary full of grace now bowed low with outspread

wings, whilst on all sides the blissful court responded
in such a way that each face shone with deeper peace.
"Holy father, you who have left that sweetest place
where you sit by eternal lot, undergoing
time spent away from the timeless... who is gazing
with such utter love into the eyes of our queen
he seems entirely fire?" Thus I appeal again
to the knowledge of one whose beauty's from Mary,
just as the morning star's resplendent clarity
is a gift of the absent sun. "Both fearlessness,"
he said, "and a felicitous spirit such as
is surpassed by no other single angel, no

human soul, subsist in him; we would have it so,
for he's the messenger who carried down the palm
when the Son of God intended to be or seem
burdened with our brutal cloak. Now peer round slowly
as I speak, and *see* the justice and clemency
of the greatest patricians of His empire. Those
two near Augusta are the roots of our white rose...
the one to her left is that ancestor whose taste
of the gleaming fruit has embittered man the most,
and on her right is the venerable father
to whom Christ entrusted the keys to this flower;
beside him sits the one who saw, before he died,

all the grave sufferings of the exquisite bride
bought with the nails and lance, and beside the other
shines Moses. See Anna, so glad to gaze at her
daughter that as she sings she barely moves her eyes,
then Lucy opposite the human family's
first patriarch... she sent your lady when you bent
your fateful brow. But, like the tailor whose garment
is measured to his cloth, I must here make an end;
the time draws near when a sleeper shall be wakened.
We now direct our minds to Love, navigating
as far as we dare into primal light, each wing
kept from backsliding by that grace derived from prayer.

Attend to what I say... follow with your heart's desire."

33.

"Daughter of your own son, calm and vestal mother –

ah how could I, how could I dance with another? –
most humble and exalted, endlessness's goal,
who gave such nobility to the human soul
that the entire Creator entered flesh's tomb...
love was rekindled and remade within your womb,
a love whose warmth opens, in unfading silence,
the white song of this bloom's immense incandescence.
You are the world's deathless spring of hope, the daystar
of charity for us throughout heaven; you are
so powerful and prevailing, gentlest lady,
that to yearn for Him yet not turn to your beauty
is to seek to fly without wings... benevolent

not just to those who cry for help, you've often sent
your grace before the asking; you are compassion,
mercy and magnificence, the compression
within a single creature of everything best
in joy's creation. This man, who, from the lowest
pit of the universe as far as our wild rose,
has witnessed the living and the dead, heard their sorrows,
implores of you the vigour to lift his face to
ultimate salvation; and I, your Bernard, who
have never burned for my own vision more, now pray
that you dispel the cloud of his brain with a ray
of pure supplication, in order that the light

of the Most High may be unfurled inside his sight.
I also ask, fair Queen – since you possess the fire
of perfect will – that you keep his deep desire
single-pointed after the vision of such things,
preserving his soul from a multitude of cravings;
look down... see how Beatrice and numberless thousands
of the blessed are echoing my words, joining hands!"
The one both loved and venerated by the One
shows her delight in those who voice their devotion
with a dazzling glance, then turns to the zero
of eternity (into which, I believe, no
other being sees with such an unpolluted eye).

And I, approaching the end of my longings, I
now bring all longing's fire to an end within me.
Bernard gestured and then smiled, but already
I had done by myself what he required; my sight,
ever purer, pierced the beam of prolific light
more and more deeply, the shining that itself is
truth. From here on, vision passed all that languages'
trickeries parade and baffled my remembrance;
as bizarre dreams will disappear almost at once,
and yet what one felt stamps its sigil on the mind,
this wicked heart can sometimes taste or scent a kind
of quintessence of the sweetness which came to birth then...

thus, in April sun, the ice's seal is broken,
the sibyl's dark sayings are launched upon the breeze.
O supreme light, you whose glittering summits rise
way, way beyond conception, grant my memory
a mere glimpse – even if only momentary –
of how you appeared to me now, and make my voice
staunch enough to utter one spark of your glories
for the liberation of the dead and unborn.
The ray was so sharp that I knew that to have torn
my eyes away would have destroyed me, a thought
which steeled me to endure it till the gaze had brought
itself to something infinitely fine. Abundant

grace, by whom I dared to probe the radiant
blaze that illuminates but does not consume!
I saw in its depths, bound by Love in one volume,
the poem the whole universe speaks and conceals –
for God is both essence and its myriad veils –
and this solitary phrase was a simple light...
a knot which to recall makes me pulse with strange delight,
although I've forgotten much more of the instant's
splendour than every single thing that's happened since
Neptune marvelled at the Argo's flying shadow.
My uplifted mind is exponentially aglow
as it mirrors His brilliance in total stillness,

the flawless light where you're made so light that it is
inconceivable to turn your gaze away;
hence I will be as to the point with what I say
as a child who still renews his voice at the tit,
concerning even these fragments I retain of it...
the light in whom shines that Good, goal of the spirit,
beside which nebulae and worlds are counterfeit.
My sight becoming stronger as I stared, the one
phenomenon underwent a transformation
in conjunction with mine; through the profoundly clear
ground of the sentient glow there now appear
three spheres of three colours and a sole circumference,

the second cast by the iridescence
of the first – a rainbow picturing a rainbow –
and the third a flame breathed between the other two. Oh
speech falls short, frail and withered next to what I know...
and mortal thought, compared to what I *saw*, is so
meagre that no word can express such paucity.
Eternal light, truly comprehended only
by yourself, your own unimaginable throne,
and, in the blessèd union of knower and known,
engendering an ecstasy and unending
love; that reflected gleam born within you, circling,
seems in my rapt absorption to possess the same

hue as the human spirit's simulated flame;
in the face of this vision, this living miracle,
I am like he who dreams of squaring the circle
though can't find, despite ceaseless reckonings, the key...
such is my hunger to understand completely
the place where emptiness and image coexist.
These wings were not equal to that flight, yet a blast
of palest fire then annihilates the partial
mind and an infinite thirst is satisfied. All
power of representation here fails me,
but – like a golden wheel rotating steadily –
now the intellect, my will and every desire's

held by the Love that moves the sun and untold stars.

SELECT BIBLIOGRAPHY

Anderson, William. 1980. *Dante The Maker* (Routledge & Kegan Paul).

Bakhtiar, Laleh. 1976. *Sufi: Expressions of the Mystic Quest* (Thames & Hudson).

Barnes, Jonathan, ed. 1987. *Early Greek Philosophy* (Penguin Classics).

Bates, Catherine, ed. 1994. *Sir Philip Sidney: Selected Poems* (Penguin Classics).

Berenson, Bernard. 1967. *The Italian Painters of the Renaissance* (Phaidon).

Cary, Rev. Henry Francis. 1889. *The Vision, or Hell, Purgatory and Paradise of Dante Alighieri* (Frederick Warne & Co.).

Dryden, John. 1997. *Virgil's Aeneid* (Penguin Classics).

Durling, Robert M. and Martinez, Ronald L. 1996, 2003, 2011. *Inferno, Purgatorio, Paradiso* (Oxford University Press).

Fulcanelli. 1971. *Le Mystère des Cathédrales: A Hermetic Study of Cathedral Construction* (Neville Spearman).

Guenon, René. 1972. *The Reign of Quantity & the Signs of the Times* (Penguin).

Hall, Manly P. 2003. *The Secret Teachings Of All Ages* (Tarcher/Penguin).

Maritain, Jacques. 1939. *Art & Scholasticism* (Sheed & Ward).

O'Brien, Elmer, ed. 1964. *The Essential Plotinus* (Mentor Books).

Pound, Ezra. 1938. *A Guide To Kulchur* (Faber & Faber). 1952. *The Spirit of Romance* (New Directions).

Schuon, Frithjof. 1982. *From the Divine to the Human: Survey of Metaphysics and Epistemology* (World Wisdom Books).

Schwaller de Lubicz, R.A. 1988. *Sacred Science: The King of Pharaonic Theocracy* (Inner Traditions).

Sinclair, John D. 1961. *Inferno, Purgatorio, Paradiso* (Oxford University Press).

The Bible: Authorized King James Version with Apocrypha

Catechism of the Catholic Church: The CTS Definitive & Complete Edition

Chambers Dictionary of Etymology

THIS BOOK WAS SET IN
CASLON WITH FUTURA
TITLING BY CARCANET